LAW AND DISORDER IN CYBERSPACE

LAW AND DISORDER IN CYBERSPACE

*Abolish the FCC
and Let Common Law
Rule the Telecosm*

PETER HUBER

Oxford   New York

OXFORD UNIVERSITY PRESS

1997

Oxford University Press

Oxford   New York

Athens Auckland Bangkok Bogotá Bombay
Calcutta Cape Town Dar es Salaam Delhi
Florence Hong Kong Istanbul Karachi
Kuala Lumpur Madras Madrid Melbourne
Mexico City Nairobi Paris Singapore
Taipei Tokyo Toronto

and associated companies in
Berlin Ibadan

Library of Congress Cataloging-in-Publication Data
Huber, Peter W. (Peter William), 1952–
Law and disorder in cyberspace: abolish the FCC
and let common law rule the telecosm / Peter Huber.
p. cm.   Includes bibliographical references and index.
ISBN 0–19–511614–3
1. United States. Federal Communications Commission.
2. Telecommunication—Law and legislation—United States.
3. Antitrust law—United States. I. Title.
KF2765.H83 1997 343.7309'94—dc21 97–3345

Poem Number 1263, first line "There is no frigate like a book"
from The Complete Poems of Emily Dickinson, edited by
Thomas H. Johnson Back Bay Books, 1960, p. 553 is reprinted,
by permission, from Little, Brown and Company.

2 4 6 8 9 7 5 3 1

Printed in the United States of America
on acid-free paper

For Stephen Anthony

There is no frigate like a book
To take us lands away
Nor any coursers like a page
Of prancing poetry.
This traverse may the poorest take
Without oppress of toll
How frugal is the chariot
That bears a human soul.

EMILY DICKINSON

Contents

Preface

The story begins like this: Herbert Hoover had a problem. As a Republican, he liked free markets and private property. But as an engineer, he wanted things nice and tidy. Markets aren't tidy. He had to choose. He chose wrong.

Hoover wasn't president yet—he was still secretary of commerce. The critical choice he had to make concerned a fascinating new industry called broadcasting.

Westinghouse had inaugurated the first radio station, KDKN, in Pittsburgh in 1920. AT&T put a station on the air in 1922. Hundreds of stations were popping up all over the country. And no one was regulating them at all. They registered with Hoover's Department of Commerce, in much the same way as ships registered. But that was it. Nobody could stop you from going on the air.

What happened when an AT&T station tried to broadcast on a frequency already used by Westinghouse? The companies went to court. Courts were just beginning to develop rights of private property in spectrum, relying on familiar, common-law principles developed over the centuries in connection with real estate. But the common law is a messy business—as messy as the marketplace. Hoover, the engineer, wanted order.

Order had already come to telephones. In 1902, telephones had been messy, too. Half of all cities had two or more competing phone companies. They didn't connect with each other. That was a nuisance.

In 1913, antitrust litigators had hit on a solution. A consent decree forced AT&T to connect its long-distance network to independent phone companies. But by then it was already too late. People much like Herbert Hoover had taken charge. They solved the interconnection problem by abolishing competition. With only one phone company in town, it wouldn't have to connect to anyone but itself. That was tidy.

So by 1927 Hoover knew what he had to do. With the help of Congress, he nationalized the airwaves completely. He handed all the ether over to a brand-new Federal Radio Commission. From then on, private ownership of any part of the airwaves was strictly forbidden. Market forces were banished. Private users operated only under short-term licenses, under close federal supervision. The logic for this radical collectivism? Spectrum was too scarce to be owned privately.

And so in 1934—while Stalin, Hitler, and Mussolini were proving to the world the remarkable efficiency of national socialism, and while George Orwell was formulating his gloomy views about Big Brother—we in the United States folded all federal authority over both wireline and wireless communication into a new, superpowerful communications commission. We called it the Federal Communications Commission—the FCC. Germany got an FCC, too, even bigger and more efficient than ours. They called it the Bundespost. Joseph Goebbels loved it.

Our own Commission never got that bad, but it got bad enough. Our airwaves were about as free as a high-school newspaper. Anybody lucky enough to get a broadcast license took care not to offend the Commission. You wanted that license renewed.

And telephones? Well, in 1954 the FCC invoked the full majesty and authority of the federal government to block sales of the Hush-A-Phone. It was a small metal cup sold by a tiny independent company. The cup attached to the mouthpiece of a telephone, providing a bit of privacy and quiet in crowded offices. The FCC said it was a "foreign attachment," a competing network that was attempting to interconnect with Bell. And competition was illegal. Interconnection was forbidden. There was talk of outlawing private sales of plastic slipcovers for phone directories.

The years passed. And then suddenly we woke up one day, and who did we find on our telephone network? Markus Hess. Hess was a teenage mutant ninja. Hess was a hacker. He was Joseph Goebbels, turned inside out. His 1986 exploits would be recounted in Clifford Stoll's bestseller, *The Cuckoo's Egg.*

Using pseudonyms like Pengo, Zombie, and Frimp, Hess and others like him were bent on creating electronic anarchy. Several of them had set up the chaos computer club in Hannover, Germany. They despised phone monopolies. They called Germany's the Bundes-Pest.

So they began throwing electronic bombs. They attacked computers in Germany, Switzerland, France, and then the United States. For a while they seemed able to go anywhere they liked. And they did it all over the phone wires.

What had happened? One day you can't sell a slipcover for a phone book. The next, people with names like Zombie and Frimp are ambling down the international phone lines and into the most private recesses of your computer.

Two things had happened. First, Bell Labs had invented dial tone for computers. It was an operating system called Unix, designed for computer networking.

Second, in the 1970s the FCC had finally grown fed up with the silliness of regulating slipcovers. And so the commission began instructing Bell to connect with its most direct rivals: first the competition's phones, modems and computers, then with long-distance competitors like MCI, and then with on-line servers—the building blocks of the Internet. Big pieces of telephony were being handed back to the competitive marketplace.

Consumers were startled. We'd been living under rigid state control for half a century. We didn't know a thing about free enterprise in this arena. We were like the Russians in 1992, trying to learn how to handle the free market. For a while hustlers like Zombie and Frimp swept in and conned us.

Discipline was collapsing in the airwaves, too. The FCC had grown tired of running high-school newspapers, so it pretty much told broadcasters to broadcast what they liked. We got Jenny Jones and Rikki Lake—the Zombies and Frimps of the airwaves. They elbowed their way into our living rooms with tales of lesbian headhunters' preteen incest. We were too stunned even to turn the dial.

Herbert Hoover gave us the state, and when the state began to crumble, Markus Hess gave us a taste of anarchy. It is time now to return to where we started: common law for the telecosm. It is the closest we will ever come to utopia.

Acknowledgments

My two best friends are Michael Kellogg and John Thorne. Together, we have written three legal treatises: *Federal Telecommunications Law* (Little, Brown, 1992, and Supp. 1995), *Federal Broadband Law* (Little, Brown, 1995), and *The Telecommunications Act of 1996* (Little, Brown, 1996). It was in working on those books, with those two excellent colleagues, that I developed the ideas contained in this one.

I would also like to thank two young attorneys, Evan Leo and Gonzalo de Dios, for their invaluable assistance on all my telecom-related writing. Laura Haefner coordinated legal research and production of the final manuscript with consummate skill and patience. I am also very grateful for the research assistance provided by Elizabeth Anderson, Danielle Briggs, Sara Elder, Todd Kichn, Jason Kowal, Anne Mauboussin, and Jonathan Shiffman. I received first-class secretarial support from Marilyn Leeland, Joyce Cannon, Danelle Fortune, and Heather Knight.

LAW AND
DISORDER IN
CYBERSPACE

1

Introduction

Until 1996 the telecosm was governed by laws written half a century ago. The rules for the telephone industry dated back to 1887. They had been written at a time when land, air, water, and energy all seemed abundant, while the telecosm seemed small and crowded, a place of scarcity, cartel, and monopoly, one that required strict rationing and tight, central control.

In the last decade, however, glass and silicon have amplified beyond all prior recognition our power to communicate. Engineers double the capacity of the wires and the radios about every two years, again and again and again. New technology has replaced scarcity with abundance and cartels with competition.

The electronic web of connection that is now being woven amongst us all is a catalyst for change more powerful than Gutenberg's press or Goebbels's radio. Every constraint of the old order is crumbling. The limitless, anarchic possibilities of the telecosm contrast sharply with the limits to growth we now encounter at every turn in the physical world.

In early 1996 Congress passed the most important piece of economic legislation of the twentieth century. The Telecommunications Act of 1996 runs some one hundred pages. The Act's ostensible purpose is to open markets to competition and deregulate them. It may eventually have that effect. The process of deregulating, however, seems to require more regulation than ever. The FCC no longer aspires to immortality through its work. Like Woody Allen, it aspires to immortality through not dying.

It is time for fundamental change. It is time for the Federal Communications Commission to go.

The Future and the Past

The telecosm—the universe of communications and computers—is expanding faster than any other technocosm has ever expanded before. It is the telephone unleashed, the personal computer connected, and the television brought down to human scale at last. Its capacity to carry information has expanded a millionfold in the last decade or two. It will expand another millionfold in our lifetime—or perhaps a billionfold. No one really knows. The only certainty is that the change will be enormous.

This change is characterized by a paradox: It is both fragmentation and convergence.

The old integrated, centralized media are being broken apart. Terminals—dumb endpoints to the network—are giving way to "seminals"—nodes of equal rank that can process, switch, store, and retrieve information with a power that was once lodged exclusively in the massive switches and mainframe computers housed in fortified basements. This is the fragmentation.

At the same time the functions of these nodes are coming together. In digital systems a bit is a bit, whether it represents a hiccup in a voice conversation, a digit in a stock quote, or a pixel of light in a rerun of *I Love Lucy*. This is the convergence.

Then there is the law. Until 1996 most of telephony was viewed as a "natural monopoly." The high cost of fixed plant, the steadily declining average cost of service, and the need for all customers to interconnect with one another made monopoly seem inevitable. The broadcast industry was viewed as a natural oligopoly. It depended on inherently "scarce" airwaves, and was therefore populated by a small, government-appointed elite.

The FCC and comparable state-level commissions were established in the 1920s and 1930s to ration the scarcity and police the monopoly. The administrative structures, their statutory mandates, and the whole logic of commission control reflected the political attitudes of the New Deal. Markets didn't work; government did. Competition was wasteful; central planning was efficient. A fateful choice was made: Marketplace and common law were rejected. Central planning and the commission were embraced.

The common law evolves from the bottom up. Private action comes first. Rules follow, when private conflicts arise and are brought to court. Commission law was to be top-down. A government corps of managers, lawyers, economists, and technicians would settle in at the FCC first. Private action would follow later, when authorized. Common law is created by the accretion of small rulings in discrete, crystallized controversies. Commission law would be published in elaborate statutes and ten-thousand-page rule books; while these were being written, the world would wait. Common law centers on contract and property, legal concepts that are themselves creations of the common law. Commission law would center on public edicts, licenses, and permits. Common law is developed and enforced largely by private litigants. Commission law would come to court only at the end of the process, when public prosecutors filed suits against private miscreants.

Common law would have suited the American ethic of governance far better, particularly in matters so directly related to free speech. But between 1927 and 1934, when the FCC was erected, the winds of history were blowing in the opposite direction. National socialism, right-wing or left, seemed more efficient, the only workable approach to modern industrialism. Around the globe, people in power persuaded themselves that the technical complexities of broadcasting, and the natural-monopoly economics of telephony, had to be managed through centralized control. The night of totalitarian government, always said to be descending on America, came to earth only in Europe. But America was darkened by some of the same shadows. One was the FCC.

Once in place, the FCC grew and grew. Today it has 2,200 full-time employees and a $200 million budget—more offices, more employees, and more money than at any other time in its history. As competition increases, monopolies fade, and the supposed scarcity of spectrum is engineered into vast abundance, the Commission just gets bigger. An institution created to ration scarcity now thrives by brokering plenty. It is an Alice-in-Wonderland sort of world, in which the less reason the Queen has to exist at all, the more corpulent and powerful she becomes.

For the next several years at least, the FCC will have the most important mission in Washington. Wireline and wireless telephony, broadcasting, cable, and significant aspects of network computing together generate some $200 billion in revenues a year. For better or worse, the FCC will profoundly influence how they all develop. And in so doing it will exert a pivotal influence over the entire infrastructure of the information age and thus the economy, culture, and society of the twenty-first century.

The faster that power is dissipated, the better it will be for America.

Deconstructing the Telecosm

The beginning of the end was cable television. Cable demonstrated that spectrum could be bottled, and made abundant. Cable refused to be merely "broadcaster" or merely "carrier." It threatened all the old regulatory paradigms. It was just too capacious and flexible for regulators, even with the relatively primitive technology it used at that time. Now cable is moving into telephony. Meanwhile, by boosting the capacities of their wires, phone companies are poised to move into video. They already carry most of the Internet traffic, which is television in slow motion.

Wireless services are changing even faster. Once dedicated largely to feeding the idiot box, wireless is now the flourishing center of cellular telephony, direct broadcast satellite, wireless cable, and personal communications services. Spectrum is gradually being privatized and dezoned. The new owners are using their wireless bandwidth to provide whatever services they like, to whichever customers they choose.

The fundamentals of deregulation are now clear. The concepts are simple. They can be implemented quickly.

First, throw open the markets. For wireless, this means privatizing the critical asset—spectrum— by giving it away or (better still) selling it. For wires, it means letting anyone deploy new metal and glass alongside the old. Contrary to what Congress assumed for half a century, no commission is needed to protect against "wasteful duplication," "ruinous competition," or "inefficient deployment of resources." Markets take care of that.

Second, dezone the bandwidth. On wire or wireless, a bit is a bit. No government office should zone some bandwidth for pictures, some for voice, some for data. The market can work this out far better than any central planner.

Won't new robber barons then buy up all the wires, corner the spectrum, jack up prices, ruin service, and impoverish consumers? With the entire industry in ferment, with engineers doubling the capacity of every medium every few years, and with the telecosm expanding at big-bang rates, these fears are utterly implausible. But in any event, the traditional antitrust laws will remain in place. For all practical purposes, antitrust law is common law. It addresses specific problems in courts, not commissions. It is decentralized, adaptable, and resilient. Sclerotic commissions just get in the way. Indeed, for decades the FCC has legitimized telecom practices that antitrust courts would never have tolerated in its absence.

Ironically, the Commission can justify much of its current frenetic activity by blaming its predecessors. If the airwaves hadn't been nationalized in 1927, they wouldn't have to be sold off today. If the FCC hadn't spent half a century protecting telephone monopolies, it wouldn't have to dismantle them now. If the Commission hadn't spent so long separating carriage from broadcast, broadcast from cable, and cable from carriage, it wouldn't have to be desegregating those media today. If it hadn't worked so diligently to outlaw competitive entry back then, it wouldn't have to labor so hard to promote it now.

I-broke-it-then-so-I'll-fix-it-now has a certain logic to it, even if the confession of past breaking is always much less emphatic than the promise of future fix. But the fixing somehow always seems to take as long, or longer, than the breaking. And while the Commission plans and plans for perfect competition, competition itself waits uselessly in the wings.

The telecosm would be vastly more competitive today if Congress had just stayed out of session in 1927, in 1934, in 1984, and again in 1992—if Congress had never created the Federal Radio Commission, never folded it into the FCC, never extended the Commission's jurisdiction to cable, and never expanded the Commission's powers over cable further still. The 1996 legislation guarantees that the Commission will grow in size and influence for the rest of this decade while it uproots the anticompetitive vineyard planted and cultivated by its predecessors.

But the uprooting should be done quickly. Five years is time enough; ten would be too long. And then? Then the Commission should shut its doors, once and for all, and never darken American liberty again.

Common Law for the Telecosm

Who, then, will maintain order in all these areas when the Commission is gone? Private actors and private litigants, common-law courts, and the market. It is the Commission that must go, not the rule of law.

We still need laws to defend the property rights of people who lay wires and build transmitters, to enforce contracts and carriage agreements, to defend the freedom to speak and to listen, and to protect copyright and privacy. Anarchy works no better in virtuality than in actuality. The question is not whether there will be rules of law, but where they will come from.

Commissions proclaim the "public interest, convenience, and necessity." They issue general edicts. They publish rules in a massive Code of Federal Regulations. Common law, by contrast, evolves out of rulings handed down by many different judges in many different courtrooms. The good rules gain acceptance by the community at large, as people conform their conduct to rulings that make practical sense. In this kind of jurisprudence, constitutions and codes provide, at most, a broad, general mandate to develop the law by adjudication. They operate like the Bill of Rights or the Sherman Act.

Commission law has been tried. Not just in the telecosm but in command-and-control economies around the globe. Like Communism, commission law has failed. It is rigid, slow, and—despite all the earnest expertise of bureaucrats—ignorant. Market forces, mediated by common law, elicit information faster and more reliably. Markets constantly probe new technology, try out new forms of supply, and assess demand with a determination, precision, and persistence that no commission can ever match. Property-centered, contract-centered, common-law markets allow people to get on with life first and litigate later, if they have to. Most of the time they don't. Rules evolve spontaneously in the marketplace and are mostly accepted by common consent. Common-law courts just keep things tidy at the edges.

The one strength of commission law is that it reduces uncertainty all around. But only because the market must wait for the commission to invent a whole framework of law up front. That often takes years, and the framework is always rigid and inadequate. In a universe where technology transforms itself every few months, where supply and demand grow apace, where new trillion-dollar economies can emerge from thin air in a decade or so—in such a universe, uncertainty is a sign of health and vigor. In a place like that, nothing except common law can keep up. The law must build itself the old-fashioned way, through action in the market first and reaction in the courts thereafter.

If that suggestion seems outlandish, it is only because the FCC has been around so long that people can no longer imagine life without it. Once Henry the Eighth's licensing of printing presses had become routine, it would have seemed equally outlandish to suggest that such an unfamiliar, complicated, and important technology might be left to open markets and common-law courts. When it was created in 1887, the Interstate Commerce Commission seemed essential to proper management of railroads. But when it was abolished in early 1996, hardly anyone even noticed. We never did create a Federal Computer Commission. The computer industry has nonetheless developed interconnection rules and open systems, set reasonable prices, and delivered more hardware and more service to more people faster than any other industry in history.

Now, in the 1990s, with the telecosm growing explosively all around us, with the cacophony of free markets already drowning out the reedy proclamations of a senescent Commission, the only outlandish proposal is that we should keep it.

It is time to finish the job. The Commission must go.

I

THE FUTURE
AND THE PAST

2

Technologies of Freedom

As Lenin once remarked on the subject of tanks, quantity has a quality all its own. Even things old and familiar can be transformed beyond recognition by the raw power of size.

A painter of miniatures developed the essential elements of an electromagnetic telegraph in 1835. Then he devised a code to represent letters and numbers by combinations of short and long pulses. A decade later Samuel Morse transmitted the message "What hath God wrought" from Baltimore to Washington. Alexander Graham Bell added the microphone and speaker. These were the origins of all wireline communication, first by electricity, then by light.

Wireless communication can be traced back to 1864, when James Clerk Maxwell demonstrated theoretically that electrical disturbances propagate through space at the speed of light. Guglielmo Marconi read of electrical experiments that had been conducted by Hertz, grasped the possibilities, and produced the first practical "wireless telegraph" in 1895. The following year, just as Bell's patents on the telephone were expiring, Britain granted Marconi the first patent on a radio. It came to be named for what it wasn't. It was the "wireless."*

Wire and wireless define the two halves of a boundless telecosm. From a physicist's perspective, they are not very different. Radio waves come in an infinite range of frequencies. AM radio is low on

---

*Years later, Guglielmo Marconi was asked to explain how his new gadget, the radio, differed from a telegraph. "A telegraph is like a dog," Marconi replied. "You pinch the tail at one end, and it barks at the other. My radio is just the same, except there's no dog."

the dial. Ruby-red laser light is high. Fiber-optic transmission is just radio on speed, the oscillating crystal of an old-fashioned radio replaced by an oscillating cavity of gas called a laser. The only real difference between wireless and wire is the "wave guide"—the wire itself. An ordinary radio transmitter shines outward in all directions; it "broadcasts." An electronic or photonic transmitter points its signal into a shielded tunnel of metal or glass; it "drills."

The tunnel solves the problem of interference. Any number of "radios" can transmit side by side on wires; when one strand is filled, another can be unrolled next to it. The wire also excludes dust and rain, so the signal is more dependable. A wire can turn corners, dodge buildings, or track the curvature of the earth. And a wire can be more private. The National Security Agency much prefers glass to air.

Does wire, and particularly glass, therefore have a decisive edge over wireless? Not always. Wireless is often more efficient for one-to-many communication, and it is essential for mobility. It is less private, but the whole point of broadcasting is to reach lots of people. Overall, wired networks offer more capacity and privacy but are most efficient only for stationary, "narrowcast" connections.

Townships in the Telecosm

Networks may be built mostly of radios or of glass, but at least half the circuitry is still paper—that is, law.

The communications laws of the 1920s and 1930s were written, unimaginatively, around the technological paradigms of the day. Broadcasting at that time was wireless and truly "broad"; there was no cable and no scrambling. Common carriage—telephony—was wired and used overwhelmingly for public carriage; there was no dial-a-porn audiotext, no dial-up video, and no virtual private networks. Private networks were wholly private; they didn't interconnect as nodes on the Internet do now. Cable, which today supplies a messy mix of carriage and broadcast, had not been invented. Digital broadband was beyond imagination.

The laws were written accordingly. Private entities could do what they liked, so long as all their facilities and communications remained strictly private. Carriers were to provide transport, no more. Broadcasters were to supply a fully integrated package of wireless transport and content, no less. Other quarantines and proscriptions followed. Telephone companies were to stay out of computers and video. Broadcasters were forbidden to "broker" their airtime by chopping it into small slices and selling it to any willing buyer. Players, media, and services were to occupy separate townships. It was apartheid for the telecosm.

If the laws had been written a generation earlier, the boundaries of the townships might have been drawn quite differently. Alexander Graham Bell originally expected his telephone to be used for what we would now call "cable radio"—the broadcast of music, news, and other information to a mass audience of paying subscribers. In 1893 Hungary's Telefon Hirmondo began running such a service in Budapest, supplying a goulash of concerts, news, and novels. Marconi, by contrast, expected radio to provide point-to-point messaging. In the 1920s AT&T tried to run one of the early radio stations by selling small slices of time to all comers. By the 1930s, however, telephone was mostly common carriage and radio was largely broadcast. The Communications Act of 1934 was drafted accordingly, with little thought that technology and markets might radically change.

For six decades the telecommunications industry grew within these legal confines. Today the average American household is deluged with electronic signals. Ninety-four percent of households have telephones. Over 98 percent have television, and 83 percent of those receive at least seven television broadcast channels. Cable, which passes 97 percent of television households and connects to 65 percent, delivers an average of fifty-three video channels. Direct broadcast satellite (DBS) began broadcasting to the United States in 1994; the signals reach almost everyone, and as of this writing some 4.5 million subscribers have bought dish antennas to receive them.

Yet despite the torrents of electronic information cascading into our offices and homes, the telecosm is still young and, in critical respects, unformed.

Along one dimension, television is broad and telephone narrow. Broadcast television delivers high bandwidth—it transmits an enormous amount of data very fast. Telephone lines are a thousand times narrower. Along a second dimension, however, telephone is broad and television narrow. There are about 150 million telephone lines in the country, but only about 1,500 TV broadcast stations. From this perspective, television is a hundred thousand times narrower than the telephone network. Television is a one-way technology, connecting the few to the many. Telephone gives everyone both a transmitter and a receiver.

The missing parts of the network create a remarkable financial paradox. The narrow connections, which are consumed too sparingly, are far more lucrative than the broadband ones, which are consumed in profligate excess. In round numbers, the Super Bowl attracts a hundred million viewers and $100 million in sponsors' cash. The game lasts four hours. That's about twenty-five cents per viewer-hour. While sports enthusiast Jane Doe watches the big game, John prefers to chat with his college roommate on the phone. The connection is still very narrow. Yet for entertainment that good, John is willing to pay about $12 an hour to his long-distance phone company.

Multiply these numbers across 150 million households and offices, and you arrive at a comparatively small TV entertainment industry and a much larger telephone industry. Though they provide a broadband signal—sound and full-motion color video—and occupy the average American many hours every day, broadcast and cable combined generate revenues of $56 billion a year. Though each telephone line is used only about twenty-five minutes a day, local telephony alone generates about $103 billion a year. Long-distance calling generates another $45 billion. In total, then, telephony generates more than twice the revenues of video.

Broadcast delivers a great deal, but the network behind it is steeply hierarchical. Telephone is narrow but egalitarian. That simple difference accounts for the two-way telephone's two-for-one revenue edge over one-way television. If we have to choose, thin, two-way connectivity is worth far more than a fat but one-way channel.

But we don't have to choose anymore.

The End of Scarcity

Our demand for bandwidth has grown rapidly, and without interruption, since the days of Morse, Marconi, and Bell. A good Morse-code telegraph operator could transmit about twenty-five words per minute, or about three characters per second. A character today is represented in binary code by eight bits. So the telegraph supplied a bandwidth of about twenty-four bits per second (bps). Voice conversation, converted into digital form, requires about sixty thousand bits per second (60 Kbps)—two thousand times more. An uncompressed color television picture requires another ten-thousand-fold increase in bandwidth—roughly 100 Mbps. High-definition television (HDTV) requires two to six times more than that.

Though our notions about abundance will seem pitifully narrow to our grandchildren, about fifty million bits per second is typically what we mean today when we speak of "broadband" communication. That's about five complete newspapers a second, a compact disk every minute and a half, or five simultaneous channels of color television. Visionaries speculate about holographic three-dimensional television with a virtual Rambo or Barney sitting next to you in the den. That would take gigabits per second (billions), or perhaps terabits (trillions).

But even these standards derive from the worlds of speech and entertainment, the wrong points of reference. Human eyes and ears can process incoming bits only so fast; intelligent machines face no similar limitations. Computers, not humans, will be the ultimate consumers of bandwidth. There is no reason to suppose that their appetites will ever be satiated.

The technology to supply almost limitless bandwidth is now at hand. Broadband networks already occupy the top tiers of the telephone network, operated by regional and national telephone companies, and the top tiers of the broadcast networks, operated by video carriers. Only the last mile remains to be conquered.

Coaxial cable—a single copper wire at its center, surrounded by an outer cylindrical shield (typically aluminum), with polyethylene foam between—was originally developed to provide high-capacity telephone trunks. In the 1940s it began to be used to import television signals into areas that couldn't get good over-the-air reception. Entrepreneurs then set up microwave towers to pipe in more-distant signals to the head ends of their cable networks. Ted Turner followed in 1975. His independent UHF Atlanta station, WTCG (now WTBS), was already using microwave to distribute programming to cable operators. Turner began using satellite to create the first national "superstation."

Today, with compression technology at both ends, a single coaxial cable can carry hundreds of channels. Information retrieval, Internet, and other interactive services head the list of services cable operators expect to offer their customers in the 1990s. The FCC has backed cable's right to provide telephone service as well. Cable still has years of life left in it.

But cable is gradually giving way to fiber-optic glass, a truly remarkable technology. The idea is simple; it is like children sending messages to each other by blinking a flashlight in the dark. A tiny laser, flashing inconceivably fast, sends signals through unimaginably pure glass at the speed of light. Every year or two some engineer, somewhere or other, doubles the blink rate, and that doubles the potential capacity of every existing strand of glass. The carrying capacity of fiber-optic cable increased a millionfold between the mid-1970s and the early 1990s. Another millionfold increase will occur in our lifetimes. Or perhaps a billion.

Ounce for ounce, glass is the most capacious broadband medium now operating. There is nothing faster, broader, more secure, or more interactive. The U.S. long-distance telephone networks are almost all glass already—a remarkable transformation from only a decade ago. Glass is now tunneling toward every node on the telephone network that generates large volumes of traffic. Local phone companies use it for all their heavy-duty hauling. Cable companies are glassing all but the very ends of their local distribution plant.

Eventually we will all be glassed. But not immediately. Running new fiber-optic glass cable right down to every home and office in America would cost some $100 to $300 billion, or around $1,000 per household. If installing glass were the only expense, every new line would already be glass today. But splicing into glass is much more difficult than splicing into metal, and the interfaces between glass and the ubiquitous electronic hardware of telephones, televisions, and computers still often favor the metallic status quo.

The capacities of wireless media are growing almost as fast. Because it is high in the sky, satellite is the broadest of the broadcast media, geographically speaking. Terrestrial cellular radio uses nearby transceivers with small footprints; satellites operate at a great distance with a footprint to match.

As a result, satellites can be extraordinarily efficient for delivering the same message (the Super Bowl, say) to everyone. For that reason, satellite has taken over the long-distance delivery of broadcast content—video (for network television), voice (for network radio), and data. By providing cost-effective networking to hundreds of otherwise separate local cable networks, satellites made possible the phenomenal growth of that industry.

Broadband satellite is now making the transition from wholesale to retail markets. Direct broadcast satellites transmit at two to ten times the power of a conventional bird, and their signals can thus be received on pizza-sized dishes. DirectTV successfully launched a sixteen-transponder DBS satellite, DBS-1, in December 1993; in August 1994 DBS-2 went up. DBS is now one of the fastest-growing consumer services in U.S. history.

Other wireless media are being reinvented, too. Until the late 1970s microwave transmitters were used almost exclusively for point-to-point transport of long-distance telephone calls—hence the *M* in MCI. Soon after the 1984 Bell breakup, however, Sprint began running advertisements that showed microwave towers being dynamited to the ground, to be replaced by glass. Microwave frequencies are now used by pay-TV and "wireless cable" providers—multichannel multipoint distribution services (MMDS) and local multipoint distribution service (LMDS). CellularVision, the leading LMDS licensee today, uses an innovative microwave technology to transmit video signals within small "cells," much like those used for cellular telephony. Signals ricochet off buildings and other surfaces and are picked up by flat receivers. The FCC approved commercial implementation of CellularVision in December 1992.

The electronic linchpin for all these advances is the highway-in-a-box—the silicon-charged intelligent terminal at the end of the wire or antenna. Smart ends widen the channel itself—and can widen it indefinitely.

By the narrow standards of 1878, telephone service was astonishingly broad—telephone represented a huge increase in transmission capacity over the telegraph. Yet both telegraph and telephone transmitted a variable electric current over the same kind of wire. The difference was the telephone itself, which increased the bandwidth of the wires from the speed of the human finger to the speed of the human tongue.

The digital microprocessor uses that same alchemy to open up vast new possibilities. Improvements in the box—the telecomputer itself—can be much greater, and can be deployed far faster, than improvements in the wires that connect one box to the next. Year by year, mathematicians and programmers double and redouble our ability to convert cataracts of raw data into trickles of highly compressed information. There are mathematical limits to how much signals can be compressed with no alteration or loss whatsoever. But there are no theoretical limits to the "lossy" compression of picture or sound in ways undetectable by human eyes or ears. Improvements in microprocessors alone will double the effective capacity of all our networks every few years from now into the indefinite future. Those same processors are also the key to effective scrambling, which maintains both privacy and property rights in intellectual content.

Deconstructing the Telecosm

The original "broadcasters" were farmers. The word is in fact centuries old. To broadcast seed is to scatter it over the whole surface of the earth; the alternative is drilling, where seeds are planted in rows. The 1934 Communications Act understood these two paradigms and embraced them. Telephone was wires, and wires drilled. Broadcast was wireless, and wireless landed everywhere.

But the engineers and the entrepreneurs just wouldn't pay attention to the lawyers.

When the FCC opened the skies to competitive communication satellites in 1972, it expected to promote competition in long-
distance phone service. At that time, AT&T also distributed most of
the video programming for national TV networks, over landline circuits. As competing satellites began to be parked in orbit, however,
long-distance telephony was moving back down to earth. Satellites
turned out to be the ideal medium for distributing video channels to
the new cable industry. Cable had started life as a carrier, a "community antenna," a passive retransmitter of broadcast TV. Fed by satellite, cable operators now became major video programmers, too.

The satellites evolved as well. They were supposed to be carriers for
cable, but rural householders began setting up their own six-foot
backyard dishes; that made the satellites "direct broadcasters," too.
Entrepreneurs soon launched higher-powered satellites whose signals could be picked up on smaller dishes. The difference between
satellite "carriage" and satellite "broadcast" is thus 100 watts (one
light bulb).

By scrambling signals and then selling decoders, broadcasters become narrowcasters. Both radio and television broadcasters also use
parts of their spectrum to provide carriage. Paging is a common-
carrier service, but it uses the subcarrier frequencies of FM radio stations to locate travelers. Cellular technology narrowcasts a radio
transmitter right down to the point where it becomes a telephone.
Microwave has moved in the opposite direction. AT&T developed it
for long-distance telephone service. When glass displaced it, entrepreneurs began using microwave frequencies for "wireless cable."

Local phone companies are already into broadcasting of sorts. A
dial-a-porn 976 service is a topless, for-pay radio station, even if we
still style it as a phone call. Sooner or later, video dialtone services will
do for video what 976 services did for voice. And on top of the phone
lines, of course, we already have the World Wide Web.

On the Internet today, a single telecommunicating conduit contains
virtual newspapers, virtual television stations, and virtual carriers. Using these platforms, anyone can become a broadcaster simply by connecting a personal computer to a telephone line. When the bandwidth of the wires increases another hundredfold or so, which will
happen before long, computer screens will become as animated as
television. Any teenager in his basement will be able to compete head-
to-head against Peter Jennings. Nielsen, not the FCC, will decide
who is the broadest among tens of millions of casters.

But we won't speak of broadcast anymore. With high bandwidth, on
the one hand, and scrambling technology, on the other, all broadband
digital communication, wired or wireless, will be drilled. Telephone

networks will keep their narrow-cast capabilities but add bandwidth. Broadcasters will keep their bandwidth but add scrambling to narrow their cast. The digital trumpet sounds. All the walls of the old regulatory townships will come down.

Making Connections

If Bill Gates alone could own a telephone, he wouldn't want to. There is a "network externality" here—my telephone makes his more useful, and vice versa. Telecom services are "club goods:" Instead of sharing a pool and golf course, we share our compatible, interconnected telephones, fax machines, and computer bulletin boards by linking them to a common network. Up to a point, a similar arithmetic works in broadcasting. The Super Bowl is worth more, not less, because it has become an obligatory cultural event. The treasure is in the sharing.

So connectivity is good. Other things being equal, we want more of it. But how much, and to whom? We clearly need more outbound connectivity than we currently have from factories, offices, and hospitals—wherever people work rather than lounge. Here, the power to send information is as important as the power to receive it. Enabling people to order a pizza by telephone in Pavlovian response to TV advertising will not be enough. In other contexts, most of the demand is for more inbound bandwidth—more entertainment, or faster links to the Web.

Simpleminded highway metaphors don't help the analysis. Solid things like cars obey immutable laws of conservation—what goes south must come back north, or you end up with a mountain of cars in Miami. Information is completely different. It can be replicated at almost no cost, so every individual can (in theory) consume society's entire output. Rich and poor alike, we all run information deficits. We all take in more than we put out.

Efficient networks will be designed accordingly. They may provide a very broad inbound channel over one medium (satellite, glass, or coaxial cable) but close the loop over a different, narrower-band medium (a digital telephone channel, perhaps). Markets will be segmented, too. A bank and an insurance company do not need the same lines as a library or a home; a hospital needs something different again. Most workplaces will need capacious outbound channels, just as factories need loading docks. Schools will need more bandwidth in than out.

With bandwidth, one size does not fit all. The elderly and the unemployed consume vastly more information in their homes than they produce. A child parked in front of a cable-connected television swallows a Niagara of junk bits with every minute of connection to the Cartoon Network, and is the poorer for it. By comparison, a cyber-nerd on the Internet uses tiny amounts of bandwidth to send e-mail or transfer a file to the office. Telecommuters already manage today with channels a thousand times less capacious than the ones used for television. The difference is that they are producing meat-and-potato bits, not just inhaling Twinkies.

The only prescription for meeting such heterogeneous and varied needs is not to prescribe anything. Networks must simply intercon-nect, wireless to wireline, broadband to narrow. The Web is probably the best model at hand for the broadband architecture of the future. It is already the world's largest communications system, the data arch-ipelago of the planet. It spans the national, regional, and local com-munications networks used by commercial, government, and educa-tional organizations worldwide. It is also, at the same time, an array of independently owned and managed networks, separately funded, sep-arately developed, and separately maintained, with no single entity or agency in charge of managing everything.

It is, in short, the model of the future. A broadband Web will offer decentralized and nonhierarchical connectivity, but not simplicity or uniformity. It will be an inelegant mix of glass, coax, and copper, of terrestrial transmitters and satellites. No one technology will prevail. Bandwidth and two-way capabilities will constantly improve. The technological mix will constantly change.

Bandwidth and connectivity will proliferate, but so will complexity and unpredictability. It has been suggested that the airwaves and the landline network are trading places—that everything that now goes by wire will go by air, and vice versa. But what is really going on is a hybridization of technology, not a simple exchange of chairs. Both wireless and landline technologies can provide broadband links; the choice will therefore depend on such factors as the need for mobility, population densities (which sharply affect the relative costs of wire and wireless), and overall network economics. The market will use broadband media in unexpected ways, if regulators will let it find them. Unforeseen synergies between different broadband media—satellite and cable, for example—will create entirely new markets and wholly new categories of services.

The Marketplace of Ideas

In a charming 1945 essay, "Poetry and the Microphone," George Or-well reflected gloomily on the prospects of radio. People had come to associate radio exclusively with "dribble," "roaring dictators," or "genteel throaty voices announcing that three of our aircraft have failed to return." This was not because there is something inherently vulgar, silly, and dishonest about the whole apparatus of microphone and transmitter, but because all broadcasting happened to be under the control of governments or great monopoly companies.

No more. The telecosm is being transformed into a network of networks, an intricately interconnected matrix of wireless, satellite, copper, coaxial, and glass, with multiple overlapping and complementary providers, and no single dominant center. As Ithiel de Sola Pool recorded in 1983, these are indeed the technologies of freedom.

3

The Commission

George Orwell said it would happen like this. The network, the two-way video terminals, the entire telecosm, would end up ruled by the Ministry of Love, headquarters of the Thought Police. By 1984 the Ministry would tower over central London, "vast and white above the grimy landscape," an "enormous pyramidal structure of glittering white concrete, soaring up, terrace after terrace, three hundred meters into the air." It would contain "three thousand rooms above ground level and corresponding ramifications below." The Ministry of Truth—the state propaganda office—would occupy an identical megalith next door.

We got the Federal Communications Commission instead. It officially came into existence on June 18, 1934, at much the same time as Orwell was forming his gloomy views about telescreens, Big Brother, and the Thought Police. It never has amounted to anything quite so fearsome as Orwell imagined. It just gradually coalesced over the course of a century, a hodgepodge of bureaus, divisions, titles, missions, and powers.

Telephone

The idea of telephony, from the Greek "far speaking," has tantalized humanity since time immemorial. Alexander Graham Bell, grandson of a professor of elocution,* son of a linguist who taught speech to the

---

*According to legend, the expertise of Bell's grandfather in eliminating Cockney accents inspired George Bernard Shaw's character of Professor Henry Higgins in *Pygmalion*.

deaf, produced his first rough plans for a "harmonic telegraph" in 1872. Within a few years he had developed the "phonautograph," which translated sounds into visible markings. In 1875 Bell discovered the basic principles of the electromagnetic microphone and speaker. He transmitted the famous words "Mr. Watson, come here, I want you" to his assistant on March 10, 1876, and inaugurated commercial telephone service the following year. Bell was confident that someday "a telephone in every house would be considered indispensable."

Telephones were first installed in point-to-point pairs; then telephone companies grasped the possibilities of a telephone exchange. The exchange—at first a simple switchboard, with human operators—made possible calls between any pair of phones connected to it. Newark, New Jersey, boasted the first semiautomatic switching system in 1914.

By that time, however, the Bell Telephone Company's patents had been narrowly construed by the courts or had expired. Thousands of independent telephone companies had been formed. By 1902 451 out of the 1,002 cities with telephone service had two or more companies providing it. When a telephone census was taken in 1907, the independents owned nearly as many telephone stations as Bell.

Competitive exchanges seemed to defeat the key advantage of a centralized switch—universal connection. A second problem was interexchange, or long-distance, connection. While Bell had lost its original patents on the telephone, it had acquired new ones, covering "loading coils" and the "audion"—the first vacuum tube amplifier. These patents gave Bell a critical edge in providing good long-distance connections.

At about this time, Theodore Vail, a brilliant administrator, took over at Bell. Vail believed passionately in "universal service," to be supplied by one company, his own. Bell therefore offered its superior long-distance service only to its own local affiliates. It refused to provide interconnection even to independents that did not directly compete with it. In rapid succession, independent phone companies either merged with Bell or folded.

Bell's activities attracted the attention of antitrust lawyers at the U.S. Department of Justice. In a 1913 agreement with the U.S. Attorney General, a Bell vice president (N. C. Kingsbury) agreed that Bell would cease acquiring independent telephone companies and would permit the remaining independents to interconnect with Bell's long-distance arm. But local exchange monopolies were left intact, still free to refuse interconnection with any local competitor. Nor was there any provision to accommodate competition among long-distance carriers.

Thus the markets were carefully divided up: one for each of the monopoly local telephone exchanges, large or small, and one for Bell's monopoly long-distance operations. Bell might not own everything, but either Bell itself or some sibling monopolist would own each discrete market. Regulators of the day had no objection. All they wanted was to keep the commercial monopolies at a size that they could manage.

Vail understood that well. Bell's actual slogan was One Policy, One System, Universal Service.

The Commission

Sidney Burleson, the postmaster general in President Wilson's cabinet, began lobbying Congress to nationalize the phone system. Liberal congressmen backed the idea enthusiastically. They demanded the "postalization of telephones and telegraphs."

When the United States entered World War I, the federal government took over the railroads. Congress then held hearings to consider taking over communications. Postmaster Burleson was heard at length. AT&T wasn't invited. Congress passed a joint resolution, and President Wilson took legal control of the network. AT&T still ran things, but now it was under the post office's direction. Rates immediately rose sharply. The war ended a year later, and the phone network was returned to its own management and shareholders.

Postal authorities and others still favored tight federal control. State and local governments hoped to end "inefficient competition" and expand service. Bell itself wanted to consolidate its dominant position and legitimize its monopoly. Vail spoke publicly in favor of regulation, sounding an anticompetition theme—"cream skimming"—that would become a Bell System rallying cry for the next half a century. "If there is to be state control and regulation," Vail declared, "there should also be state protection—protection to a corporation striving to serve the whole community . . . from aggressive competition which covers only that part which is profitable." Monopoly telephone service came to seem inevitable.

Federal authorities had already been regulating railroads for decades. Congress figured that regulating phones would be much the same. The Mann-Elkins Act of 1910 placed interstate telecommunications under the jurisdiction of the Interstate Commerce Commission. The Act defined telephone companies as "common carriers" and obligated them "to provide service on request at just and reasonable rates, without unjust discrimination or undue preference." The ICC could set aside "unjust or unreasonable" carrier rates. In a landmark 1930 decision, however, the Supreme Court required state and federal regulators to allocate telephone assets between intra- and interstate uses and divide their authority over them accordingly.

As it turned out, the ICC of the 1910s and 1920s was too busy pursuing railroads to worry much about telephones. In twenty-four years of oversight, the ICC presided over only four telephone company rate proceedings. In 1921 the ICC was authorized to approve telephone company consolidations; thereafter it approved almost all of them.

By the late 1920s support began to emerge for tougher oversight. State authorities wanted an effective federal counterweight to AT&T. The interests favoring new regulation converged; the voices in favor of unregulated competition fell silent. On February 26, 1934, President Roosevelt asked Congress to create a separate federal communications commission. Both houses passed legislation, and the president signed the Federal Communications Act of 1934 into law on June 18.

Most of the Act's telephony provisions were drawn directly from the Interstate Commerce Act. Railroad regulation conceived in 1887 was thus formally extended to telephones, under the aegis of a new commission. Federal communications law would not be fundamentally revised until 1996, just a few months after the century-old Interstate Commerce Commission was abolished.

Broadcast

Marconi produced the first practical radio in 1895. He had conceived of radio as a messaging system for ships. Radio communication of human speech first occurred on Christmas Eve, 1906, between Brant Rock, Massachusetts, and ships in the Atlantic Ocean. Soon the vacuum tube amplifier—the "audion"—would improve radio transmission as dramatically as it improved telephony. In 1909 Bell's chief engineer sought research funds to put the company "in a position of control with regard to the art of wireless telephony, should it turn out to be a factor of importance."

The military was interested, too. In a 1910 letter to Congress, the navy denounced the "chaos" prevailing in the airwaves. Various government departments, the navy observed, had "for years sought the enactment of legislation that would bring some sort of order out of the turbulent condition of radio communication." The navy wanted all wireless stations placed under federal control. A 1918 congressional bill proposed to do just that. Radio, Secretary of the Navy Josephus Daniels would explain, was "the only method of communication which must be dominated by one power to prevent interference." "My judgment is that in this particular method of communication the government ought to have a monopoly." "There is a certain amount of ether, and you cannot divide it up among the people as they choose to use it; one hand must control it."

Private broadcasters multiplied anyway. With the early technologies, radio's great advantage was not in point-to-point messaging like telephone, but in point-to-everywhere broadcasting. David Sarnoff, who started as a telegraph operator for the Marconi Wireless Telegraph Company of America, was the first to recognize this. In 1916 he submitted his idea for a "radio music box" to the management of Marconi. Within six years, both Westinghouse and Bell put radio stations on the air.

Hundreds of stations began broadcasting in the 1920s. A spontaneous market order began to evolve. The early broadcasters were settling the airwaves in much the same way as pioneers on the prairies had created private property out of unbounded space, by settling on the land and putting it to use. The chaos of the airwaves began gradually to crystallize into an orderly, functioning market.

The Commission

This ad hoc privatization met with fierce resistance from government officials. A 1925 Senate resolution declared radio spectrum to be "the inalienable possession of the people of the United States." In July 1926 a joint congressional resolution announced that no license should be granted for more than ninety days for a broadcasting station, or for more than two years for any other type of station.

In contrast to telephones, however, radio broadcast services did not readily fit any established models of regulation, either state or federal. The closest analogy to broadcasting is a newspaper, as to which the First Amendment declares: "Congress shall make no law."

Congress made a law anyway. It enacted the Wireless Ship Act, in 1910, after the navy complained that distress calls from vessels at sea were being lost in the "etheric bedlam" of numerous unregulated stations. Two years later Congress gave the Secretary of Commerce authority to register broadcasters. Certain segments of spectrum were zoned entirely for maritime or military communications; the rest were left open. Most empty airspace could still be occupied by the first comer, however. Homesteaders just had to register their claims with the Department of Commerce.

Conflicts were inevitable. In 1920 the Intercity Radio Corporation initiated a "wireless telegraphy" radio service between New York and other cities. It registered its claim and was duly issued a license to operate for twenty months. When the license expired, Secretary of Commerce Herbert Hoover refused to renew it on the grounds that Intercity's operations were interfering with other government and private stations. Intercity insisted it had a right to go on broadcasting anyway. A federal appellate court agreed. The 1912 Radio Act was just a registration law, "substantially the same as that in use for the documenting upward of 25,000 merchant vessels." Commerce could choose the wavelengths on which stations would operate, but it could not deny registry.

Hoover responded by enlarging the allocation of spectrum. He continued to ration licenses, and, in defiance of the *Intercity* ruling, refused to process a string of applications. The first radio station began broadcasting in 1920. By 1922 more than five hundred stations held federal licenses. By 1924 radio reached twenty million listeners.

Three years later a federal court in Illinois took *Intercity* a step further and ruled that Commerce had no power even to impose restrictions as to frequency, power, and hours of operation. Hoover sought clarification from the Department of Justice, which advised that licensees were indeed free to decide these things for themselves. Hoover then abandoned all efforts to regulate. More than two hundred new broadcasters began operation in the next nine months. Problems with interference multiplied.

A sensible solution began to materialize in late 1926. Applying common-law principles, an Illinois state court delineated rudimentary property rights in spectrum. WGN, an established Chicago broadcaster, complained that a newcomer was wrongfully trespassing on its frequency. The state court agreed, declaring, "priority of time creates a superiority in right." Had the courts been given time to develop it methodically, this simple idea would have created property rights in the ether, much as the common law had created property rights in the land beneath it—rules of trespass, easement, nuisance, and the like that define the bounds of ownership in real estate.

In 1943 Justice Frankfurter would look back at radio in the early 1920s and describe that period as one in which the industry was "veering toward collapse." It wasn't. Despite interference problems, the industry of the 1920s was growing phenomenally fast and successfully.

The three main broadcasting networks were successfully launched in the middle of this "chaos." With the help of the courts, an orderly free market in broadcast properties was crystallizing out of thin air.

But Congress had other ideas. In 1926 it required anyone granted a license to waive any ownership right in the ether. President Coolidge called for comprehensive new legislation. Industry incumbents united in support of the idea. Major broadcasters, already well established, were eager to enlist government in protecting their incumbency against the next round of upstarts.

The logic for a government takeover of the airwaves seemed strong. Spectrum, it was said, was inherently "scarce." Two radio stations could not broadcast simultaneously in the same area without interference. There was, it was said, some natural (though never defined) physical limit to how many radio stations could be on the air at the same time. Spectrum was like a commons, a smallish national park. The federal government would have to be the national owner and trustee. Rights to graze would be doled out sparingly, and only to the most worthy of citizens.

The result was the Radio Act of 1927. It nationalized all wireless spectrum and placed all aspects of radio broadcasting under the ultimate control of the newly created Federal Radio Commission. The Commission was empowered to license every last transmitter in the land. It would assign frequencies for public use and decide who could use them. It would classify radio stations, prescribe service limits, assign wavelengths, approve the locations and power levels of transmitters, and regulate networks. Its power to grant, renew, deny, or revoke licenses was unlimited. The Commission was merely exhorted to advance the "public interest, convenience or necessity."

Those words, it soon became apparent, allowed the Commission to do whatever it pleased. The Commission promptly issued licenses to all established major broadcasters, shut down marginal competitors, and sharply curtailed new entry.

Seven years later the 1927 Radio Act was folded intact into the Communications Act of 1934. The Federal Radio Commission was absorbed into the new Federal Communications Commission.

Satellite and Cable

The 1934 Act thus extended FCC power to everything of any significance that touched on interstate communication. The public operations of both carriers and broadcasters were solidly under FCC control. Title II set out the Commission's authority over common carriers—entities that offer service to the general public and do not control the content of what they transmit. Title III codified the Commission's authority over wireless broadcast. Private connections of any kind were covered expressly in Title III (if wireless) and implicitly in Title I (if by wire). Wireless carriers (like today's satellite carriers and cellular phone companies) could be regulated under both Titles II and III simultaneously. Only wireline "broadcasters" (like today's cable operators) were not addressed at all.

Ever since, new FCC powers have been created as needed, mostly by stretching out the old ones. When satellites offered a new platform for radio, the Commission's authority to regulate them was already in place. The satellites were just newfangled radio stations, located a hundred million feet higher than Congress contemplated in 1927. For good measure, however, Congress passed the Communications Satellite Act of 1962.

Cable television was harder. The 1934 Act assumed clean technological and economic divisions between common-carrier telephony and publisher-like broadcast. Cable is a bit of both, and the mix keeps changing. "Community Antenna TV" was viewed at first as a local carrier—a passive transporter of broadcast, and thus a candidate for strictly local oversight. In 1958 broadcasters asked the FCC to regulate the upstart cable industry. The Commission declined, on the grounds that the 1934 Act did not provide federal authority over cable. Cable wasn't a carrier because the operator unilaterally controlled what was transported over the wires. Cable wasn't a broadcaster, either, because cable used wire, which limited the possible audience. Viewed through the law of 1934, cable wasn't really anything at all.

Broadcasters complained vehemently about this existential vacuum until the Commission agreed to fill it. In 1962 the Commission started by regulating the microwave common carriers that were delivering to cable systems television broadcasts from distant cities. Not long after, the Commission simply announced that the sweeping introductory language of the 1934 Act gave it all the power it needed to regulate the new medium.

This required a remarkable inversion of logic. The airwaves had originally been nationalized on the theory that spectrum was scarce. Cable provided an enormously capacious substitute. By all logic, cable was the reason to begin deregulating the airwaves. Instead, the FCC announced that the airwaves were the reason to begin regulating cable. Faced with the choice between changing its mind and proving that there was no need to do so, the Commission got busy on the proof.

The Supreme Court upheld that bold new assertion of power. The Commission had plausibly (in the Court's view) concluded that cable might undermine free broadcast; the Commission could therefore crush cable, or at least regulate it, to assuage those concerns. A second Supreme Court ruling swept away virtually all remaining obstacles. A stopping point was reached only in 1976, when the FCC tried to order larger cable systems to install additional channel capacity and provide two-way capabilities like telephone. By this point, cable had been pegged as being like television. The Commission could not, therefore, require it to perform like telephone. Federal authority to do so had to come specifically from Congress.

It came in the 1984 Cable Act. The new law carved up cable jurisdiction between federal and state authorities. A second federal cable law was enacted over President Bush's veto in 1992. These two laws gave the FCC broad power to regulate cable, either directly or through local authorities acting under its directive.

Townships in the Telecosm

Thus, step by step, year by year, the Commission acquired sweeping power over the telecosm, from the airwaves in the stratosphere down to the cables buried alongside the sewers and the subway tunnels. There was no master plan, no sinister conspiracy, just relentless mission creep. The FCC's telephone authority dated back to the railroad laws of 1887, its broadcast authority to the Radio Act of 1927, its satellite authority to the broadcaster rules and to a tag-on statute enacted in 1962. Cable's rules were first squeezed out of the broadcast provisions of the 1934 Act, then codified in 1984 and 1992.

The FCC is by no means the only authority of its kind. State utility commissions and municipal franchise boards operate as little clones beneath it. Above, though far less powerful, stands the International Telecommunications Union (ITU). The same regulatory pattern is thus replicated at different scales, from the global ITU to the county cable commissions of Oshkosh and Okefenokee.

Each medium, each type of service, gets its own compendium of regulation. The rules that decide which medium will be regulated by whom, over which part of its length, and toward what purpose look like a sausage created by a fractious band of intoxicated butchers. Who's in charge depends on the medium: airwaves or wires, copper or coax, terrestrial or satellite. It depends on where the medium is deployed: on private premises, under local streets, in the air, or across state or international boundaries. And it depends on the matter at hand: franchise requirements, price regulations, carriage obligations, content restrictions, and so on.

Entry regulation—licensing—lies principally with the states for cable and local telephone franchises, but principally with federal authorities for terrestrial or satellite broadcasting. The power to regulate price lies mostly with the states for local telephone service, but mostly with the federal government for cable television and satellite services. Common-carriage obligations are determined by yet another mix of federal and state mandates. So are structural limits on cross-ownership, vertical integration, or the raw size of telecom conglomerates. Federal authorities assert control over some parts of content—political advertising and copyright, for example—while localities retain the power to define pornography.

To compound the confusion, each medium is regulated according to its own particular set of maps. The basic division for telephone is between federal and state regulators. Wireless services are under federal control, but the FCC is directed to promote "localism." Cable TV franchises typically track county lines. Direct broadcast satellites have national footprints.

A single wire can be regulated in a dozen different ways, by as many different authorities. So far as the same wire is used partly for local and partly for interstate telephone service, authority is carved up between the FCC and state regulators. But some channels on the same wire can also be used to provide cable television, and that entails a quite different division of regulatory authority, usually between the FCC and municipal franchisors. If the wire connects to a radio transmitter or antenna, jurisdictional lines of authority shift abruptly at the point where the signal switches medium. The 1996 Telecommunications Act attempts to rationalize some of the lines of regulatory authority. It creates as much new confusion as it resolves.

This book focuses on the FCC, but virtually everything I say applies equally well to its alter egos above and below. I do not even mean to be especially hard on the FCC. Many state and local commissions have performed as badly, and worse. Some significant part of the modern FCC's mission is to overrule and crowd out the reactionary, anticompetitive efforts of state bureaucrats below it, or international authorities above.

Still, the FCC is just a fairly typical and well-documented representative of its kind. As I shall argue, commissions small and large, local, state, national, and international, should have been extinguished years ago.

Orwell in Reverse

In 1934 the economic logic for centralized federal management of the telecosm was as solid and scientific as Marxism. Telephony had to be a monopoly—monopoly was cheaper, and without it, phones wouldn't all connect to each other. Broadcasting, or at least ownership of the airwaves, had to be monopolized, too, otherwise stations and receivers would connect in such profligate excess as to create "etheric bedlam." This was why we needed an FCC. And it was the advent of FCCs and the like that so horrified George Orwell. He knew they would grow and grow. By 1984 all control of all communication would have been totally centralized at last, in the Ministry of Love.

And yet, there was something deeply paradoxical about Orwell's ministry and our own, more modest realization of it. Bureaucracies do indeed gather things together. But why should bureaucratic impulses, which pull things into one place, prevail over the network itself, which spreads things apart? The telecosm permits people to distance themselves from bureaucratic citadels, states, and even nations, if they have to. It is the domain of the nowhere man.

So why not imagine Orwell played out in reverse? Why not a network recreating government in its own image—decentralized, egalitarian, ruled not by a commission but by common law, not by central planners but by decentralized courts, not by a tiny nucleus of political technocrats but by a vast, seething, uncoordinated mass of private citizens, associations, and corporations? Why not imagine order maintained not by a sort of federal air traffic control but the way pedestrians maintain it, through commonly accepted rules of conduct, enforced by common-law courts only if and when those common-law norms are transgressed?

4

Into the Labyrinth

Soon after printing presses arrived in England, Henry the Eighth resolved to own them all himself. In 1586 the Star Chamber limited the number of presses allowed in the kingdom. All presses had to be reported to the Stationer's Company. When unregistered presses proliferated anyway, the government tried to license books instead. Publication and importation of unlicensed books was barred by Star Chamber decree in 1637. It took independent printers until 1694—more than half a century—to put an end to this abominable licensing practice.

The framers of the Constitution learned their lesson from this. Federal licensing of the press in the United States was eliminated by ratification of the First Amendment on December 15, 1791. The Amendment blocked virtually all government attempts to impose "prior restraints" on presses or what they printed.

That takes care of paper and ink. But the First Amendment does not apply—or at least not quite so clearly courts of this century have said—to photons, phosphor, or fiber-optic glass. For electronic media, franchises, licenses, and permits remain the norm. You can't unroll the wire, turn on the transmitter, or launch the satellite until someone in government gives the nod.*

---

*Whether other, more ordinary functions should be licensed, too, is open to question, as one trial lawyer's examination of a witness revealed:
Q: Is that the only license you hold?
A: I have a marriage license.
Q: You're not a realtor or a plumber or anything else like that?
A: No. They don't require a license to have children, which they should.

Franchising Telephony

Business advertisements at the turn of the last century often carried the notation "Both Phones." As noted in chapter 3, telephone companies competed head-to-head in many markets. This was denounced as chaotic, a hindrance, a nuisance, and wasteful duplication.

Theodore Vail, the visionary president of AT&T from 1907 until his death in 1920, saw things that way, too. Monopoly was inevitable, and regulation was just fine. Vail was opposed only to outright takeover of his company by the government: "Government ownership would be an unregulated monopoly."

Regulators and economists have been justifying monopoly telephone service ever since. The benefit of connecting to the network that has the most subscribers eclipses all else. Moreover, one wireline phone company can serve a market more cheaply than two; competition just raises costs for all. If only one company is licensed, regulators can average prices and promote universal service. That's fairer, too. Or so the arguments run.

By 1934 most states had already empowered their utility commissions to shut down competition. The 1934 Communications Act specifically prohibited construction of new interstate lines unless the FCC first concluded that the specific facilities in question would serve the "public convenience and necessity." Congress spent little time agonizing whether the long-distance monopoly "was born of nature or created by its owners." Monopoly was better than the alternative. Strict entry regulation would protect against "the wastes of duplication."

In the late 1940s the Commission received several applications to construct private long-distance microwave networks. It authorized a few in areas where common-carrier service was unavailable. But it required private users to abandon their licenses once Bell caught up with private entrepreneurs. And the Commission steadfastly barred competition of any other kind.

It also refused to require Bell to interconnect with anyone else's microwave facilities. It backed and enforced Bell's own strict restrictions against piece-out and resale of long-distance services. The piece-out clauses in AT&T's tariffs prohibited anyone else from building competing parts of the long-distance network over flat terrain, for example, while reselling Bell services to carry traffic over mountains. AT&T would connect its private-line services only to ultimate customers. Customers and end users could buy AT&T's

services. Competing carriers, resellers, and operators of private networks could not.

Courts backed these restrictions wholeheartedly, sometimes with even more conviction than the Commission could muster on its own. In 1951 the Commission unexpectedly discovered a "national policy in international communications favor[ing] competition." It authorized a small radio-telegraph company to open competing circuits to Portugal and the Netherlands. But the Supreme Court ruled that the Commission had given too little attention to the blessings of monopoly. The "encouragement of competition as such," the court noted, "has not been considered the single or controlling reliance for safeguarding the public interest." In daring to authorize competition "wherever competition is reasonably feasible," the FCC had "abdicate[d] what would seem to us one of the primary duties imposed on it by Congress." Competition wasn't in the "public interest" as understood by Congress in 1934. The Commission had failed to articulate how it would be in 1951.

Franchising Equipment

"A man looks pretty small at a wedding," Thornton Wilder observed in *Our Town*. "All those good women standing shoulder to shoulder, making sure the knot's tied in a mighty public way." In due course, the Commissioners of the FCC would take on a similar role. They would stand there alongside Ma Bell herself, making quite sure there was no adulterous hanky-panky going on at the end of AT&T's wires.

In 1882 Bell acquired Western Electric, a successful manufacturer of telephone equipment. "Left to himself," Vail complained, "every manufacturer and every exchange man . . . would run off in different lines of development." That would never do. "[S]tandardizing the apparatus, and having it as nearly alike as possible for all places," he concluded, "would be a great advantage to the business generally." Bell's exchanges wouldn't connect to competitors' facilities; Bell's lines wouldn't, either.

In 1913 Bell placed "foreign attachment" provisions in all its tariffs. Connecting any non-Bell product to Bell's network was strictly prohibited. Thereafter Bell didn't sell equipment at all; it sold end-to-end service. Every particle of equipment between the mouth at one end and the ear at the other was to be supplied by Bell.

The 1934 Act casually swept equipment into the monopoly franchise along with everything else. It directed the Commission to regulate all "instrumentalities," "facilities," and "apparatus" that were "incidental to" transmission. That meant telephones, wires on private premises, and all else. Had they been around in 1934, every fax machine, every modem-equipped computer, and every video display, disk drive and keyboard beyond—every last component of what is now the Internet would have been covered by this provision, too.

In the 1950s the tiny Hush-A-Phone company began selling a metal cup that snapped onto the mouthpiece of a telephone to muffle the noise in crowded offices. Bell denounced the cup as illegal. After gravely weighing the matter for seven years, the FCC agreed. Gadgets like these might degrade signal quality or send destructive pulses of electricity through the network, it was ruled. They might impair "the quality and efficiency of telephone service, [cause] damage to telephone plant and facilities, or injur[e] telephone company personnel."

A federal appellate court eventually threw out that ruling. But it would take another thirty years to throw out the legal mandate that stood behind it and open the market to competitive manufacture of telephones, modems, and communicating computers.

Zoning Out Computers

The walls that protected Bell also confined it. Most significant, they would end up isolating Bell from the universe of computing. Newton stood on the shoulders of giants; the FCC stood on their feet.

In the 1960s bigger computers were better. Computers occupied whole rooms and had armies of attendants. According to Grosch's Law, the efficiency of a computer increased in proportion to its size. So computing for the masses depended on time-sharing. Small, dumb terminals would connect to large, central mainframes over the phone lines. "[I]t is clear," the FCC confidently declared in 1966, "that data processing cannot survive, much less develop further, except through reliance upon and use of communication facilities and services." Steve Jobs and Steve Wozniak, both youngsters at the time, apparently neglected to read this pronouncement from Washington. But their stand-alone Apple computer still lay years in the future.

Meanwhile the Commission studied whether to pull the new industry out of the wild and domesticate it within the regulated telephone franchise. The telephone itself had been invented as an improvement on the telegraph. It now appeared that the computer might dramatically improve on the telephone. The Internet and the Web weren't yet part of the vocabulary, but the possibility of such networks was already apparent.

By the late 1960s, however, the FCC was beginning to tire of phone company monopolies and all the regulatory responsibilities they entailed. It decided not to take on the regulation of computing, too. That raised a new challenge: how to draw an intelligent line between communications inside the regulated franchise and data processing outside.

The Commission decided that the only workable approach was rigid apartheid. Computer-supplied "enhanced services," the Commission declared, should not be intermingled with basic telephony at all. There was to be "maximum separation" between voice services and data processing, between telephone and computer. Like any other business, a phone company could own and operate computers, but only for its own, in-house purposes. Bell's computers, with all their power to store and compute, were to be kept completely out of sight of Bell customers.

In 1966, in its first Computer Inquiry, the FCC erected a regulatory barrier between "data processing," "hybrid data processing," "hybrid communications," and "pure communications." Litigation over that stew of regulatory words ended in 1973. Three years later the Commission launched Computer Inquiry II. This proceeding proposed two new definitions: "basic services," which Bell would be permitted to provide, and electronic "enhancements," which it would not. These rules took four years to finalize. By then AT&T had already introduced an early version of voice messaging in some of its telephone exchanges. AT&T cancelled the new service, and Bell technicians were sent in to haul the offending equipment off the premises.

Zoning Out Video

Pictures were evicted, too. In the 1950s the FCC had concluded that cable television was a strictly local business and therefore beneath the FCC's regulatory radar. Cable prospered, and by 1966 the Commission had discovered that cable was really "interstate" after all. Telephone companies therefore needed FCC licenses to do cable.

Seventeen phone companies that were already providing cable service applied for the necessary papers. In 1970 the Commission said no and made the ban universal and permanent. Phone companies would be permitted to provide video "channel service"—raw transport—but not video programming. Federal authority had been engaged only to make sure that phone companies stayed out of the new market; local regulators continued to decide who would be let in. In 1984, with no debate, Congress codified the FCC's prohibition in a new Cable Act. That completed the legal separation of telephones from televisions.

The Airwaves

In 1922 Bell had put a radio station, WEAF, on the air in New York City. David Sarnoff, Westinghouse, and the Radio Corporation of America (RCA) planned to operate radio stations at a loss to promote the sale of radios. Bell's radio station planned to sell airtime. It would sell any willing buyer—such as advertisers, perhaps—slices of time on Bell's radio. The buyers could occupy their serving of ether however they pleased.

Giving away the broadcast razor to sell the radio blade worked for a while but couldn't last. RCA and its partners had mistakenly assumed that radio could prosper in the same manner as telephony, with profits tied to the hardware at the end of the connection. But without a wire, you couldn't tie the knot. Once radio patents expired, anyone could build a radio and tune in whatever was out there. Bell's model— common carriage for radio advertisers—was the more viable approach. Bell made solid profits in the first few years of its operations, while RCA lost money.

There was one other viable option, of course—which was not to broadcast at all. Scrambling and addressing are as good as wire if you handle them right. Had Bell been allowed to stay in the business, it would surely have pushed its original scheme to its logical end soon enough. That logical end was not broadcasting or advertisers or anything like them. It was cellular telephony—a far more valuable service.

Scarcity

Broadcasting couldn't be sustained by the sale of radios because any set could pick up any signal. This was also the biggest technical problem that the young broadcast industry faced. Nobody would receive anything useful at all if two or more transmitters sent out signals on the same frequency.

The industry and the courts gradually began to hammer out property rights in the airwaves to limit interference. Once they established their own homesteads, however, radio broadcasters grew hostile to later arrivals. They didn't want to wait for interference quarrels to be resolved in court; they didn't want any more settlers on the prairie at all. They persuaded themselves, and others, that the airwaves were inherently scarce and would have to be nationalized completely—with grandfather clauses, of course, for anyone already in place.

Congress signed on in the Radio Act of 1927. It established as federal truth a simple falsehood: The airwaves had to be owned and licensed by the federal government because of inherent "scarcity" in the stratosphere.

Thereafter the licensing of broadcasters would be conceptually straightforward. First the Commission would zone the real estate, assigning large blocks of spectrum for particular uses such as FM radio or VHF TV. Then it would slice each block into smaller licenses and assign them to individual users.

The Commission chose licensees pretty much as it pleased. If you were lucky enough to win the Commission's favor, you got your license for free. But spectrum was in fact worth a lot. The Treasury could not have been more popular if it had been issuing licenses for people to help themselves at the mint. Demand for FCC licenses far exceeded supply. So the Commission held "comparative hearings"— Miss America–like pageants, complete with exhibitions of eccentric talent and suggestive posturing in various states of corporate undress. Like Miss America herself, winners didn't keep their crowns forever. The 1927 Radio Act expressly declared that licensees got no "property rights." Licenses typically expired after three, five, or seven years. They could not be transferred without Commission approval. And so far as the drafters of the 1927 Act were concerned, licenses could be revoked whenever the Commission saw fit.

The First Amendment notwithstanding, all this was perfectly constitutional. The Supreme Court itself was sure of it. It explained why in a 1943 opinion by Justice Frankfurter. "[T]here is a fixed natural limitation upon the number of stations that can operate without interfering with one another"; a comprehensive federal licensing scheme was thus needed to prevent "etheric bedlam."

It has been said that if all else fails, immortality can always be assured by spectacular error. This was how Frankfurter assured his.

Zoning Out Bell

The early radio broadcasters feared competition from others like themselves, but they were absolutely terrified of Bell. For a time, however, it had been AT&T that feared radio. Marconi had conceived of radio as a messaging system, principally for ships. The wireless telegraph had quickly evolved into a wireless telephone—radio communication of human speech first occurred on Christmas Eve, 1906, between Brant Rock, Massachusetts, and ships in the Atlantic Ocean.

With the technology of the day, however, radio's best use was for broadcasting. AT&T recognized this and got into broadcasting. Other radio companies united in denouncing AT&T's incursion onto their turf. Friends may come and go, Bell learned, but enemies accumulate. In Congress and elsewhere the alarm was sounded: no monopoly in radio. This was code, and what it really meant was no competition from Bell.

AT&T got the message. In 1926 it sold its flagship radio station, WEAF, to RCA for $1 million. AT&T agreed to get out of the local end of broadcasting entirely. RCA then used WEAF as the centerpiece of its wholly owned broadcasting subsidiary, the National Broadcasting Corporation. NBC soon came to dominate radio broadcasting almost as completely as AT&T dominated telephony.

The Radio Act of 1927 finalized the separation. It reaffirmed the general prohibition against "monopoly" of the airwaves. And it flatly forbade any operation of broadcast stations as common carriers. If an operator of a radio station had stumbled on the idea of cellular telephony in 1930 and had simply begun using its spectrum to provide such a service, it would have lost its federal license.

Zoning Out Brokers

Despite the Commission's best efforts, feckless broadcasters kept drifting toward the forbidden domain of common carriage. In 1941 the Commission announced that while some "time brokering" might be tolerated, a broadcaster could not surrender control over the content of its airwaves.

After failing to prosper with black-oriented broadcasting, an FM radio station in New Jersey began selling most of its time in large units to brokers, who resold it to numerous small, eager buyers, including many foreign-language broadcasters, producers of ethnic programming, and individuals. As it would subsequently explain in a legal brief, the station ended up broadcasting material in "Spanish (45.5 hours); Italian (35.5 hours); Greek (10 hours); Hungarian (4 hours); Arabic (2.5 hours); Polish (2.75 hours); Brazilian (2.05 hours); Portuguese (2 hours); Lithuanian (1 hour); Slovakian (55 minutes); Croatian (.5 hours); Albanian (.5 hours); Ukrainian (.5 hours); Roumanian (.5 hours); Armenian (.5 hours); Yugoslavian (.5 hours); Bulgarian (.5 hours); Norwegian (.5 hours). By 1972, WHBI also broadcast in Korean, Macedonian, Urdu, Hindi, Bengali, Japanese, and Russian."

It is not clear that all of these are real languages, but in any event, this was more diversity than "the public interest" could tolerate. In 1976 the Commission refused to renew the station's license. A station could sell a bit of its time to advertisers—even to a single advertiser that sponsors a particular show on a regular basis. The station could surrender a large part of its time to a national network. It could sell twenty-four hours of time for Jerry Lewis's telethon. But it could not sell its time retail, to numerous small, individual buyers. That would make it too much like a phone company.

Zoning Content

In 1961 FCC Chairman Newton Minnow declared himself shocked to discover that television had turned into a "vast wasteland." To paraphrase author Harlan Ellison, the state of American television today can be found somewhere between the Okefenokee Swamp and Love Canal. It is a polluted stream of tabloid lunacy. Almost everyone but broadcasters themselves knows this to be true. What is often forgotten is that this despoliation has occurred under the watchful eye of a federal commission that has had almost absolute control over the airwaves for seven decades.

As short-term tenants, broadcasters are allowed to use the premises only in ways approved in advance by the landlord. The 1927 Act didn't expressly require broadcasters to provide specific kinds of programming. But by 1930 the new Federal Radio Commission had announced that every licensee was expected to offer "a well rounded program schedule, in which entertainment, religion, education and instruction, important public events, discussions of public questions, weather, market reports, news and matters of interest to all members of the family find a place." "The tastes, needs and desires of all substantial groups among the public" were to be met "in fair proportion." In 1946 the FCC published its *Public Service Responsibility of Broadcast Licensees*, better known as the Blue Book.

The next edition, issued in 1960, described fourteen kinds of programming "usually necessary to meet the public interest, needs and desires of the community." In 1964 the Commission officially frowned on an application for a UHF TV station because the applicant had stated that 70 percent of its programming would be entertainment and 30 percent would be educational, with no airtime devoted to other categories of service. The Commission continued to tinker and fiddle with the official menu. It adopted a guideline that suggested 10 percent of programming be informational. It announced it would question any license application proposing less than 5 percent local and less than 5 percent informational programming. Broadcasters followed Commission "guidelines" with meticulous care. They all knew where they would have to go to get their licenses renewed.

When the Commission's enthusiasm for this sort of nonsense began to flag, courts reminded it of its duties. In 1970 a classical music radio station tried to sell out to new owners with other plans. Declaring that it would no longer act as a "national arbiter of taste," the Commission approved the transfer. An appellate court ordered the Commission to think again. "The Commission is not dictating tastes," the court declared, "when it seeks to discover what they presently are, and to consider what assignment of channels is feasible and fair in terms of their gratification." In a follow-up case in 1973 the Commission refused to conduct a hearing on the transfer of a radio station that was to replace classical music with top-forty fare. The appellate court overruled again. "[P]reservation of a format that would otherwise disappear, although economically and technologically viable and preferred by a significant number of listeners, is generally in the public interest."

The needs of children have been the subject of special FCC pronouncements for thirty-six years. Congress added its own exhortations in the Children's Television Act of 1990. The Commission has solemnly defined key terms such as "children" and "educational or informational" programming. *The Jetsons*, the Commission recently ruled, is not educational, notwithstanding the cogent argument that the cartoon portrays family values in the high-tech future.

All of which proves that official ignorance is never out of style. It was in fashion yesterday, it is the rage today, and it will set the pace tomorrow.* Amidst all the pompous and foolish blather, all the public-interest posturing, all the treacly sermons about the nation's youth, a single truth has never been officially uttered: "Educational television" is an oxymoron. Television doesn't fill a young mind, it drains it. Turn the set off.

Localism

Genius may have its limitations, but stupidity is not thus handicapped. The FCC did not merely promote swamp, or children's

---

*I am quoting Franklin K. Dane.

swamp; it demanded that the swamp be of local origin and manufacture. Federal regulators labored to keep broadcast close to home.

The 1927 Radio Act required no less. It divided the country into five zones. Amendments enacted a year later directed that each zone get equal treatment in the licensing arena. Licenses were to be distributed "among the several states and communities as to provide a fair, efficient and equitable distribution of radio service to each of the same."

The Commission set in place elaborate procedures to dole out spectrum accordingly. In 1933 the Supreme Court itself had occasion to note that the "deletion of WIBO and WPCC would reduce the over-quota status of the State of Illinois and the Fourth Zone by .88 unit and .45 unit, respectively, and would increase the quota of Indiana by .43 unit." To promote localism, broadcast transmitters were typically allowed a footprint with a radius of about twenty-five miles. Local stations were required to carry "responsive" programming—live shows, locally produced, using local talent and addressing local issues.

But here again, something had been missed. This time it was economic reality. Efficient programming requires a far larger scope of operation. And TV viewers in Oshkosh are more interested in sights from Hollywood than sights of Main Street, which they can already discern outside their windows. So broadcasters formed national networks. Their lawyers simply built by contract and affiliation what their engineers were not permitted to build with radios and towers. The same result would have been achieved if the FCC had simply issued national broadcast licenses directly to the networks themselves.

The Labyrinth

I have described only some of the larger and more conspicuous walls of the labyrinth. There are hundreds of others, all ostensibly there to protect America from monopoly. Taken together, the rules resemble the most intricate and incomprehensible provisions of the tax code. They are understood only by a tiny club of highly specialized lawyers, who charge exorbitant fees to steer entrepreneurs through the byzantine legal complexities.

Consider one example: The Oshkosh Telephone Company (Osh-Tel) may own WOSK, a TV station in Oshkosh, but not Oshkosh Cable. OshTel may own one but not two cellular licenses in Oshkosh. WOSK may not own WOSH, a second TV station in Oshkosh; the same goes for owning two AM radio stations, or two FM stations, or a TV station and a radio station.

But the owner of the WOSK AM radio station may also own WOSK FM; for a time the Commission positively encouraged alliances of that kind. The Commission also loosened its Waiver Standards to allow combinations of radio with UHF or VHF TV. Oshkosh Cable may not affiliate with WOSK voluntarily, but it is required to carry WOSK's signals involuntarily if WOSK so demands. Oshkosh may not own a terrestrial wireless cable alternative. But it may own Primestar or DirectTV—DBS satellite broadcasters that blanket the whole country and represent Oshkosh Cable's most immediate competitor.

Oshkosh TV is not merely permitted but is required to combine content and conduit into a single, integrated service; uncoupling the two by way of schemes such as "time brokering" is strictly prohibited. WOSH AM radio may not affiliate with the *Oshkosh Daily News*, but may affiliate with General Electric, a $60 billion-a-year corporation that owns NBC.* Oshkosh Cable, by contrast, is permitted to affiliate with the *Daily News* but not with NBC—even if NBC has no broadcast affiliate in Oshkosh. Or that, at least, was the rule until 1996.

Other Commission rules outlaw corporate obesity. In the 1940s the Commission forced NBC to spin off one of its two broadcast networks. Later the Commission prohibited joint ownership of more than six FM radio stations, three television stations, or seven AM radio stations. In 1984 the Commission repudiated most of these limits as "anachronistic" but left in place an interim twelve-station rule. The 1996 Act contains intricate limits on how many commercial radio stations a party may own or operate in various markets (anywhere from five to eight, depending on how many other stations operate in the same market). The FCC may waive any of these rules if it determines

---

*Consider one more eye-glazing example, straight from 1996 legislation that was supposed to deregulate things. OshTel may not own Oshkosh Cable—unless the town of Oshkosh has fewer than thirty-five thousand inhabitants and lies outside an urbanized area, as defined by the Bureau of the Census. There is an exception to the exception if OshTel already serves too many cable households in Okefenokee. And an exception to the exception to the exception: If Oshkosh is not one of the top twenty-five cable markets and is already served by two cable systems, OshTel may buy the smaller one—provided three other requirements are met. And a further exception: OshTel may buy into any cable system that serves no more than twenty thousand cable subscribers if no more than twelve thousand of those subscribers live within an urbanized area and if Oshtel earns under $100 million a year (Telecommunications Act of 1996 §302(a) (to be codified at 47 U.S.C. §652(d)(1–5)). And a further completely discretionary exception: the FCC may waive any of these proscriptions if enforcing them might entail "undue economic distress" or would bankrupt Oshkosh Cable, or if the deal generally serves the public interest, or "the convenience and needs of the community to be served," and if local authorities concur (Telecommunications Act of 1996 §302(a) (to be codified at 47 U.S.C. §652(d)(6)).

that higher concentrations of ownership will increase the number of radio stations in operation.

Another FCC rule of the 1980s prohibited joint ownership of TV stations that reached over 25 percent of households nationwide. Today's rules allow common ownership of twenty AM, twenty FM, or twelve television stations, but still subject to a 25 percent overall limit. No similar rules were extended to cable, however, until Congress called for them in the 1992 Cable Act. Now the rule is that no single cable operator may reach more than 30 percent of U.S. households.

The 1996 Act swept aside several existing ownership limits on broadcast TV stations and created a new one: No terrestrial TV network may own stations that reach more than 35 percent of the national audience. But any operator of a direct broadcast satellite lawfully reaches 100 percent of the same market. The 1996 Act also codifies a rule permitting a single entity to own up to half of all radio stations in markets served by ten or fewer commercial radio stations, but no more than eight stations in markets served by more than forty-four stations. No known economic theory explains why a 50 percent market share is acceptable in Oshkosh, while 18 percent is tops in Chicago.

Apartheid in the Telecosm

The power to license gave the FCC a double-layered power to regulate. First, the Commission could control entry. It could maintain telephone as a monopoly. It could exclude AT&T from broadcasting. It could admit new wireless providers when it felt like it, and not before. Second, the Commission could limit and condition licenses as it pleased. It could zone computer services and video out of telephone lines and time brokers off the airwaves. It could force phone companies to provide nothing but pure transport and force broadcasters to provide a fully integrated bundle of transport and content. The Commission did all of these things, again and again.

Each little wall in the labyrinth was erected with good intentions— to promote localism, competition, diversity, new technology, or the welfare of children. But taken all together, in all their pathological complexity, they created paralysis. They immobilized bandwidth, wired and wireless, in a stifling cocoon of regulation. Each little walled-off industry became corpulent, complacent, and grotesquely uncompetitive, like a prize pig confined to a tiny sty. The more the

Commission claimed to protect consumers from monopoly, the more it in fact protected monopoly from competition.

It is now clear beyond serious dispute that the Commission's schemes for maintaining apartheid in the telecosm have cost the national economy hundreds of billions of dollars. The losses continue to mount to this day, at a rate of tens of billions of dollars a year.

II

DECONSTRUCTING
THE TELECOSM

5

Cable

The growing telephone industry needed fatter wires. Bell installed its first coaxial cables in New York in 1936. "Coax" could carry huge amounts of information with high fidelity. It would supply many of the high-capacity trunks of the telephone network until the end of World War II.

Bell began using cable to distribute network programs to local television affiliates in the late 1940s. Private entrepreneurs soon came up with an even better idea: A cable that could feed video to TV stations could feed it straight to homes. In 1948 John Walson began running coax cable from residences in Mahonay City, Pennsylvania, to a large hilltop antenna that could pick up broadcast signals blocked by nearby mountains. This was the first "community antenna." Entrepreneurs like Walson then began installing microwave systems to beam in broadcast signals picked up even farther afield. And then satellites.

At first the FCC viewed cable as a strictly local matter, too parochial to be of federal concern. Cable was broadcast without spectrum, and so no one in Washington could take it very seriously; it was like surfing in Nebraska.

Yet right from the start, cable offered something radically different. Until then TV channels in any given area had been counted in the single digits. Now suddenly there could be dozens. The broadcasters were taken aback, much as someone humming in the bath would be taken aback to be suddenly joined by the massed choirs of the Russian Army. The broadcasters made their discomfort known to federal authorities. The Commission abruptly announced it would regulate cable after all.

The Commission lacked the resources, however, to oversee the deployment of new wire networks in every city and town in the country. It decided to become a regulators' regulator instead. Each local authority would franchise a cable operator for its community. The FCC would set out general rules for all. Congress eventually codified this management plan in 1984.

Cable was on track to become yet another telecom utility, just like telephone. It would get protection from competition—along with tight limits on how cable itself would compete.

Franchising for Profit

Local authorities soon discovered they could prosper by diverting cable's monopoly profits to themselves. In the 1970s and 1980s would-be cable operators competed fiercely for the monopoly privileges, pledging millions of dollars to support services favored by local worthies. The FCC took on an unfamiliar role, trying to limit just how far other regulators could go. From 1972 on, the FCC insisted that local regulators seize no more than 5 to 10 percent of cable's gross revenues.

So local authorities began to accept noncash payments instead— free wiring of school systems, studios for local high schools, free channels for politically favored organizations, and free TV sets for city officials. Contenders for a local franchise retained prominent citizens to back their case. Companies bidding for a cable license would hand out stock to political insiders. Community groups were bought off with promises of cash, video equipment, or future access to channels. Influence peddling, bribery, and other forms of graft proliferated.

The FCC realized that regulating noncash deals was impractical. Congress codified the 5 percent cap in 1984 but made no attempt to restrict other forms of payment. It simultaneously stripped the FCC of most authority to address franchise fee disputes. None of this addressed the root economic problem. Cable monopolies were creations of local regulation. All the haggling was about how the take would be divided up between people who operated the monopoly wires and people who enforced the monopoly laws.

The Exclusive Franchise

A cable operator who shared generously got in return full protection from competition. In the 1960s some franchises contained an express commitment that no other applicant would be licensed. By the 1980s exclusivity had become the almost universal (though often unwritten) practice. A 1992 survey found head-to-head competition in only fifty communities across the country.

The owners of apartment buildings, hospitals, and hotels could readily compete if allowed to. They simply set up their own rooftop antennas and satellite dishes and deployed their own private cable. This Satellite Master Antenna Television (SMATV)—"private cable"—can often be offered much more cheaply than public cable. Subscribers are clustered together, private property is more secure, and you don't have to give free service to the mayor.

Franchise authorities denounced all forms of private cable as "cream skimming," an antisocial threat to universal service. For a period the courts agreed. One common way to thwart new entrants was to require every cable operator to provide service on day one to every home in the franchise area. Cable, the authorities declared, was a natural monopoly. Competitive eruptions on private premises were inefficient and therefore illegal.

In one early and influential appellate decision, the ordinarily sensible Judge Richard Posner accepted this reasoning and so rejected a First Amendment challenge brought by an unfranchised SMATV operator. Exclusive franchising of cable was justified because it enabled the franchise authority to grant "the most efficient competitor" a monopoly in exchange for a promise "to provide reasonable service at reasonable rates." Competition would end up in monopoly in any event. There would be "wasteful duplication of facilities" in the interim.

Backyard satellite dishes skim the cream one household at a time. Private dishes began popping up like huge metallic mushrooms outside hotels, bars, and individual homes. Over 40 percent of dishes were sold to households that could have subscribed to cable. Some states and local authorities tried to ban private dishes, ostensibly for aesthetic reasons.

The FCC gradually curtailed local authority over private master-antenna cable systems. Then the Commission began chipping away at zoning rules aimed at suppressing competition from home dishes. The Commission thus found itself in the unfamiliar but dignified position of promoting competition by suppressing other commissions located lower in the regulatory food chain.

All the while, however, the FCC kept firmly in place the most anti-competitive restriction of all. Telephone companies had invented coax; they presented a far graver competitive threat to cable than a satellite dish in somebody's backyard. The Commission had driven telephone companies out of the video business in 1970, and Congress had codified that quarantine in 1984. It would remain in effect until 1996.

Zoning Out Distant Signals

Early cable operators faced a second big problem: They had no programming of their own. What they did have was the power to import broadcast television from far away. In effect, cable could thus force local TV stations to compete against each other in ways the FCC licensing authorities had never contemplated or intended. Boosted by cable, a New York station could reach residents of Boston, and the sleepless in Seattle could watch late night television from San Francisco. Before cable, local broadcasters had operated within a comfortable, closely knit oligopoly. Most communities received only a handful of over-the-air stations. With cable, they could receive dozens.

But for the Commission, competition would have unfolded quickly. Cable operators would have negotiated with distant broadcasters for permission to deliver signals to distant viewers. Many broadcasters—those affiliated with the big three networks—would have refused at first. The networks would not have chosen to upset relations with their local affiliates by putting one affiliate into competition with another. But the independent stations, particularly those in the UHF band, would have had no such qualms. And the networks themselves would eventually have arranged to let cable operators import distant signals into communities where the networks had no broadcast affiliate at all.

Before long the networks would have recognized that their local broadcast affiliates weren't so essential after all. They would have begun to treat broadcast and cable as alternative delivery vehicles for national programming. The tight contracts and exclusive dealing between national television networks and local broadcasters would have eroded. Cable and broadcast would have competed fiercely for the right to carry the national networks.

But none of this happened. Market forces were crushed by a single disastrous ruling from the Supreme Court and by the FCC's equally disastrous reaction to it.

In a landmark decision in 1968 the Supreme Court concluded that over-the-air broadcasts were supposed to be free. For that reason broadcasters, and the networks behind them, couldn't enforce copyrights against cable-company pirates. Cable could retransmit broadcast television with impunity.

That, however, threatened the entire economic underpinning of advertiser-supported broadcasting. National commercials for Coke or Pepsi might be equally effective in Seattle or San Francisco, but advertising by local used-car dealers wouldn't be. If broadcast signals were retransmitted over cable willy-nilly, residents of Seattle could tune in to *I Love Lucy* without ever being enticed to visit Gordon's Give-Away Pontiac—*Lucy's* sponsor in San Francisco. San Francisco viewers might watch the same program together with commercials from the Greater Buick Association of Seattle. The value of broadcast advertising in both cities would plummet.

The FCC responded by hounding cable out of any competition of that sort. To begin with, the FCC insisted that cable carry local TV stations first and foremost, in privileged positions, low on the TV dial. That single directive swallowed up more than half the channels available on the early cable systems, commensurately reducing the number of possible imports. Then, as I discuss further in chapter 15, the Commission adopted a slew of "nonduplication," "syndicated exclusivity," and "anti-leapfrogging" rules. These barred imports that would duplicate local broadcast fare.

As intended, the effect was to cripple cable as a direct, competing distributor of broadcast-network programming. Cable, the Commission effectively decreed, was to complement broadcasting, not substitute for it.

Both mistakes grew directly out of the legal framework created by Congress in the Radio Act of 1927. The Supreme Court would never have messed up copyright law so badly if Congress hadn't first sanctified the whole edifice of free broadcasting. And the FCC then would have had far less cause to suppress cable so vehemently if copyright laws and network contracts had stayed in place to protect the broadcasters' legitimate interests.

Zoning Out Cable Programming

Cable's second major competitive opportunity was as a programmer in its own right. As CNN, ESPN, and dozens of other cable networks would subsequently confirm, the new cable industry was poised to challenge the news desks, sports anchors, and sitcom producers of the national networks and their local affiliates. For two decades, however, the FCC suppressed that too.

No fundamental law of economics declares that consumers must pay for TV programming only through their purchases of Devil Dogs and Doritos. As early as 1952 applicants sought FCC licenses to provide pay-TV on scrambled UHF or VHF signals. But the FCC had learned never to rush into a job without a lifetime of consideration. Tomorrow always held the possibility for new technologies, astounding discoveries, and a reprieve from the Commission's obligations. There was always next year.

In 1961 the Commission finally authorized one tiny trial—a three-year study to be conducted over a single local UHF station in Hartford, Connecticut. The trial was doomed by regulation before it even began. The station was to be subject to all broadcast television regulations and was required to air at least twenty-eight hours of conventional television programming each week. In 1968 the Commission finally authorized permanent pay-TV operations, but subject to equally crippling restrictions. Pay-TV was permitted only to operate as a "beneficial supplement" to free television; it was not to be "duplicative of the programming of free TV." Programs, audiences, and talent were not to be "siphoned" away from free television, because the public already had a "tremendous investment . . . in television receivers based on the expectation of free service." With conditions like these, the Commission might just as well not have bothered. It didn't want the trials to succeed.

As the Commission saw it, cable television presented all the same antisocial perils as pay-TV. In 1968, however, a federal appellate court casually upheld broad FCC regulation on that basis. "Indiscriminate [cable] development, feeding upon the broadcast service, is capable of destroying large parts of it," the court reasoned. "The public interest in preventing such a development is manifest."

Soon after, the FCC extended its anti-siphoning rules to cable. The rules baldly reserved all the most popular programming for the broadcast networks. Cablecasters were strictly forbidden to bid for popular feature films, sports programming, or series programming like soap operas. Broadcast, the beer-and-pretzel distributor, was to be protected from cable, which—the Commission was quite sure of this—would cater only to consumers of Campari and canapes. To crown it all, the Commission proscribed most advertising on pay cable channels. Advertiser-supported cable, it appeared, might become too cheap and so threaten free television even more.

Separating Broadcast and Cable

The FCC had slotted cable into the one narrow market niche that the Commission believed it was destined to occupy. Cable's lot in life was to serve as fancy rabbit ears for the fancy rich. It would be required to carry broadcast television before it carried anything else. And it would be forbidden to outbid broadcast television for anything at all.

In these circumstances, one would have supposed, cable companies would have been encouraged to team up with local broadcasters. Since the two weren't going to compete, they might as well cooperate, perhaps even merge. But that too was outlawed. In 1970 the FCC categorically forbade joint ownership of broadcast television and cable systems in the same market. Like the cable/telephone ban, this ban was codified by Congress in 1984.

If all the other rules that barred competition between them had not been promulgated first, separating broadcast television and cable would have made some sense. In 1970 cable still operated largely as a community antenna. The community antenna boosted the effective power of broadcast stations; cable's main effect was thus to promote competition among broadcasters by pulling in distant signals to compete against local ones. There was, therefore, some reason to permit alliances between cable and out-of-area broadcasters while forbidding similar alliances within a single service area.

But the out-of-area alliances were forbidden, too. In 1974 the Supreme Court upheld cable's right to pirate distant broadcast signals, just as it had already accepted cable piracy of local broadcasts. The FCC responded with an array of rules designed to prevent this piracy from getting completely out of hand. And it reaffirmed cable's duty to fill half or more of its channels with local TV broadcasts.

In effect, the Commission thus required cable to do under duress what cable had been forbidden to do by choice. Cable was strictly forbidden to collaborate directly with local broadcasters on any mutually agreeable terms. Cable was strictly required, however, to collaborate with local broadcasters on terms prescribed by the Commission. As a result, 60 percent of U.S. households can today receive eight or more television channels both over the air and by wire. This represents a phenomenal waste of transmission capacity, all brought about by the

Commission that was established in 1927 to husband the nation's desperately "scarce" spectrum.

Cablecasting and the First Amendment

Why didn't the First Amendment protect cable operators from all
these constraints on what cable could "publish"? For the first two
decades of its life, cable's freedom of speech was simply lost somewhere in the arcane interstices of the 1934 Communications Act.

The Act had given the FCC virtually complete control over broadcasters. But for wireline carriers, the Act left a lot of authority with
the states. After some early equivocation, the FCC decided that it
didn't want states to manage cable; federal authorities would do the
job better. But to place control over cable completely in federal
hands, the Commission had to classify cable as just a variation on
over-the-air broadcasting. And the trouble with that—for cable operators—was that by the time cable arrived on the scene, broadcasters
had already pretty much lost all their First Amendment rights.

Justice Felix Frankfurter had so declared in his spectacularly misguided 1943 ruling, the one rationalized by the specter of "etheric
bedlam." Spectrum was "scarce"—that justified federal licensing and
all manner of other regulation of content, fairness, and so forth.
When cable operators first began claiming free-speech rights in the
late 1960s, courts simply analogized cable to broadcast, quoted
Frankfurter, and threw the operators out.

They kept coming back, however, and courts at last woke up to the
obvious. Whatever one might say about spectrum, there is nothing
inherently scarce about metal wire wrapped in plastic. Regulating
wire because spectrum was "scarce" had it exactly backward. Cable
marked the end of scarcity. Deregulating cable would replace scarcity
with abundance.

In 1977 the FCC's anti-siphoning policies—the rules that said cable
could not bid against television for the best movies and sports
events—arrived before an appellate court in Washington, D.C. "In
these proceedings," the court dryly noted, "the Commission has
changed its vocabulary from the pejorative 'siphoning' to the more
neutral term 'migration.'" They might call it pasta, but it was still
spaghetti; a new vocabulary was not enough. The Commission could
not outlaw siphoning without strong evidence that it was a real problem. The Commission didn't have any. Its rules had been based on
mere "speculation and innuendo." Moreover, the anti-siphoning
rules couldn't be reconciled with the First Amendment. Virtually

identical rules had been upheld in the context of pay-TV, but that was broadcast. The scarcity logic might apply there, but it didn't apply here. No argument based on economic scarcity or natural monopoly could justify the rules, either. The anti-siphoning rules had to go.

The FCC now radically changed its course. The anti-siphoning rules were eliminated, and cable flourished.

A simple economic fact quickly become apparent: Viewers value programming more than advertisers value viewers. Subscribers might be willing to pay a dollar or more per viewing hour to see a recent feature film, while advertisers were willing to pay only three cents per viewer. Thus a cash-paying audience of one million could easily buy a film away from a Doritos-crunching audience of ten million—if distribution markets made possible this kind of contest. Cable did. It could therefore outbid in-the-clear ("free") broadcasters for almost any kind of programming.

Every student of the industry has since learned what any competent economist would have predicted decades earlier: Letting people buy and sell things doesn't create scarcity, it creates plenty. We could require newspapers to be supported by advertising alone, but by permitting readers to pay for the *New York Times* we get more newspaper overall, not less.

Any pay-as-you-go policy is politically hard to swallow, however, when consumers have grown accustomed to things being free. Regulation-minded politicians have therefore persisted in their crusade to limit what for-pay media may buy. As recently as 1984 some local authorities were still trying to forbid cable to bid for certain sports events. In 1992 Congress considered empowering local authorities to set rates for pay-per-view championship sports events, but ended up just directing the FCC to "investigate and analyze." The Commission duly announced in 1993 that migration of programming was not much of a problem, but it also insisted that "widely popular sports events [must] remain available to the public via free, over-the-air television." The Commission vowed "to take appropriate regulatory action" if the American citizen's right to watch interminable hours of free sports should ever be put in jeopardy by the intolerable intervention of free markets.

So far no one has tested that promise against the First Amendment. When someone finally does, the Commission will lose. No comparable law would pass constitutional muster if it limited *Time* magazine's right to bid for a Pulitzer-prize-winning novel. Time-Warner's bidding to buy the Super Bowl for cable is constitutionally indistinguishable.

The Inclusive Franchise

Courts have now established that cable operators, unlike broadcasters, have real First Amendment rights. In winning these cases, however, cable inadvertently opened a second door it would have much preferred to have left closed. If a commission can't keep one newspaper from publishing what it likes, it can't bar a second newspaper from publishing, either. Why should cable be any different?

The watershed case was brought by Preferred Communications, Inc. (PCI), a cable operator, against the City of Los Angeles. PCI had not participated in the city's franchise auction, through which Los Angeles had issued a single, exclusive cable franchise to serve each major area of the city. A federal appellate court agreed with PCI that exclusive franchising was constitutionally indefensible. The city's franchising procedures created an unacceptable risk of discrimination against cable operators who didn't cater to city officials in their choice of programming.

The case went up to the Supreme Court, which affirmed on narrower grounds and sent the matter back down for further fact-finding. Lower courts then declared invalid the city's exclusive franchising policy. The city need not offer unlimited access to its rights of way, but it may not limit access to just a single cable operator either. Two might suffice to pass First Amendment muster; one would not.

The FCC then curtailed the power of state regulators to interfere with Satellite Master Antenna alternatives. Cable operators challenged the order. Unleashing SMATV, they argued, was irreconcilable with a national policy to promote universal service. A federal appellate court disagreed. Local regulators could no more require SMATV operators to provide universal service by installing dishes everywhere than they could require these operators to install television sets or telephones on private property.

Exclusive franchises are not quite dead yet, but they are fading fast. A 1990 FCC report concluded that second entrants should be temporarily exempt from any universal service obligations, in order to encourage competition. The 1992 Cable Act prohibits "unreasonably" exclusive franchises. Some regulators will continue to insist that a natural-monopoly rationalization for an exclusive franchise is reasonable. But reasonableness does not suffice to make it constitutional.

And in any event, as I discuss in chapter 6, there is no natural monopoly. Cable is now being delivered without the cable, and without a local license, either.

Cable Retransmission and Cable Carriage

As cable matured, Congress was finally forced to correct the dreadful mistake the Supreme Court had made in 1968. That was the ruling that had permitted cable to pirate over-the-air broadcasts with impunity. In 1976 Congress revised the Copyright Act. Then in 1992 it revised cable law. As I discuss in chapter 15, these changes returned to broadcasters a considerable measure of control over the retransmission of their signals.

By simply reaffirming private rights in private property, Congress made it possible for the FCC to sweep aside the clumsy edifice of regulatory alternatives it had erected as substitutes. The FCC no longer had to cripple cable's right to import distant television signals. So long as they can secure permission from people who own programming, cable operators may buy programming wherever they like. They may program as much as they please. Or they may return to their origins as the community antenna, delivering only content created by others.

As cable shakes loose from the last of its quarantines, it will invade telephony and common carriage. Cable telephony is already booming overseas. In Britain, the incumbent local carrier is losing fifteen thousand subscribers a month to cable services, provided in large part by U.S. cable television companies working in collaboration with U.S. local telephone companies.

On this side of the Atlantic, the legal picture remained muddled until passage of the 1996 Act. When the FCC (in 1970) and Congress (in 1984) had barred phone companies from entering cable, they implicitly barred cable from entering telephony as well. The 1996 Act makes clear, however, that cable operators may provide voice, just as phone companies are now permitted to provide video. The walls between these two functionally interchangeable media have finally come down. One must wonder, in retrospect, why they were erected in the first place.

Metamorphosis

Cable began life as a community antenna, really more a carrier than anything else. But what it carried was the signals of broadcasters. This greatly confused federal and local regulators, whose respective spheres of authority had been defined and divided around the traditional models of pure carrier (telephone) or pure broadcaster (radio and television). From the 1960s to the 1990s the authorities took the worst of both regulatory models and piled them high on top of cable, to the point where they almost killed it.

How could good regulatory intentions lead to such bad regulatory policies? How has a single, quite simple medium—coaxial cable—succeeded in sowing such total confusion among so many intelligent lawmakers?

It was the proliferation of possibilities that left the Commission so confused. Like telephone, cable began as a local wireline network, and so it would be franchised by local authorities. Like television, however, cable was a one-to-many mass medium, and federal regulators had plenary authority over broadcasting. But cable also had plenty of room for its own programming, and that was not like anything that had come before. Cable was simply too capacious. It could do too many different things. It could evolve from one application to the next too quickly. Cable's regulators were creatures of the narrowband past. Cable was the prototype of the broadband future.

The old, orderly categories of technology and service codified in the 1934 Communications Act didn't fit, and couldn't be made to. They will never fit again. The simple, two-tier structure, carriage in one tier and broadcast in the other, has been demolished. Technology and the marketplace have walked away from the rubble. Only obsolescent laws and senescent commissions remain.

6

The Airwaves Unbound

Even the earliest cable systems could carry twelve channels. But there weren't twelve broadcast networks to pirate. So cable owners bankrolled Ted Turner to develop made-for-cable programming.

The new networks needed an efficient way to get *Gone with the Wind* from Turner in Atlanta to thousands of independent cable networks scattered across the country. The most efficient way, it turned out, was a new kind of broadcast.

And that, it turned out, marked the beginning of the end of broadcast regulation.

Mirror in the Sky

A relay satellite is a mirror in the sky. With more-powerful transmitters or more-sensitive receivers, the moon itself would serve, if only it didn't drift so much across the heavens. When parked in the right orbit, communications satellites stand still. An uplink transmitter sends a signal to a satellite transponder. The signal is regenerated and sent back down. It's really just plain old broadcasting, but from a mast twenty-three thousand miles tall. From that height, the transmitter's footprint spans one third of the globe.

Turner was the first to grasp the possibilities. He was already using microwave to distribute programming from his independent UHF Atlanta station to nearby cable operators. In 1975 Turner used a satellite to create the first national "superstation." For years the FCC had promoted the oxymoronic idea that broadcasting's mission was local-ism. Turner offered Miami and Seattle television from Atlanta.

The FCC slowly began cutting satellites loose from its regulatory tether. It authorized private launches and adopted an "open skies" policy for transmissions to the U.S. market. Satellite operators still needed a license from the Commission, but satellites communicate in the microwave bands, and there was plenty of spectrum available.

Wireless Cable

Satellites didn't compete against cable at first. They just delivered new channels that cable operators could pluck out of the air and de-liver to subscribers. But individual homeowners, apartment land-lords, hospitals, and hotels could pluck and deliver, too. They began setting up dishes and connecting them to their own networks—fifty feet of cable from the backyard to the den. Cable, the original pirate of other people's broadcasts, was now being pirated itself.

As I discuss in chapter 15, cablecasters eventually solved that prob-lem by scrambling. For broadcasters, however, satellites compounded the cable disaster. Most galling of all, the new attack came not from wires but from a new generation of broadcasters. The new guys had just found a taller mast.

There was one last legal card to play. It was already marked as a loser, but the broadcasters had nothing else.

In the 1950s broadcasters had persuaded the FCC not to let pay-TV encroach on free television. When the Commission had grudg-ingly approved limited trials, broadcasters and theater owners had gone to court. Pay-TV was unlawful, they had argued, because the 1934 Act didn't authorize scrambled broadcasts. Pay-TV also violated the First Amendment because it discriminated against the poor. Rules against siphoning were essential to protect free television for the poor, but these same rules would also infringe unconstitutionally on the pay-TV operators' First Amendment rights. It was, in short, im-possible to promulgate lawful pay-TV rules of any kind. An appellate court had handily rejected all three arguments.

In 1982 broadcasters raised them all again, this time in a last-ditch attack on the newest generation of satellite technology—direct broadcast satellite (DBS). Millions of rural homeowners had al-ready deployed backyard dishes. But the dishes were very large. To get satellite broadcasts into the suburbs and city would require more-powerful satellite transmitters, whose signals could be picked up on smaller dishes. This was DBS.

DBS, the broadcasters claimed in their lawsuit, had no legal right to exist. The 1934 Congress had said broadcast licenses were to be distributed "among the several states and communities." Localism was the law; national footprints had no place in this scheme of things. DBS would rob local television of its advertising revenues and undercut coverage of local interests. A federal appellate court characterized these arguments as "Luddite" and rejected them all.

The old world of broadcasting midgets—a baby-shoe world of twenty-five-mile transmitters—thus gave way to giants with footprints three thousand miles across. The war between localism and telecommunications was over. Telecommunications had finally won.

Today two DBS satellites provide several hundred national broadcast channels continent-wide. The number of channels transmitted over the air to every community has increased fiftyfold, and the signal quality of the digital DBS broadcasts is immeasurably better.

DBS is completely beyond the reach of local authority. This is why entrepreneurs favor DBS so overwhelmingly in Europe and East Asia. Securing permission to lay wire is close to impossible when authority is fragmented among countless local functionaries, in political environments hostile to change of any sort. Securing a single regulator's permission to broadcast from a satellite is easy by comparison. And one country's satellite broadcasts can often be viewed from many other countries.

In the United States the licensing of satellites themselves is straightforward. The FCC, to its credit, has entirely deregulated the dishes used to receive satellite signals. Consumers are embracing the new technology fast.

Unbroadcasters

The deregulation-minded FCC of the Reagan years decided not to regulate the content of satellite broadcasts, either. It did so with perfect Washington logic, declaring that the new superbroadcasters— the broadest broadcasters on the tallest towers—would not be called "broadcasters" at all.*

In 1982, when it put in place rules for DBS, the Reagan FCC simply left it to the operators themselves to pick their own legal labels from the fine print of the 1934 Act. Those that opted to operate as carriers would supply transport to independent customer program-

*"I can't explain myself, I'm afraid, sir," said Alice, "because I'm not myself, you see." "I don't see," said the Caterpillar.

mers, much as a phone company supplies transport to psychics and sex-talk artists on 976- and 900-number platforms. Who, then, would be the "broadcaster" subject to the full panoply of regulation under the 1934 Act? In a brilliant deregulatory stroke, the Reagan FCC announced that nobody would. The chicken had not merely crossed the road, it had (as Ralph Waldo Emerson said) transcended it.

Flabbergasted, the conventional broadcasters summoned their lawyers yet again. The same court that had dismissed them as Luddites on the question of localism was a touch more sympathetic on this narrow point. Cutting everyone loose from the "broadcaster" label did not seem to square with the expansive definition of that term the Commission had adopted in the past. The Commission was told to take another look.

It did, and it went even further. It reclassified all subscription TV services, however delivered—everything that isn't wholly advertiser-supported—as "non-broadcast services." This approach was upheld in court. Congress halfheartedly reimposed some broadcaster duties on DBS in the 1992 Cable Act. But it was all foam, no beer. The battle was over.

The upshot is that by the end of the 1990s tens of millions of homeowners will receive hundreds of television channels—CNN, C-Span, the whole lot—over the air, but without the intervention of anyone legally labeled a "broadcaster." The underlying satellite carrier literally broadcasts the channel but does not choose it. The programmer, who selects between Julia Roberts and William F. Buckley, is not physically broadcasting anything. Instead of applying to the FCC for bandwidth, this unbroadcaster applies to a cable company, a satellite operator, or a telephone company's video dialtone sales office. Ms. Roberts still travels through the ether into the living room, but there is no "broadcaster" anywhere in legal sight.

She must be scrambled, of course. The FCC and the courts have agreed that broadcasting is what is made available free to the general public. But in the intelligent tele-puters that will soon be found in every home, scrambling will be just a few lines of software, distributed at almost no cost. If payment of some kind is still needed to satisfy legal formalities, it may amount to a box top from a package of Froot Loops. The moment a Loop-top is tendered, broadcasting regulations no longer apply.

Beneath this legal sleight of hand lies something fundamental: a radical break from the kind of broadcasting defined into federal law in 1927. From new technology and a cauldron of legal mumbo-jumbo there has emerged a radically new legal category: none of the above. The providers of subscription video services are privatecasters, narrowcasters, or unbroadcasters. They occupy the twilight between broadcasters and common carriers. They are nomads. They have no obvious home in existing regulatory structures. As traditionally understood, broadcasting is finished. It has been deconstructed into its component parts, carriage and content. The regulation of broadcasting is finished, too. The wheel may still be spinning, but the hamster is dead.

Satellites Dezoned

The carrier itself is deconstructed at the same time. A satellite typically bears not a single radio station but twenty-four, each separate transponder operating on its own frequency. The owner may supply common carriage to independent programmers on six transponders, broadcast its own video programming on several others, use some for satellite telephony, sell some others outright, lease some under long-term contract, and keep several to serve the profitable spot market for smaller slices of satellite capacity. The owner can thus supply carriage, broadcast (if advertiser-supported), unbroadcast (scrambled and sold for cash or Loop tops), and purely private transport—all at the same time. And the mix may be changed as the owner pleases.

This is perfectly sensible. It is also a radical break from half a century of Commission policy. The satellite broadcaster is the first spectrum licensee that has been told, in effect, to use its assigned spectrum for any useful purpose it likes. It is as simple as that. And it works just fine. The only pity is that to enjoy this much freedom, broadcasters must locate their transmitters twenty-three thousand miles from downtown Washington.

Cells

Cellular telephony was launched at about the same time as the first DBS satellites, but on a smaller rocket. Instead of placing the radio high up, with a continent-wide footprint, it would be placed on a low tower, with a footprint of only a few miles—far smaller than a conventional broadcast station.

The idea of a radio telephone was not new. But a key problem with early systems was that there just didn't seem to be enough spectrum available to allow simultaneous use of very many of them. A few dozen stations pretty much fill up the dial of a radio—and radio telephone requires radio stations in pairs to maintain two-way conversation.

In the 1940s researchers at Bell Labs proposed an ingenious solution. Radio telephones should be low-power, short-range devices. The same frequencies could then be reused again and again, just as they are today with cordless home telephones. A city would be divided into many separate "cells," each one served by its own small transmitter. The capacity of a cellular system could then be increased almost indefinitely, by shrinking cells and increasing their number.

The FCC had never thought of this before; the Commission never thought of anything useful on its own. It thought only by infection, catching an opinion like a cold, only much more slowly. It took the Commission four decades to catch this one. The FCC finally approved commercial cellular telephone systems in 1981. The industry grew explosively, and by 1995 it was serving an estimated twenty-five million users. A remarkable economic fact had emerged: The airwaves could be used much more profitably for carrying the intelligent conversations of ordinary Americans than the inane babble of *Roseanne.*

Both television and cellular telephony use broadcast technology: a pocket cellular phone, like a TV station, transmits outward in all directions. A television station uses 6 MHz; a cellular telephone network uses 25 MHz. In 1981 the Commission decided to license just two cellular carriers in each market. Thus a city with eight VHF and UHF stations and two cellular networks uses about as much spectrum for TV (48 MHz) as for wireless telephony (50 MHz). The cellular carriers, however, create not a single, broad, one-way video channel, but thousands of narrow, two-way voice channels. Though still in its infancy, and still growing at breakneck speed, cellular telephony already generates revenues of about $30 billion a year. Broadcast television, though mature, generates about $26 billion a year—and that total includes the value not just of the transport but of the content, too. Within a few years cellular's revenues will dwarf broadcast's. The airwaves thus progress toward one definition of communication: mind over chatter.

After watching a decade of meteoric growth in cellular, Congress and the FCC allocated another 400 MHz of spectrum to be used for wireless telephony and other related services. At least five wireless providers will now have sufficiently large blocks of spectrum to compete head-to-head in the provision of voice services in every geographic market.

All of this is a triumph—but of the marketplace, not the FCC. Cellular telephony was conceived in 1947; AT&T began operating its first experimental system in 1962. The FCC did not issue the first cellular licenses until 1983. Nationwide cellular service could have been in place at least a decade earlier; consumers lost at least $85 billion because it wasn't. Six years of FCC-imposed delay in licensing a next-generation wireless phone service (PCS, personal communications services) cost consumers a further $9 billion.

So far, cellular technology has been used mostly for voice. In the next decade, however, data and even video applications will develop rapidly. Cellular data networks are also already in widespread use.

Like DBS operators, the new wireless companies ride on a federal ticket; state regulators can't stop them. Like the DBS operators, the new wireless carriers can fit themselves into the familiar regulatory category of common carriage. But they themselves, or their customers, can use the facilities to provide any mix of pure carriage, pure broadcast, subscription services, or anything in between. Like the DBS operator, the new wireless licensees are told, in effect, to use their assigned spectrum for any useful purpose they like.

It is as simple as that. It works just fine. And cellular transmitters need not travel twenty-three thousand miles first. They may operate even in Washington.

Broadcasters Dezoned

Subscription television, satellite, video dialtone, and cable services have all been defined to lie outside the regulatory definition of "broadcaster." But someone has to be left inside, or the definitions will have effectively repealed a major part of the 1934 Communications Act. The first to arrive at the regulatory dance—the original broadcasters—must be the last to leave.

But even they are slowly breaking free. They have already begun slipping some carrier-like services into their transmissions. Radio stations transmit paging services using the subcarrier portions of their assigned frequencies. Television stations broadcast electronic newspapers, data, computer software, and paging services within the otherwise unused vertical blanking interval of their spectrum. Had the Commission permitted FM subcarrier frequencies to be used for services other than broadcast services in 1948 instead of in 1983, the economy would have gained nearly $2 billion.

The FCC has gradually backed away from regulating program content as well. In 1976 the Commission reconsidered its role in resolving program format disputes and boldly concluded it shouldn't have any at all. An appellate court disagreed. In 1981, however, the Supreme Court finally accepted that the Commission had the discretion to leave program formats to the marketplace. The FCC then abandoned its main programming guidelines for both radio and broadcast television. The Prime Time Access Rule, which required network affiliates to devote at least one of the four daily prime time hours to non-network programming, was finally repealed in 1995. The Commission continues, however, to monitor programming to ensure responsiveness to local needs. Every radio and television broadcaster must give "significant treatment" to five or more community issues each quarter. But nobody takes this too seriously any longer.

The FCC no longer worries much about time brokering, either. As recently as 1991 the Commission reiterated that a licensee must not "assume[] the passive role of a common carrier." In 1992 the Commission revisited the question and decided that time brokering was a sort of joint venture that would generally be approved, at least for radio. All licensees must, however, still "reserve to themselves the ultimate editorial discretion." So it is still illegal to use broadcast spectrum to provide pure carriage, like cellular phone service.

The 1996 Telecommunications Act makes a few halting attempts to dezone broadcasters, but also reaffirms some of the old rules. The Act's "Broadcast Spectrum Flexibility" section addresses use of new blocks of spectrum to be allocated to broadcasters for "advanced television services." Existing television broadcasters are the only eligible recipients of these licenses. They may offer "ancillary or supplemental services"—such things as wireless voice or data—on the new channels, but only if they do so alongside advanced television.

It appears that old-style broadcasters will carry the regulatory baggage of the 1934 Act for another decade or so. Early in the next century, however, this dismal regulatory era will finally come to an end. Broadcast spectrum will be dezoned. *Roseanne* will have to compete for airtime with the more civil, uplifting, and profitable expressions of ordinary people talking on wireless phones. For the first time since 1927 broadcasters will truly own their airtime.

Philosophers have noted that it is better to be a human being dissatisfied than a pig satisfied. As the FCC fades from the scene, broadcasters will have their first chance in half a century to make a honest business as honest electronic publishers. They will prosper, if they can, by catering to consumers, not commissions.

Giving Away the Goods

Though nobody yet says so openly, broadcasters are reclaiming ownership of the airwaves. True to the ways of Washington, nobody gets an actual deed of title. They just get all the legal essentials of private property.

The concept of property implies a right to hold on to a good indefinitely, use it as you please, exclude trespassers, and sell it if you wish. Beginning around 1970 the Commission gradually streamlined and then all but eliminated the hearings it conducts when spectrum licenses come up for renewal. The 1934 Act plainly didn't intend this at all, and for a while the courts resisted. Renewal rights slowly solidified nonetheless. Today the FCC recognizes the "renewal expectancy" of any licensee that is found to have provided "meritorious," "superior," or "substantial" service. To lose a license, the service record has to be "minimal or nonexistent." In 1981 Congress increased the term of television licenses to five years, and radio licenses to seven. The 1996 Act curtails the Commission's discretion to deny renewal and sharply limits the rights of would-be competitors to challenge license renewals.

A creeping giveaway of this kind raises no cash for the government. It is progress nonetheless, because it solidifies private control over a very valuable resource. The new de facto owners have strong incentives to develop and improve what they own. If they do not know how to use the resource well, they sell it in the secondhand market to someone who does. At least prime un-real estate ends up in the hands of able developers, rather than being left to grow weeds and accumulate trash.

For this reason, the 1996 Act's giveaway of new spectrum to incumbent TV broadcasters is merely bad, not abominable. Every incumbent is to be given a second 6 MHz license, on which it is to begin offering "advanced television services." Ten or more years later, the licenses currently held by the incumbents are to be returned to the Commission. By Washington lights, this looks like a reasonable trade, designed to smooth the transition from analog to digital television—even though the right to broadcast on two TV channels rather than one during the ten-year transition is worth somewhere between $10 and $100 billion.

Selling Un-Real Estate

The other alternative—an attractive one for an owner several trillion dollars in debt—is to sell the goods. That too is a process already well under way.

In 1993 Congress for the first time authorized the FCC to auction off licenses for "personal communications services," a new generation of cellular-like networks. The Commission began by defining vast slabs of spectrum in bubble-like territories across the country. The first PCS auctions, conducted by the Commission in 1994, allocated ten nationwide narrowband licenses. These licenses were sold for more than $600 million—about ten times preauction projections. The Commission conducted a second wave of narrowband auctions later that year. Final bids for the thirty licenses topped $490 million. Another auction—by far the largest—began on December 5, 1994, and revenues exceeded $7 billion. The latest round of bidding concluded in May 1996 and netted $10 billion. Spectrum auctions were initially expected to net as much as $12 billion between 1994 and 1998, but auction revenues had already topped $15 billion by mid-1996.

These numbers confirm the obvious: Spectrum is a valuable commodity. If all extant spectrum were simply leased by the federal government to current users, it would generate revenues estimated at $10 billion to $20 billion a year. This compares with $3 billion currently generated from offshore oil and gas leases and royalties and $28 million generated from federal grazing fees. The FCC and other government agencies are sitting on billions of dollars' worth of additional spectrum, much of which remains completely idle.

Auctions generate public revenue. They eliminate the elaborate and politically charged procedures of comparative hearings. They sharply reduce government's incentive to condition licenses in ways that control content. But so far, at least, Congress has shown little inclination to replace FCC commissioners with auctioneers from Sotheby's. As other media ascend and broadcast declines, Congress will eventually come to understand that it may just as well take the money and run.

Privatizing the Airwaves

A general strategy for repealing the 1927 Radio Act and getting the FCC entirely out of the radio business is now crystallizing. The federal government must privatize in the 1990s what it nationalized in 1927. In much the same way, and for much the same reason, as the Russian government is privatizing in the 1990s what it nationalized in the 1920s. The airwaves should be privatized, quickly and irrevocably.

This idea is far from fanciful. In the United States spectrum is already bought and sold, though only in the secondary market. New Zealand and Britain have already moved a significant way toward selling off their spectrum.

What does it take? First, a standard parcel. The government has to sell the goods in pieces, just as it sells rights to drill for oil in specific parcels of land or seabed. Standard units of size have already been established for radio (10 kHz, AM; 200 kHz, FM), television (6 MHz), cellular (25 MHz), and PCS (40 MHz). Those units can be used to define standard bandwidth parcels for sale. Standard geographic territories already in use—twenty-five-mile contours for television broadcasts, for example—can be used to define standard geographic footprints. There is no need to worry too much about the details here—downstream markets will subdivide or consolidate these units to create the most efficient packages for delivering usable services.

Once the standard parcels are defined, they can be sold to the highest bidders. To keep for how long? Forever. Just like land. As for already established broadcasters, cellular carriers, and others, they would simply be given title to the spectrum they already occupy. Existing licensees—AT&T, for example—paid for their spectrum when they wrote their checks ($17 billion in AT&T's case) to primary licensees like Craig McCaw. At this point there is no fair or politically feasible way for the government to reclaim those licenses.

Giving these downstream buyers clear title would simply let them get on with putting spectrum to the best possible use. If we authorized one UHF television station in Los Angeles to transfer its spectrum to a third cellular provider, the overall public gain would be about $1 billion, or so the government itself estimated in 1992. Nextel was created in just this way, by an entrepreneur who bought up taxi dispatch licenses and then persuaded the FCC to rezone them for digital radio services. Deleting a few lines of legal boilerplate from all outstanding FCC licenses would create tens of billions of dollars of new national wealth.

All spectrum, old and new, would be dezoned. Existing owners and new buyers alike could use their wireless territories to carry, to broadcast, or to provide any mix in between. They could alter uses at will, subject only to the contractual commitments they might make to their private customers. This model is familiar, too. It is already used for DBS and PCS.

Might some conniving monopolist end up owning all the spectrum nationwide? That fear is ridiculous. It would take hundreds of billions of dollars and a complete suspension of the antitrust laws. Moreover, an airwave monopoly is no monopoly at all when wires provide vastly more bandwidth to precisely the same markets.

What of problems of interference among all the private transmitters? They would be handled just as they are now, but without the inefficiency of a commission bureaucracy standing in the way. Trespassing is not a new problem, and it is always more of a problem on public land than on private. Courts would still be required to help decide who has trespassed on whom and what the remedy should be. That is exactly what courts do today. If a pirate station begins broadcasting one morning on channel 5 in Washington, D.C., the channel 5 licensee doesn't wait around for the Commission to notice the problem. It locates the offending transmitter, races to court, and secures an order directing the sheriff to seize the pirate equipment and shut it down. None of that would change.

In 1927 Congress believed that interference problems could be solved only by nationalizing all the airwaves under the authority of a single federal commission. Congress was wrong. Private property rights in spectrum would have served better. They still can. They will.

The Airwaves as Commons?

And then . . . then, technology and the market may transform the airwaves back into a public commons after all.

Private markets create shared spaces, too—golf courses, country clubs, Disney World. No, they aren't free, but Central Park isn't free either, except for people who pay no taxes. The free market creates such spaces, and assesses private taxes to support them, for assets that are best used collectively rather than in strictly private isolation.

Telecom visionary and free-market guru George Gilder has developed a cogent argument for deprivatizing the airwaves. His case centers on the remarkable capabilities of new spread-spectrum technology. In the old, analog world, communication breaks down when two users attempt to occupy the same piece of spectrum at the same time. But with new intelligent digital radios, interference problems are quickly mediated and resolved by the machines themselves. The computer behind the radio constantly monitors for open space, much as a pedestrian hurrying along on a crowded sidewalk uses his eyes in tandem with his feet. Trains, which aren't agile or intelligent, require exclusive use of separate tracks. Cars don't, because steering wheels and drivers let them dodge and weave. Spread-spectrum digital radios have electronic eyes and the power to maneuver.

Intelligent digital radios are now at hand, and their prices are plummeting. With this kind of technology, Gilder argues, exclusive private tracks just get in the way. In the old world of analog, narrowband radio, every transmitter could be effectively shut down, for a moment at least, by any passing spray of radiation. The new digital broadband world is much more robust. Errors are corrected, and lanes are changed continuously to avoid other traffic. Instead of auctioning off any more exclusive lanes, the FCC should begin shutting down high-powered, blind transmitters—the obsolete technology that demands the whole beach and excludes everyone else from the surf.

And Gilder may well be right. But the one certain thing is that true wisdom in matters this complex does not emerge from centralized commissions, nor even from visionary pundits. Wisdom emerges from markets. Markets find ways of reassembling private pieces into public spaces when that is the most profitable thing to do. They may take more time than an omniscient central authority, but finding omniscient central authority takes even longer. For now, the thing to do is to get the spectrum out of government hands, however it can be done, and leave it to the market to re-create the public commons. It will, if the economics are there.

The End of Scarcity

Whether or not Gilder is right, the 1927 Congress was wrong. There is no inherent scarcity of spectrum, no law of physics that limits how much information can be transported through the air or through any other medium. Since 1927 we have increased by at least a millionfold the amount of information moving through the airwaves—and still we have not run out of space. We would have increased the amount ten-million-fold, or a hundred, if the airwaves had been left in private hands all along.

With airwaves, as with all other media, the more you spend, the more you can send; it all comes down to engineering and smart management. But there are few incentives to stretch the airwave dollar, because there is no dollar. The FCC issues broadcast licenses for free and prescribes exactly what the licensees may transport. The dollars are therefore spent on lawyers and lobbyists, political contributions, and influence peddling. Demand for free licenses far exceeds supply. Commission management creates a new bedlam, the Washington kind, the highest insanity of all. Scarcity is something manufactured and maintained by commissions. Markets deliver plenty.

It was never necessary to nationalize the airwaves; private ownership would have served better. It was never necessary to regulate program formats to promote diversity; deregulation has supplied far more varied news and entertainment. It was never necessary to zone bandwidth to ensure a supply of different kinds of service; the market would have found its way to both *Roseanne* and McCaw far sooner without help from a commission. It was never necessary to police strict lines between broadcasters and carriers; the market has brought them together and returned the best alternative of all, the unbroadcaster. No federal commission was ever needed to prevent bedlam in the airwaves; property rights and smart technology do the job far better.

This whole litany of unnecessaries sprang from the one great fear, that of scarcity, and one grand conceit, that central authority would manage it wisely. But central management maintained scarcity itself, in U.S. airwaves just as on Russian wheat farms. Private property and free markets eliminate scarcity and tame bedlam far better than a federal commission.

7

Wires Unbound

Even in the shelter of its anointed monopoly, the Bell System remained a for-profit enterprise. If it provided better, faster, and cheaper service, its revenues and profits would grow.

The company had been founded on technology, and technology had remained its strength. In Murray Hill, New Jersey, it established the greatest peacetime scientific research program that the world has ever known: Bell Laboratories. Its scientists set off in pursuit of better telephones, better networks, and better switches. It was the search for a better switch that led to the greatest discovery of all.

It is by opening and closing a whole chain of switches that a single continuous circuit is set up between Romeo in San Francisco and his Juliet in New York City. The technology of telephone switches had languished after the first electromechanical switches began to be used in 1889. As late as 1951 operators were still being used to connect almost 40 percent of long-distance calls. The operators sat in front of panels and plugged in wires—one end into this hole, the other end into that one. They opened and closed conduits call by call, much like soldier ants forming living bridges across a stream. Switches, as it happens, are also the heart of a computer. By shifting on and off, switches can keep track of numbers, and numbers can keep track of everything.

In 1936 the director of research at Bell Labs discussed with physicist William Shockley the possibility of creating electronic telephone exchanges. Electronic switching, however, required a better amplifier than a vacuum tube. While each tube was capable of electronically opening or closing a single circuit in a telephone switch, an exchange handled thousands of circuits. Tubes used too much power and generated too much heat to be packed together in the numbers required. Shockley, together with his Bell Labs colleagues Walter Brattain and John Bardeen, set off to find something better.

They found it in 1947—the transistor. A Nobel prize followed in 1956. The transistor was a wonderfully compact, energy-efficient on-off switch. The new transistor soon came to the notice of Jack Kilby, an engineer who had been designing compact systems for hearing-aid companies. In 1958 Kilby moved to the Dallas headquarters of Texas Instruments. Transistors were being made on silicon by then. Kilby had a brainstorm. Why not make resistors and capacitors out of silicon, too, and thus manufacture entire circuits all at once, in one process, on one substrate? Why not, in other words, manufacture an "integrated circuit"? Robert Noyce, another alumnus of Bell Labs who was then working at Fairchild Semiconductor, would soon radically improve on Kilby's design. In 1968 Noyce and a colleague set up their own new company, Intel. Intel would eventually become master of the microprocessor. Their computer-on-a-chip would fundamentally transform all of telephony, computing, and broadcasting.

Terminals Unbound

Developments in computers, radios, modems, fax machines, telephone handsets, and all the other varied progeny of the transistor made competition inevitable in markets where it had not been seen for decades. Competitors arrived, first in ones and twos, then in legions. They demanded permission to install equipment and supply services all around Bell's citadel.

At first Bell responded along familiar lines. Alien attachments to Bell's network were as welcome as vampires at a blood bank. By the 1960s, however, the pressure from the market had grown too intense for the FCC to ignore. The Commission grudgingly reconsidered the advantages of end-to-end exclusive franchises.

It began by authorizing various types of electronic terminal equipment on private premises. Beginning with its *Carterfone* ruling in 1968, the FCC progressively eliminated all "foreign attachment" prohibitions from Bell's tariffs. Standard interfaces between customer equipment and the network were established. The network now had something that it had not had before: jacks, empty sockets, open plugs in the wall. Any humble citizen could plug pretty much anything into them, with hardly a by-your-leave from Bell or the FCC.

The FCC discovered a new power it had never thought to exercise before. It would carefully define some segment of the market—terminal equipment, say—then expel state regulators by declaring the turf to be under exclusive federal control. Then it would expel itself from that same segment by announcing that it would "forbear" from regulating the space at all. The Commission had discovered, at long last, that occasional flashes of silence might make its conversation perfectly delightful. Had the Commission permitted consumers to buy their own telephones in 1956, when it first considered the issue, instead of 1975, when it finally said yes, consumers would have saved over $3 billion.

After two more decades of fighting, the equipment rules eventually spawned a new competitive market for enhanced services. If customers could connect their own telephones and answering machines to the network, private entrepreneurs could connect their own electronic publishing, data processing, voice mail, or dial-a-porn services, too. All of these services simply involved connecting new equipment to the existing wires.

"Terminal equipment" need not terminate; it can serve instead as the starting point for another network—long distance, cellular, cable, or computer. The entire ferment of the Internet of the 1990s can be traced back to a single courageous decision to stop regulating in 1968.

Long Distance Unbound

Broadcast engineers of the 1940s pushed their way up the radio dial and vastly expanded the carrying capacities of their transmitters. By the 1950s they were transmitting the huge volumes of information required for television. Bell, however, had been barred from the radio broadcast business by the Radio Act of 1927.

But not all radio waves spread out like ripples on a pond. With the right antennas and wavelengths, radio signals can be made to move in straight lines, like beams of light. Bell recognized early on that it might use radio waves in its own core telephone business. Its scientists searched for equally high-capacity—broadband—radios to serve as conduits for telephony.

This led them to microwave. Harold T. Friis and his colleagues developed the horn-reflector antenna, now a standard fixture on microwave towers. Unlike their longer-wavelength cousins on the dial of a car radio, microwaves—short-wavelength radio waves—can be precisely focused. Because of their comparatively high frequency, microwaves can also carry far more information; even early systems were designed to carry up to a thousand voice circuits. Microwave towers could be placed thirty miles apart: that made them cheap, especially for crossing difficult terrain. They bypassed local regulatory obstructions, too; with a license from the FCC, AT&T didn't have to negotiate with a sheriff or landowner in Alabama. By 1959 microwave systems comprised a quarter of Bell's long-distance network.

Microwave radically changed the economic picture. Previously long-distance service had used wires in much the same way as local service. If local markets were "natural monopolies," long-distance markets certainly were, too, probably even more so. Now long-distance markets were shifting rapidly to radio, and the economics of radio were quite different. Wire networks became progressively more efficient and economical as traffic volumes increased. Radio networks didn't. The costs of boosting capacity on radio networks rose in step with the volume of traffic carried. Two competitors could set up links between Boston and New York at much the same cost as one monopolist.

Demands for competitive alternatives came first from large businesses; they wanted to deploy microwave to supply strictly private, point-to-point links. In 1959 the FCC concluded there was enough spectrum to let them do so. In 1963 a small start-up firm, Microwave Communications, Inc. (MCI), applied to the FCC to construct a microwave line between St. Louis and Chicago. MCI told the FCC it would offer business customers "interplant and interoffice communications with unique and special characteristics." What MCI really had in mind was plain old long-distance phone service.

Other MCIs came clamoring to the FCC's door, demanding tickets of their own. Prodded repeatedly by the courts, the FCC slowly let them in. In 1980 the Commission at last adopted an open-entry policy for all interstate services. Had the Commission authorized full long-distance competition when it was first proposed in 1968, consumers would have saved $16 billion.

Without ever quite describing the policy in these terms, the FCC largely defranchised the long-distance telephone market. Ironically, as I discuss in chapter 9, these policy changes were finalized just as microwave itself was being driven out of long-distance markets by still newer technology—fiber-optic glass. But by then the policies favoring competition had taken hold. The Commission extended open-entry policies down the wires of the network, as far as its jurisdictional arm would reach. "Interstate" wires must, of course, run into the states themselves. Facilities that provide access to the interstate network can thus be defined as interstate, too. The FCC has pinned that label on them, thus trumping state regulators who might otherwise have blocked deployment of these "competitive access" networks. Dozens of entrepreneurs have since deployed fiber-optic rings and microwave systems to provide competing connections between business customers and interexchange carriers in every large city in the country.

The Inclusive Local Franchise

By 1996 most state regulators were already following the FCC's lead. They were already preparing to authorize competition for in-state long-distance services or had already done so. The 1996 Act took care of the holdouts. It broadly preempts most state laws to the extent that those laws explicitly bar competitive entry. It specifically affirms the right of cable operators to compete head-to-head against local telephone companies. The legal path has been cleared to allow electric utilities and gas companies to build communications networks, too.

Wireless providers had won similar freedom years earlier. Once they secure a license to use spectrum, they face no other federal or state entry requirements and no rate regulation of any consequence. And vast new tracts of spectrum are being allocated to local wireless telephony every year.

For wireline and wireless competitors alike, one of the first and most lucrative targets will be short-haul toll markets—a curious halfway house of the long-distance market concocted by lawyers in the course of breaking up Bell. In deference to state authorities, the drafters of the breakup papers allowed the local Bell companies being spun off by AT&T to retain their traditional monopolies over toll markets close to home. These mostly in-state toll calls currently generate about $9 billion a year, or about 15 percent of all toll revenues nationwide.

By 1995 states had already begun opening these major markets to full competition; the 1996 Telecommunications Act sets up a process for finishing the job. Established long-distance carriers like AT&T and MCI will be allowed into the short-haul toll markets at the same time as local phone companies are allowed into long-haul toll. The endpoint will be a single huge toll market—worth some $54 billion a year—in which all players are finally allowed to compete on fully equal terms.

Intelligent Networks

When the FCC completed its second Computer Inquiry in 1980, a new universe of integrated circuits and the personal computer was just beginning to unfold. The mainframe computer was giving way to the desktop micro; the economic imperative was to multiply and disperse electronic intelligence. Microprocessors were destined to become integral components of all telecommunications equipment, from the simplest telephone handsets to the large phone companies' switches.

Computers built into the telephone network could radically improve network capabilities and the quality of service. But the Commission had just announced that local phone companies would be permitted to provide only basic services. "Basic," it turned out, meant "as in 1982." The Commission had just issued an edict telling phone companies to sit out the revolution in computers.

Almost before the dust of the second Computer Inquiry had settled, the Commission had to begin tearing it down. The FCC launched Computer Inquiry number three. By 1986 it was ready to abandon the policy of "maximum separation" of telephones and computers entirely. Accounting and other safeguards, the Commission now declared, would ensure that enhanced services supplied by phone companies paid their own way. An entirely new regulatory philosophy now began to take shape. The old regulatory pair—exclusive franchise and strict quarantine—would give way to a new one: equal access and competition all around.

The quid pro quo for allowing phone companies to enter outside markets would be new flexibility in the way outsiders entered the phone companies' markets. Telephone companies would be required to unbundle their networks and offer the basic elements of service to all outside providers at tariffed rates. Outsiders would be permitted to interconnect with the public network on the same terms offered to telephone company affiliates. There would be a fundamental change in the way that local phone companies offered basic services to independent providers of enhanced services. The phone network would be rebuilt, step by step, on an "open network" architecture—one that afforded outsiders easy interconnection at many levels. That transformation is now well under way, impelled largely by market forces. The regulatory superstructure is still being litigated in the courts.

Video by Phone

The video ban is gone, too. In 1986 the Reagan FCC began questioning the rule it had put in place sixteen years earlier. But Congress had codified it in the interim, and in the 1992 Cable Act it passed over the opportunity to eliminate the restriction.

The Commission began to chip away at the video quarantine anyway. In 1992 it released a video dialtone order intended to give telephone companies a toehold in providing video services if they would also provide a network platform to distribute video fare for others. But 1984 Cable Act forced the Commission to cap telephone company occupancy of their own video facilities at 5 percent. Layers of torturous detail were added later, and after long delays the FCC approved only a handful of applications.

Meanwhile, however, phone companies had gone to court. In 1993 Bell Atlantic had filed a pathbreaking case in Alexandria, Virginia, claiming a First Amendment right to deliver "speech" of its own choice over its own wires. No phone company had previously challenged the video ban as an unconstitutional infringement on free speech. But a federal judge in Alexandria promptly knocked down the ban in its entirety. A federal appellate court affirmed. This marked a startling change in the legal landscape.

Other phone companies immediately filed copycat suits. Every other court that considered the constitutionality of the ban—six federal trial judges and three federal appellate courts—reached the same conclusion: the law was baldly unconstitutional. The case was argued before the Supreme Court in December 1995.

The phone company's position was straightforward enough. Congress cannot casually ban speech; at the very least it has to make a good case for doing so. Whatever scarcity logic might justify regulation of broadcasters doesn't apply to regulation of wires. Nor will it suffice simply to announce that cable is a natural monopoly or that other economic factors create a condition of scarcity. Neither Congress nor the FCC had articulated compelling reasons for the ban, nor had they made any attempt to draft a narrowly tailored law to serve whatever reasons they did have.

As best as one can judge from the oral argument, the phone companies were set to win the votes of all nine Justices. But no decision was ever announced. The 1996 Telecommunications Act eliminated the video ban and swept aside the FCC's tangled video dialtone jurisprudence before the Justices could issue an opinion.

Had the Commission authorized phone companies to begin competing directly against cable in 1984, cable consumers would have saved between $3 and $7 billion a year between 1983 and 1992.

Dark Fiber

In 1994, a year after the phone companies' first constitutional victory, they won a second, equally important ruling on technical statutory grounds. At issue this time was a carrier's right to provide less than plain common carriage, rather than more.

Ordinarily a carrier provides transport on uniform terms to all comers. Southwestern Bell, however, had begun leasing "dark fiber" under individual contracts to a few large business customers. Dark fiber is just the fiber-optic line itself, with none of the optoelectronics at the end to generate and modulate the laser light that transports the signal. Rather than including its own content on its lines, like a cable television company, Southwestern left it to lessees to supply even the most basic illumination needed to make the glass carry anything at all.

Everyone was happy, apparently, until the FCC decided that dark fiber should be supplied to all comers, just like a common-carrier service. The Commission ordered Southwestern to file tariffs. The phone company reluctantly did, the FCC did not like the prices it saw, and Southwestern then discontinued the service entirely. An irate FCC announced that the phone company had no right to pick up its ball and leave the field. Under the 1934 Act, carriers that need FCC permission to start a new service also need the Commission's permission to stop.

The controversy went to court; Southwestern prevailed. The critical fact for the appellate court was that Southwestern had never offered dark fiber as a common-carrier service at all. Granted, most of its other services were offered as common carriage. But this one had not been. Common-carrier status was to be decided one service at a time. A provider like Southwestern may be a common carrier for some purposes and something quite different for others. The important thing is not who but what. The licensing provision of the Communications Act simply did not apply to the withdrawal of a private service offered by a sometime common carrier.

This was all arcane legalese, of course, of a kind that only lawyers would bother with. But the practical implications were enormous. Phone companies that had struggled for years against stifling common-carrier regulation were suddenly offered a wide-open exit—an exit that could be used one service at a time.

Un-Phone Companies

So now phone companies had before them two open doors, both leading away from FCC regulation. By bundling content and transport, a phone company could define a service up into the realm of cable. By narrowing the scope of what it offered, and to whom, the same company could move service down into the realm of private carriage—which is not common carriage, either. As discussed in chapter 6, broadcasters escaped from the coils of broadcast regulation by redefining themselves as subscription services. Telephone companies now have other labels at their disposal as well. They too can now pursue deregulation by definition.

Opportunities for verbal prestidigitation of this kind abound. Each of the 1934 Act's main Titles avoids overlap with others by reference to the services regulated, not the providers that supply them. The FCC is expressly forbidden to regulate as common carriers persons "engaged in broadcasting." A provider of cable service is not to be regulated as a common carrier "by reason of providing any cable service." These "exclusive jurisdiction" clauses refer specifically to services, not providers. They apply to channels, not to wires or cables, and still less to entire entities.

Thus phone companies—or cable operators, for that matter—can escape from local regulators by setting up their video services as strictly common-carrier services. That means creating a video dial-tone platform through which anyone (the phone company included) can then offer video programming. In 1992 the Commission announced that video dialtone was exclusively under federal jurisdiction. And since the unadorned transport provided to all comers is plainly common carriage, not cable television, the Commission declared that it was to be licensed exclusively under the common-carrier licensing provisions. Incumbent cable operators complained that this would unfairly relieve phone companies of local licensing burdens, franchise fees, and the like. The FCC sent them packing. A federal appellate court agreed that the cable operators had no valid complaint. Conventional cable operators that move into common carriage can escape in similar fashion. Common carriage is licensed and regulated under common-carrier rules, regardless of who provides it.

The 1996 Act directs the FCC to promulgate rules defining an altogether new category of video service, provided on "open" video systems. The operator may not occupy more than one third of the available video channels. It may be required to pay local franchise fees at the same rate as ordinary cable operators, but no more.

This proliferation of regulatory categories gives providers a choice of regulatory homes, so long as the service is packaged right. Their customers do even better: They can live outside of regulation entirely. As discussed in chapter 6, the "customer programmers" that lease channels from direct broadcast satellites are neither carriers (since they provide no transport themselves) nor broadcasters (since they do not provide a fully integrated package of content and transport). They are the nomads—the unbroadcasters. Precisely the same holds for customers of video transport offered on a common-carrier basis over wires. But from the perspective of a couch potato switching channels on TV, the customer programmer using a common-carrier video service performs precisely the same function as a cable TV operator providing its own content over its own wires.

In due course the man on the couch will have the power to become a "wirecaster" in his own right. He already has become one in the medium of videotext. Anyone can post messages on bulletin boards on the Internet or create a home page on the World Wide Web.* Tens of millions of people can then "tune in" to the posting if they choose. As the bandwidth of the network increases, still pictures will give way to moving ones. Everyone will have the same power to display face, voice, or composition to the world.

Better in the Bahamas

The FCC's original approach to wires was simple: Limit entry to a single, favored monopolist, then quarantine and zone to make sure that the monopolist provides only a narrow, specific cluster of approved services.

Cable broke free by persuading courts that wires weren't scarce. That saved cable's First Amendment rights. Telephone companies then discovered that they had constitutional rights, too. All owners of wires are now learning to locate services under the friendliest regulatory umbrella.

Phone companies began with a core business of common carriage but gradually won the freedom to move up into cable television or down into private carriage. Cable companies began as videocasters but won the right to move into carriage. The lawyers behind all the wires finally mastered the game. Any wire could be used to provide

---

*(My own home page can be located at http://www.phuber. com/huber/home.html.)

private carriage, common carriage, videocasting, and other non-common-carrier service. Moving into the right regulatory neighborhood was like moving to the Bahamas to escape income tax.

Now, with or without cooperation from the Commission, wireline bandwidth is being dezoned. Bandwidth moves voice, video, or data. Content and conduit are bundled or unbundled, and sold as wirecast, common carriage, private carriage, or dark wires. The nation would have been far better off if that freedom had been definitively affirmed a century ago.

8

Busting Trusts

When Aeschines spoke, they said, "How well he speaks." But when Demosthenes spoke, they said, "Let us march against Philip." And that, in summary, is the difference between what the FCC does for competition, and what the Department of Justice does.

In 1910 AT&T bought Western Union, the competing telegraph company. The Interstate Commerce Commission, the federal telephone commission of that day, stood by and watched. Federal antitrust prosecutors undid the acquisition three years later.

AT&T continued to grow, however. By the end of 1983 the Bell System had annual revenues of $58 billion and total assets of $138 billion. The largest private enterprise in the world, it employed over a million people.

To say that the FCC had watched it grow to these gargantuan proportions since 1934 without complaint would be incorrect. The FCC's official mission since 1934 had been to protect telephone monopolists from "inefficient" competition.

In the end, AT&T was taken apart not by the FCC or Congress but by a compact federal law—the Sherman Act. The Act was written into the federal code in 1890, not long after Alexander Graham Bell invented the telephone. It is two paragraphs long. It gives federal courts a general mandate to stop combinations and bar exclusionary practices that undermine competition. They may do so by issuing prospective orders (legal injunctions) or by awarding money damages.

The Department of Justice and the Federal Trade Commission are frequent antitrust plaintiffs. They both are large agencies, but they are nothing like the FCC. They don't license anything or anyone. If they believe a merger or practice is anticompetitive, they have to bring a formal lawsuit and convince a court. With the Communications Act, everything is forbidden until it's permitted. Under the Sherman Act, everything is permitted until it's forbidden. The Act operates only as an enabling statute for economic common law. Antitrust rules have been developed almost exclusively by judges and juries, over the course of a century of antitrust litigation.

And without doubt, antitrust law has done far more to promote competition than any commission. In the telecommunications arena, the single largest impediment to effective antitrust enforcement has been the FCC itself.

Closed Networks

Even with the FCC at its most accommodating, Bell had to worry about the antitrust lawyers. Antitrust plaintiffs—manufacturers of telephones, answering machines, and other kinds of terminal equipment—kept suing. The Department of Justice sued, too, in 1949. It demanded that AT&T divest itself of its manufacturing arm and break it into three pieces. The case was settled in 1956. AT&T agreed, among other things, to manufacture only equipment used in providing telephone service and to stay out of all businesses other than common carriage. This was at a time when the FCC still backed AT&T's attempts to stop Hush-A-Phone from selling a cup that connected to the mouthpieces of AT&T handsets.

It was when the FCC finally began to tire of monopoly, too, that the antitrust floodgates opened. One case attacked restrictive technical standards Bell had imposed to limit interconnection with non-Bell equipment. That suit ended in 1983, with a $277 million verdict. AT&T fiercely litigated and won some other suits based on similar theories.

In March 1974 MCI sued Bell for monopolizing long-distance communications. Six years later a Chicago jury awarded MCI $600 million, trebled to $1.8 billion, then cut to $113 million on appeal. Sprint fared less well. Its predecessor (Southern Pacific Communications) filed suit in 1978. After a thirty-three-day bench trial, federal Judge Charles R. Richey accepted Bell's defense chapter and verse, and an appellate court affirmed.

The most interesting part of that last case is the one least remembered. Sprint's case had originally been assigned to Judge Joseph C.

Waddy. Judge Waddy had also been assigned the federal government's case against Bell. But Judge Waddy died in 1978. Sprint's case was reassigned to Judge Richey, who then ruled in Bell's favor. The federal government's case was reassigned to Judge Harold Greene. Had the docket assignments been reversed, Sprint might be a good bit richer, and the Bell System might still be intact today.

Judge Greene, however, quickly took control of the government case he had inherited. In ruling on Bell's motion to dismiss, he telegraphed where he was headed. The gargantuan Bell System was too large; something had to be done. Bell, a company with some understanding of telegraphs, took the hint. It capitulated.

As I discuss below, a massive decree jurisprudence evolved in the years thereafter, with the Department of Justice's lawyers performing—abominably—as a shadow FCC. But the breakup itself was clean. And while debatable as a matter of public policy, divestiture did indisputably cut AT&T into parts that could compete against each other. Today AT&T stands as the most threatening potential entrant into the local markets still dominated by its former affiliates. And they present powerful new competitive threats in a long-distance market still dominated by AT&T.

Closed Hardware

The agreement to break up AT&T was announced on Friday, January 8, 1982. On the same day the federal government agreed to dismiss its antitrust case against IBM. This put an end to almost eight decades of litigation. It was a major victory, too. Not because the government won, but because it didn't.

The old Bell System had been conceived and built by Theodore Vail. IBM's patriarch-monopolist was Thomas J. Watson. Early in the century, Watson trained as a salesman at National Cash Register. NCR's president and several other executives—including Watson— were convicted of antitrust violations in 1912, though the government later dropped the case on appeal. Watson then became general manager of the Computing-Tabulating-Recording Company.

Invented (at almost the same time as the telephone) to speed data analysis for the 1880 U.S. Census, the tabulating machine was an electromechanical device that processed information stored on punch cards. A few years after joining NCR, Watson gained total control of the company. In early 1924 he changed its name. "National" became "International." "Cash" became "Business." "Register" became "Machines."

IBM soon won a complete monopoly in the market for commercial data processing. Much of IBM's market power lay in the humble punch card itself. A large customer typically processed millions of these a year. The investment in cards, and the plug-board configurations needed for handling them, grew in step with the business itself. After a while, replicating the data in some other format became prohibitively expensive.

This was exactly as Watson intended. To function properly, calculating machines required central provision, maintenance, and oversight. Like Bell, IBM would not sell its machines at all; it would sell service, with machines provided only under tight lease. IBM customers were strictly forbidden to buy blank computer cards from anyone else.

The Department of Justice brought its first antitrust suit to overturn this practice in 1932. IBM responded that bad cards from independent suppliers would likely damage the machines IBM owned and serviced. IBM's punch card case went up to the U.S. Supreme Court, and IBM was forced to open the door to its market a crack. A subsequent round of antitrust litigation, settled in 1956, forced IBM to divest itself of part of its capacity to manufacture punch cards.

By the 1960s IBM had come to dominate the new market for electronic computers. Punch-card economics seemed to be engaged again. Once a customer had committed to IBM, a switch to another vendor entailed a prohibitive new investment in software. With the largest base of customers, IBM also offered the largest library of application programs. IBM understood this and aggressively froze out competitors. The company adhered rigidly to "closed," proprietary architectures, a policy readily enforced when all its machines were supplied (like Bell's) only under lease. Competitors were eager to sell "plug-compatible" peripherals—card readers, printers, disk drives, monitors, and so on—that would hook into the IBM machines. IBM was determined not to let them.

In 1969 government antitrust lawyers launched their third and last major attack on IBM. The objective now was to break up the company. This was the suit that was finally abandoned in 1982, on the same day that the Bell breakup was announced. One of the eight fragments of the old Bell System—the surviving AT&T—was to be freed from antitrust quarantines and permitted to enter the computer business. By this time Intel was already over a decade old. Apple was growing fast. And IBM had just introduced a brand-new machine, based on an Intel microprocessor. Big Blue's new machine—its "personal computer"—was small and beige.

Dropping the IBM suit was one of antitrust law's finest hours. By 1982 the competitive outlook was clear. The market was finally accomplishing what the antitrust litigators were after. Between 1985 and 1992 IBM shed a hundred thousand employees. IBM's stock, worth $176 a share in 1987, collapsed to $52 by year's end 1992. In 1992 the *New York Times* would announce "The End of I.B.M.'s Overshadowing Role." In a desperate scramble for survival, IBM began breaking itself up into autonomous units and spinning off some of its more successful divisions.

A Federal Computer Commission would undoubtedly be regulating IBM to this day. The applications of Apple and Microsoft to enter the market would still be under careful consideration.

Closed Software

Apple rose and fell without hindrance or help from federal authorities. Microsoft rose and rose, so high that by 1990 it was a company worthy of an antitrust investigation of its own. Competitors complained that Microsoft had included undocumented features in its Windows software for the special advantage of its in-house developers of applications like word processors.

In early 1993 the Federal Trade Commission deadlocked 2–2 on whether to sue. The Department of Justice then initiated its own investigation. A settlement agreement, which addressed issues other than the matter of operating system leverage, was announced in mid-1994. Not long after, the Justice Department successfully blocked Microsoft's attempt to acquire Intuit, another software company best known for its checkbook program.

That antitrust lawyers are making only equivocal progress against Microsoft is as it should be. It is far from clear what more Microsoft could reasonably be required to do. There is no clean line between operating systems and applications. If valuable enough, today's fancy applications invariably migrate down to become tomorrow's basic utility. From the consumer's perspective, this is simply progress.

Antitrust claims against Microsoft will continue to be raised, however, for as long as Microsoft dominates any critical segment of the computer industry. And that too is as it should be. Commissions and acts of Congress can provide only simple and one-time answers—the last thing needed in a marketplace as complex and fast-changing as the software industry is today. Nothing more centralized or stable than antitrust-law jurisprudence can keep up. This is not to say that every antitrust prosecutor or judge will make the right call; there are bound to be mistakes. But the mistakes will be limited to a particular issue and case. Good calls will be made, too, and the small legal principles that they establish will be accepted by the industry and will endure. The development of law in this arena will be messy, but no messier than the underlying competitive realities.

What might a Federal Computer Commission have done to make sure that software markets developed "in the public interest"? The FCC's three Computer Inquiries spanned three decades. While the FCC pondered, phone companies were simply barred from deploying any computer-based services at all. An infant Microsoft forced to enter into any such labyrinth of lawyers would never have been seen again.

Content Bottlenecks

By 1945 over half of the 1,800 daily newspapers published in the United States, representing over three quarters of the total circulation, were under Associated Press contracts. AP refused to sell its service to any paper serving a market already served by another AP member. The Department of Justice sued, demanding that the bylaws be changed. The Supreme Court upheld an antitrust decree directing AP to halt the exclusive dealing.

The Justice Department sued Hollywood at about the same time, on a similar theory. The big studios were buying up local theaters and were refusing to provide movies to anyone else. In 1949 the studios were forced to divest themselves of many of their theaters. The advent of cable eventually changed the market conditions fundamentally. In the early 1980's Loew's, one of the original *Paramount* defendants, petitioned to vacate the original 1949 consent decree. The Reagan administration agreed that the time was ripe, and the decrees began to vanish.

The alternative federal watchdog for the Associated Press in 1945 would, of course, have been a Federal Newspaper Commission. Mercifully, there never was one. Hollywood escaped a Federal Movie Commission. The broadcast networks did not escape.

The early FCC did in fact launch one major, antitrust-like set of rules. These forced NBC to sell its second, "Blue" network and some of its stations to candy manufacturer Edward J. Noble on October 12, 1943. This network later became ABC. Antitrust courts could have achieved the same, with one critical difference. In affirming these FCC rules, the Supreme Court (per Justice Frankfurter) articulated its notorious "scarcity" theory, which all but eviscerated the First

Amendment rights of broadcasters. That affirmed the legitimacy of FCC regulation of the content of broadcasting—"fairness," advertising, children's television, indecency, prime time access, and all the rest—for decades to come. In affirming the Commission's power to mimic antitrust lawyers, the Supreme Court casually affirmed the Commission's power to mimic censors as well.

From then on, the Commission and the well-tamed broadcasters got along nicely. The most important structural supervision of the industry reverted to the Department of Justice.

A suit filed by the Justice Department in 1974 ended up limiting the power of ABC, CBS, and NBC to combine with the studios that create prime-time entertainment. All three networks signed consent decrees that incorporated the FCC's weaker rules on the subject and added stricter conditions. Unlike the FCC rules, however, most elements of the consent agreements were to sunset in 1991. The remaining provisions were vacated on November 8, 1993, by which time the networks' hegemony was clearly in decline.

Most recently government antitrust litigators have gone after the video affiliates of cable operators. Two 1993 consent decrees barred cable operators from unduly favoring affiliated programmers and cable-affiliated programmers from refusing to supply content to competing video distributors like satellite broadcasters. Again, the decrees duplicate and extend rules promulgated by the Commission in response to the 1992 Cable Act. But they are targeted precisely at the few key players that pose real anticompetitive concerns.

Piling on Patents

Some of the most creative applications of antitrust law have concerned copyrights and patents. Intellectual property rights are supposed to create monopolies of sorts. But when it comes to impeding competition, nothing is more potent than a great aggregation of ingenuity. Sometimes a single, very creative colossus like Bell Labs simply makes one pathbreaking discovery after another, and its patents pile up. Sometimes a number of incumbent players pool their patents to create enormous entry barriers against outsiders. Either way, control of key intellectual resources may translate into control of much more. Even legal monopolies can be pushed too far. Antitrust laws have provided the main line of defense.

The early motion picture industry coalesced around a patent pool. In 1908, led by Thomas Edison, industry leaders merged their companies and formed the Motion Picture Patents Company. The group pooled all licenses and patents held by its members, then brought numerous lawsuits against infringers. The first motion picture antitrust action stripped the trust of its power.

The next major trust involved the audion—the first vacuum tube electronic amplifier. For the first half of the century this single device, the predecessor to the transistor, was the electronic linchpin for all telephony, broadcast, and eventually the first-generation electronic computers. When the navy decreed a wartime moratorium on lawsuits over radio patents in 1917, manufacturers pooled their patents. AT&T, GE, RCA, Westinghouse, and others continued pooling more than four thousand patents after the war. In 1930 the Department of Justice charged them with conspiracy to monopolize radio manufacturing and transmission. Two years later the parties entered into a consent decree that effectively dismantled the trust.

The Bell System's enormous power likewise derived in significant part from its thousands of patents. The Department of Justice's 1949 suit against AT&T alleged that the company had attempted to monopolize telecommunications equipment and services through acquisition and licensing of patents. In the 1956 settlement AT&T agreed to grant nonexclusive licenses to all comers.

Antitrust law reacted in similar fashion to the pooling of copyrights. In response to the rise of radio, the music industry created performing-rights societies—clearinghouses for collecting royalties from radio stations and others prone to use copyrighted material without permission or payment. The first of these, the American Society of Composers, Authors, and Publishers (ASCAP), was formed by composers such as Victor Herbert and John Philip Sousa in 1913. Antitrust officials eventually concluded that all the good music was being bottled within ASCAP. An antitrust consent decree followed, empowering the decree court to prescribe a "reasonable fee" for all the musical compositions in ASCAP's repertory if the parties were unable to agree to one.

Conspiracy by Commission

The single largest obstacle to effective antitrust enforcement is a commission. The grander the commission, the greater the obstruction. Commissions sanitize conduct that would be baldly illegal under the Sherman Act. They establish, shelter, and prop up far more monopoly than Vail or Watson ever dreamed of grasping.

Counties and municipalities, which typically license cable systems, ordinarily are subject to antitrust laws in much the same way as private citizens. But state governments are not. And by formally delegating their powers, states can immunize local political entities, too. The Supreme Court has upheld the antitrust immunity of franchise authorities even in cases where local authorities had been overtly corrupted. Criminal misconduct under state law (bribery, say) does not open the door to antitrust liability. A municipality suitably empowered by the state does not face antitrust liability even when it owns the monopoly cable system itself. The FCC itself is wholly immune from any accountability under the antitrust laws.

Private parties acting under any of these regulatory umbrellas receive a considerable amount of shelter, too. Often the immunity is explicit. In 1921, for example, Congress gave the Interstate Commerce Commission (and later the FCC) authority to immunize local telephone mergers from antitrust scrutiny. The 1934 Communications Act assumed that telephone was a natural monopoly and empowered the FCC to restrict licenses accordingly, protecting the incumbent from all challengers. The established monopolist did not have to connect up with encroaching networks, either, unless the Commission so ordered.

In 1986 a federal court would thus rule that the old Bell System was immune from antitrust charges that it had manipulated private-line rates to drive small providers of alarm services out of business. Several other appellate courts accepted a limited immunity for good-faith denials of interconnection required by a carrier's "concrete, articulable concerns for the public interest," and ruled that a tariff approved after an FCC hearing should be much less vulnerable to antitrust attack than one merely filed but never reviewed. The 1996 Telecommunications Act at last eliminated one small piece of antitrust shelter formerly provided by FCC approval of mergers and acquisitions.

At the state level, utility commissions and municipal franchise boards can confer complete immunity from federal antitrust laws if they play their legal cards carefully. In a key 1943 holding, the Supreme Court ruled that the Sherman Act was not intended to prohibit states from establishing private monopolies if they chose to. The Court reiterated that conclusion in 1985. A private firm following state policy is immune from antitrust attack if the policy is "clearly articulated and affirmatively expressed." Once a state regulatory commission formally anoints a monopolist, that is the end of the matter so far as antitrust law is concerned.

Even when they do not receive complete immunity, regulatees that comply meticulously with commission regulation receive a good bit of practical protection. Where a direct conflict between antitrust and regulatory mandates seems likely, courts will generally suspend antitrust proceedings to allow the regulator a first chance to resolve it. And every antitrust defendant is, at the very least, entitled to demonstrate that regulation is an important "fact of market life" in its industry, one that reasonably shapes its business conduct. The fact-of-life defense may explain away overwhelmingly dominant market shares, for example.

Or it may refute the inference that monopoly proves monopolistic intent and exclusionary conduct. The Communications Act requires carriers to meet all demands for service; a firm that complies with that mandate cannot then easily be sued for having expanded to serve the whole market. The Filed Tariff Doctrine provides broad antitrust immunity against any customer's claim for antitrust damages alleged to result from payment of tariffed rates. And in all other cases the endorsement of monopolistic practices by a large, expert federal agency acts as a powerful anesthetic on both judges and juries.

With Bell, it was not until the Commission swung around to favor competition that the company began losing to private antitrust plaintiffs. Cable operators likewise began losing antitrust suits only after the FCC started actively opposing the attempts of local regulators to protect monopolies.

Finally, and most perversely, the monopoly-building tendencies of regulatory commissions sometimes impel antitrust authorities to outlaw competition itself. Understanding their reasons requires a brief excursion into economic theory. A telephone monopolist ordinarily has little incentive to mess around in adjacent, competitive markets, unless it has some truly competitive product to offer. Otherwise its best bet is simply to milk the home monopoly—telephones wires— and let others compete freely to provide complementary inputs like telephone sets or modems. Usually there is no extra profit to be gained by suppressing competition in competitive markets nearby.

But that changes once a commission begins regulating the price of the wires. Unable to earn its monopoly profit back home, the monopolist then does have an incentive to try to capture it in the neighbor's yard. By regulating monopoly prices, a commission thus creates the main antitrust rationale for quarantining the anointed monopolist. Confronted with the antitrust horrors of a commission, the antitrust prosecutor ends up erecting market-dividing walls that would themselves amount to criminal violations of the antitrust laws if set up by private agreement.

Commission by Decree

At their worst, the guardians of those walls end up building a commission, too. They pluck a commission from the womb of a court order and staff it with their own lawyers and economists. The new commission's charter is a decree—often a decree written by the Department of Justice's lawyers themselves.

For decades after, the Department of Justice and the court may then rule by waiver, modification, exemption, and enforcement proceeding. The new, judge-made commission issues the legal equivalent of licenses, regulates carriage and interconnection, oversees prices, monitors advertising, and promulgates rules to protect customer privacy. The forum is new, but all the rest is old. The best of antitrust law degrades into the worst of commission.

These degenerate antitrust bureaucracies may endure for very long periods. In 1915 George Eastman and the Eastman Kodak Company were found to have monopolized amateur photography. The first antitrust decree was issued in 1916. The Department of Justice sued again in 1954; Kodak settled. Not until 1994 were the two decrees finally vacated, and then only over the government's strong objection. The government's crusade against IBM took on a similar life of its own. The first suit was filed in 1952, and the case was assigned to federal Judge David Edelstein in New York. The parties signed a consent decree in 1956. The Justice Department sued again in 1969; that case was dropped in 1982, over Judge Edelstein's vehement objection. Only in 1995 did an appellate court finally remove Judge Edelstein from the case.

The most notorious example of commission by decree is the one created by the breakup of the Bell System. The clean, compact breakup was orchestrated by a twenty-page consent decree. That should have been the end of it.

The settlement divided Bell's local phone companies from its manufacturing and long-distance arms. The latter businesses, inherited by the new AT&T, were thought to be competitive, or at least potentially so. So far as antitrust officials were concerned, AT&T was free thereafter to compete as it pleased. The seven Baby Bells, by contrast, were to be strictly quarantined. They would be forbidden to provide long-distance service and information services, or to manufacture telecommunications equipment. Instead they were required, under pain of criminal sanction, to supply equal access to independent suppliers of these services.

The proposed settlement was duly presented to Judge Greene. He took charge, created a system for granting waivers to the decree quarantine, and then ran that system for the next fourteen years. His courtroom operated as a shadow FCC, an independent authority that scrutinized, cajoled, hectored, and prosecuted. There were hundreds of motions, complaints, and other requests to enforce, modify, or interpret. The Justice Department issued thousands of advisory letters. The court received over six thousand briefs. Thirteen groups of consolidated appeals were carried to a federal appellate court in Washington. The Supreme Court received half a dozen divestiture-related petitions for review. The decree developed its own lore, common law, unique traditions, precedents, procedures, formalities, and technical vocabulary.

Getting an answer to a simple question often took years. Some requests for interpretation were simply met with enduring silence. In March 1988, for example, the Department of Justice recommended that South Central Bell be allowed to provide interexchange private-line service between Northwest Alabama Junior College and its off-campus extension in Tuscumbia, Alabama. Nine months passed before the private-line service was authorized. Waivers were approved one local phone company at a time, and sometimes household by household: "Pacific Bell is permitted to provide telephone service to Mrs. Mary Campbell, who lives in the Plymouth exchange in the Stockton, California LATA, via the Placerville central office in the Sacramento, California LATA"; "Wisconsin Bell may provide inter-LATA cross-boundary foreign exchange service to Ms. Vicki Millard and Mr. Ricky Schultz, as directed by the Wisconsin Public Service Commission." Judge Greene approved twenty or so such requests every year.

A 1995 Justice Department proposal to grant limited relief to two local phone companies in Chicago and Grand Rapids occupied twice as much paper as the entire original decree that broke up the national Bell System. This Son-of-Sam decree addressed network information, billing services, and customer lists. It devoted four paragraphs to regulations for marketing services to business customers and another three to marketing to residential customers. The Justice Department itself was to review and approve a written script used by Ameritech to sell interexchange service. Two paragraphs were required to spell out how Ameritech would list local competitors in its white pages.

The 1996 Telecommunications Act put an end to all this. It transferred authority over the key line-of-business restrictions to the FCC, and it established a process and timetable for getting rid of them all.

Until the Constable Arrives

The commission-by-decree problem notwithstanding, antitrust law remains by far the best instrument for policing economic behavior in the telecosm. It has been said that a screwdriver is not very good for driving a nail, but the question must be, compared to what? Compared to a banana it is pretty good. Much the same holds for antitrust law. It is not a perfect instrument for promoting competition, but it is vastly better than a commission.

The FCC tries to work out most things in advance—and while it frets, the market waits. Antitrust lawyers attack specific problems retrospectively, after they have been presented as concrete facts. And when problems are fixed, or fix themselves, the antitrust lawyers leave. The Bell decree created a quagmire, but only because its authors so feared the monopoly-building proclivities of commissions. If the commissions had been swept aside much earlier, the commission-by-decree nonsense would never have been contemplated at all.

Most antitrust suits are prosecuted outside the shadow of commissions, and most reach compact conclusions. The defendant is vindicated, or the jury returns a verdict commensurate with the plaintiff's economic injury. Any money verdict is automatically trebled; this acts as a powerful deterrent for the defendant and anyone else engaged in similar business practices. If the subject of the suit is a proposed merger, either the merger is blocked or it goes through. If the suit involves charges of attempted monopolization, specific anticompetitive practices may be proscribed. If the suit involves charges of actual monopolization, the monopolist may be broken up into two or more pieces.

These verdicts are usually clean. The ones with the fewest words—pure monetary verdicts—often speak the loudest. MCI's first suit against AT&T culminated in a treble-damage verdict of $1.8 billion, serious money even by AT&T's standards, still serious even after it was cut to $113 million on appeal. The AT&T divestiture decree, which took effect a year after a federal appellate court affirmed the MCI award, merely built on what private suits were already accomplishing. Even if AT&T had never been broken apart, the MCI verdict, and the threat of an indefinite chain of others like it, would have forced Bell to open up its networks quickly enough.

The antitrust verdicts with the most potential for mischief are those that order an end to anticompetitive practices. Prospective orders require ongoing enforcement. But even these can be comparatively simple to administer, and their enforcement can remain largely in private hands. There is no commission on the scene, no permanent bureaucracy, no army of federal employees hanging around indefinitely to meddle and mess up.

Noncommission decrees have successfully addressed virtually every issue discussed in the remaining chapters of this book. They can require interconnection and thus enforce principles of common carriage. They can require unbundling of content and conduit or the dissolution of patent pools. They can force copyright owners to give access to their copyrights. Anything that an economic commission can order, an antitrust court can order, too. The difference is that the antitrust court acts on a specific complaint against specific parties. It bases its judgment on a solid record of things that have already happened, not things that might (or might not) someday come to pass.

Even the most ambitious antitrust decrees don't try to solve everything. Commission-centered laws carve up and segregate the entire telecommunications universe into fixed settlements and townships. Antitrust law is applied case by case, to a specific enterprise in a specific market, to Oshkosh Telephone but not Okefenokee Cable. This creates more uncertainty than rules codified by a commission. But it allows for much more flexibility and a much more precise focus on concrete problems. Consent decrees normally sunset automatically after ten years. They can be vacated sooner.

When the FCC gets paralyzed by an excess of lawyers or simply grows senile or indolent, entire industries grind to a halt, because permissions to get on with life are no longer forthcoming. Under the antitrust laws, economic life goes on, albeit not always perfectly, until the constable arrives. Economic life organized under functioning antitrust laws allows the law-abiders to grow and build while the pursuit of wrongdoers is under way. The social costs of paralysis-by-analysis in the FCC far outweigh the costs of possible paralysis among antitrust prosecutors.

In any event, we can certainly stop worrying that dismantling the FCC will leave the marketplace naked and vulnerable. Eliminating the commission created in 1934 would not eliminate the antitrust law codified in 1890. Quite the contrary; eliminating commissions eliminates the commission-centered defenses to the antitrust laws. And as we have seen, antitrust law can spawn a new, ad hoc commission when it needs to. This is nothing to be very proud of, for commission-by-decree is antitrust law at its worst. But the fact that shadow commissions can be convened so easily must surely allay any fear that the demise of traditional tele-commissions would end in economic catastrophe. The economic catastrophe arrived in 1934. In the six decades of its existence, the Commission has suppressed far more competition than it ever promoted.

Like Aeschines, the FCC has quite often spoken well of competition, particularly in recent years. But it took another kind of oratory to inspire a real march against monopoly.

9

The Ascent of Competition

Among economists, it has been said, the real world is often a special case. When MCI took on AT&T in the 1960s, the contest seemed laughably uneven. AT&T had a nationwide network and a national brand. MCI started with a handful of microwave towers. Competition, the expert economists agreed, was not merely inefficient; it was impossible.

Yet from the day the FCC stepped out of the way, MCI offered nationwide service. It duplicated AT&T's network on just a few, profitable routes and resold AT&T services to cover the rest. MCI then slowly built out its network.

All the theories, statutes, and regulations that said competition couldn't work have been proved false. Given half a chance, competition has confounded natural-monopoly pessimists every time.

Telephony I

The lawyers who broke up Bell in 1984 were following MCI's beacon. They assumed that telephony consisted of two discrete markets, long-distance service and local service. Local service was a natural monopoly, but long distance could be competitive. AT&T, the largest corporation in the world, was carved up accordingly.

The antitrust surgeons believed in competitive long distance for much the same reason that they believed in baptism: they'd seen it done. MCI had been feverishly building up a competitive microwave network. But the surgeons also believed in it because they had a theory. Long-distance service was (at the time) a radio market—the *M* in MCI stood for *microwave*. And it was clear that competing providers could deploy microwave towers at least as cheaply as Bell. The basic building block in microwave transmission is a radio capable of handling twelve voice calls. Long-distance networks carry a lot more traffic than that. So in microwave transmission, costs rise as traffic volumes increase. In economic terms, radio-based services are not natural monopolies.

But as the ink was drying on the AT&T divestiture decree, the long-distance microwave towers were being dynamited to the ground. Sprint ran ads showing the spectacle. Fiber-optic glass was replacing radio. The industry didn't need radio anymore—except in a little-noticed new business at the fringe of telephony called cellular.

With radio, a carrier's costs add up as traffic volumes increase. Not so with glass. The up-front cost˘ of deploying fiber-optic cable are very high. Rights of way must be secured, and laying cable is horribly labor-intensive. The costs are largely the same whether the fiber-optic cable contains one pair of optical fibers or a dozen, whether the fiber is "lit" (i.e. connected to functioning electronics) or "dark," and whether the lit fiber carries a million telephone calls or none at all. Costs are incurred at the front end and they are fixed; wire networks have almost zero (or even negative) salvage value; costs are irrevocably sunk before they generate a single dollar of revenue.

Once the glass cable is in place, though, the cost of running traffic through it is almost vanishingly small. And the carrying capacity of fiber-optic glass can be increased almost indefinitely, and at very little cost. Every few years engineers double the carrying capacity of that cable. There is, in short, every reason to believe that fiber-optic long-distance transmission is characterized by sharply declining average costs over the whole range of demand. And that is what economists have always called a natural monopoly.

For a decade after the Bell breakup, the long-distance market continued to behave much like a monopoly. Candice Bergen (a.k.a. Murphy Brown) put on a good show, but it was Hollywood, not Wall Street. When not debating former Vice President Quayle about unwed motherhood, Bergen made ads for Sprint. All the advertising by new carriers certainly gave the appearance of sharp competition. But in the first decade after divestiture, there was far less there than met the eye.

Prices did drop sharply—but largely because local phone companies were directed by regulators to slash the access charges assessed on all long-distance calls (see chapter 10). Setting those adjustments aside, long-distance prices changed little. The industry was characterized instead by "umbrella pricing"—the diminutive upstarts set their prices just an inch under the canopy maintained by AT&T. The gap in prices between AT&T and its competitors steadily narrowed, from 10 to 20 percent in mid-1984 to about 5 percent in 1987, to still smaller margins today. AT&T's ads showing a penny of difference between its prices and Candice Bergen's didn't lie. Price competition all but disappeared.

While it praised competition, the FCC enforced laws and promulgated rules that helped suppress it. AT&T was ostensibly subject to price-cap regulation by the FCC, but the cap was really a floor. In this particular arena, the Commission spent most of its time making sure that AT&T didn't lower its prices too fast; competitors rushed to court whenever AT&T's prices seemed likely to fall. The perverse upshot, as the chairman of the FCC at one point acknowledged, was that the FCC itself "afford[ed] competitors many ways to energize the regulatory process to block price reductions potentially offered by AT&T. Most importantly, this [held] prices artificially higher, and reduce[d] customer choice."

More telling still, long-distance prices remained remarkably stable. This was extraordinary for an industry characterized (as the long-distance industry is) by high fixed—but very low marginal—costs of operation. The airline industry, with a similar cost structure, was going through frequent and convulsive pricing wars. By the early 1990s, by contrast, AT&T had begun slowly raising its prices once again. As a trade group of its competitors noted, AT&T was "apparently confident that doing so will not cause it to lose business to its rivals."

After declining sharply following divestiture, AT&T's share of the overall interexchange market stabilized at just over half of all customers. AT&T ceded some market share (by keeping its own prices high) to increase short-term earnings and to win regulatory flexibility. In an age of rapidly declining costs, it was more important for AT&T to break free from regulation than to protect the last 10 or 20 percent of its market share. Costs in the industry were dropping rapidly due to advances in fiber-optic technology. It was well worth surrendering 10 percent of market share so regulators could then be persuaded to disregard 20 percent reductions in cost.

Yet with all that said, the illusion of competition served far better than what it replaced. Long-distance prices were certainly higher than they would have been if a single efficient, efficiently regulated fiber-optic monopolist (AT&T) had stayed in sole possession of the long-distance market all along. But efficient monopolists don't exist.

Efficient regulators don't, either. Without the competitive pressure created by MCI's entry, long-distance traffic would probably still travel by radio, not glass. The illusion created by Candice Bergen is, on balance, far more attractive than the old reality. That was Lily Tomlin.

And in any event, a new and far more robust round of competition is about to be launched. The biggest mistake made in 1982 was to trust economic theory—not where it predicted competition, but where it predicted monopoly. Even "natural" monopolies can be attacked by competitors; at worst, the contest for the monopoly can last for as long as it takes technologists to discover economically viable alternatives. The only companies positioned to challenge AT&T head-on today are, of course, its own children—the Regional Bell Companies. They have region-wide glass in the ground, and the corporate bulk to take on such a rival. There are seven of them, each with roughly the same revenues and resources as MCI.

When they enter long-distance markets, these local phone companies will be seen by all the incumbents, large and small, as potentially lethal competitors. Honest—and bloody—price wars will break out. Prices will fall steadily. AT&T and its Bell Company progeny will be in a pitched battle for supremacy, not only in the national toll markets still dominated by AT&T, but also in the $9 billion short-haul toll markets still dominated by the Baby Bells. MCI and its other competitors will be allied with one or more of them. Bergen, Brown, and baby will be, too.

Telephony II

At the press conference announcing the breakup of Bell, AT&T's CEO, Charlie Brown, was asked who was going to get the infant cellular properties, AT&T or the Regional Bells. He didn't know. The economists and lawyers who framed the divestiture decree had all but ignored radio, along with most of the rest of the local exchange. Brown's negotiators had made a $17 billion mistake. Cellular was theirs for the taking; they just didn't think to take it.

The breakup lawyers had it all worked out. The local exchange, being a wireline network, was a natural monopoly. Local competition wasn't possible; it wasn't even desirable. The divestiture decree made no attempt to promote it. AT&T's infant cellular operations were handed over to the local Bells without further ado. A decade later AT&T would pay $17 billion to acquire McCaw, a pioneer in cellular service.

Perhaps the experts of the day could hardly be blamed for missing something that would turn out to be so important. In 1981 radio-based telephone systems were almost unknown. The FCC had licensed the very first commercial cellular system just a couple of years earlier in Illinois. When they thought about the local exchange, the legal pundits and theoreticians thought about copper wire. To this day, the isn't-technology-keen pictures show a single strand of glass beside a huge bundle of copper wires. But the comparison is all wrong. What the glass first replaced was microwave radio in the long-distance market. Microwave radio then turned around to attack copper in the local market.

As for the antitrust lawyers back in 1982, they weren't completely crazy. Radio is indeed more competitive than wire. What the lawyers missed was that radio was finished in the long-distance industry but was just getting started back in the local exchange.

In the following five years the FCC completed the licensing of cellular systems nationwide. Competition in the cellular telephone industry rapidly filled the allocated space. The cellular industry reached the million-customer mark in 1987. The industry serves more than thirty million subscribers today. Two out of every three new telephone numbers are being assigned to cellular phones. When it was sold to AT&T in 1994, McCaw Cellular—unaffiliated with any local telephone company—was the largest cellular telephone company in the world.

With digital cellular technology the capacity of the airwaves can be expanded indefinitely, but always at a cost: More users require more cells, and more cells require more radios. That means no natural monopoly. Quite the opposite: The more crowded the airwaves, the more economically viable competition becomes. A single, very powerful, centrally owned and maintained transmitter, is economically favored only in the land of Kim-il Song or Fidel Castro, where one voice says it all. With many voices to carry, there can be many carriers.

For some years to come, the incumbent local phone companies will remain leading, and in many areas dominant, providers of local telephone services. Their businesses will continue to grow in absolute terms, because demand is growing faster than anything. But their market share will fall steadily. By analogy, AT&T's revenues have grown steadily since 1984, yet during that same period it lost some 40 percent of the long-distance market to competitors like MCI.

Pure resellers will enter first; they will focus on providing ancillary services such as marketing, billing, and operator support. Because these services do not require networks, competitors in these arenas can materialize almost overnight. Resellers will put serious competitive pressure on incumbent telephone companies even while they still rely on those companies' facilities, just as MCI put pressure on AT&T even in MCI's early years as a reseller. Resellers will exploit every price dislocation maintained by regulators, in much the same way as Wall Street arbitrageurs ferret out even the smallest price anomalies in capital markets.

One step beyond pure resale lie competitive switching and intelligent services. Switches and other forms of equipment operated by private institutional users already provide a significant volume of competitive local switching and intelligent services. Major long-distance carriers also have switches in every major community. AT&T, MCI, and others will deploy thousands of additional switches, both in their own offices and for private customers. These "switch" competitors will aim to cannibalize 20 to 50 percent of incumbent local phone company revenues, even while they still rely on phone company wires.

Competitive wires will follow. Competitive Access Providers (CAPs) provide links between long-distance carriers and large institutional customers in major urban markets. Cable operators are upgrading their networks to provide digital, hybrid fiber-coax. Electric and other utilities will attempt to enter the local market as well. With fiber-optic networks already in place, the utilities will be offering equivalent services within a few years.

Competitive wireless systems will evolve in parallel. Within a few years five or more significant competitors will be contending for share in every wireless market. Through new allocations of spectrum, the introduction of digital radio, and the shrinking of cell sites, the overall transmission capacity of wireless service spectrum bands will increase at least tenfold over the next five years, and at least a hundredfold over the course of the next decade. The price of wireless service will drop steadily. Wireless links will become competitive with wireline, for voice and some kinds of data, in the last mile of the network.

This last prediction does not look to price alone. Wireless service offers consumers a better product—full mobility. That advantage will make wireless an attractive substitute even at higher prices. For decades consumers were happy enough with free broadcast. The FCC officially scoffed at the idea that significant numbers of consumers would prefer to pay $20 a month or more for cable. But most households in fact did, because cable was so much better than the free service it replaced. Wireless and wireline telephony are now on a similar competitive trajectory.

Through McCaw, AT&T has made wireless a cornerstone of its strategy to reenter the local exchange. Cable companies will combine cable backbone networks with wireless "local loops." (WirelessCo, an alliance that combines Sprint, TCI, Comcast, and Cox, was the largest bidder for new personal communications services (PCS) wireless licenses; the consortium paid $2.1 billion for twenty-nine licenses that cover 145 million potential subscribers.) Electric utilities see wireless as an excellent fit to their extensive fiber networks and rights-of-way. The fiber and coaxial backbone networks that CAPs, cable companies, and power companies already have in place allow these enterprises to deploy simple radio base station microcells (for as little as $3,000 a site) and make efficient use of large switches in distant central offices.

The wireless-wireline battle will be much messier for competitors than for consumers. Wireless phones can readily be built to include the intelligence needed to play off one type of service against the other, drawing alternately on each to get the most convenient service at the lowest price. A smart wireless phone can simply operate as a cordless phone and lock directly into the landline network when close to a home-base unit, an entirely personal microcell. The same phone can tune in to a cellular or PCS cell to bypass whichever aspects of local wired service are priced too high. And only the wireless phone will follow the owner on the road. Phones with these capabilities are already in service. They will soon be ubiquitous.

Video and Data

Cable and data networks are converging into all-purpose networks, fully capable of providing telephony, video entertainment, and two-way data communications.

Though they can readily travel over the same networks, video, data, and voice present different demands from an engineering perspective. Video transmission requires huge bandwidth but not perfect fidelity; a lost bit here or there doesn't matter. Data networks require near-perfect fidelity, though that can be ensured largely by intelligent processing and error correction at the ends of the line. Computers are also more forgiving about timing; they can normally wait a second here or there, searching out and taking advantage of dead space, in ways that would be intolerable to people conducting a conversation or watching a movie. Voice is like video in that the consumer demands what appears to be a continuous connection but tolerates quite low fidelity; voice is like data in that two-way, low-bandwidth connections are the norm.

Broadband networks and fast packet switches transcend all these differences. Once networks can send data packets quickly enough, and intelligent terminals can assemble them smoothly enough, voice, data, and video will move side by side.

Delivering more than one form of content on a single network offers many efficiencies. Apart from the obvious business advantages of one-stop marketing and provisioning, data transport can often be provided very cheaply at the margin, as the secondary and much more flexible user of whatever extra bandwidth happens to be available.

Every major network operator will attempt to occupy the center of the voice-video-data triangle. Local phone companies will seek to enter the video market and improve their data services by increasing the bandwidth of wireline networks and developing new wireless video and data services. Cable operators, broadcasters, and wireless carriers will offer data delivery in addition to video and voice service.

By early in the next century, a third of all video traffic will move on media other than cable, and a third of all data traffic will move on media other than telephone lines. Other wire and wireless technologies will supply access to the Internet and e-mail. Cable will offer two-way digital data and extremely fast Internet access. Once customers get used to relying on cable for high-speed data services, they may migrate more readily to cable voice services. Five or six direct broadcast satellites (DBS) will use digital technology to supply one-way video, and they will also provide data services by closing the loop over telephone lines. Many cable operators are nearing the halfway point in upgrading their networks to a digital, hybrid fiber-coax architecture, capable of delivering telephone and other advanced information and two-way services.

As cable, DBS, and other technologies gain even more ground, broadcasters will look to use some of their spectrum for other telecom services. Television broadcasters already transmit data on subcarrier and vertical blanking interval channels; they too are developing digital data capabilities. The new 6 MHz blocks of spectrum that will probably be given to broadcasters, ostensibly for high-definition television (HDTV), will end up being used largely for wireless data and voice services.

From Cheops to Fuller

As competitive networks multiply, the telecommunications infrastructure is changing from a pyramid to something more like a geodesic dome—from Cheops to Buckminster Fuller. The old telephone network was a carefully tiered edifice, a rigid hierarchy of phones and switches, as solid and permanent as a great pyramid, which on paper it resembled. Broadcast was a sideshow. Cable didn't exist.

Then transistors and the microchip changed everything. Electronic switching became cheap. Switches and other intelligent nodes proliferated everywhere. Every network node sprouted new arms. Network "terminals" no longer terminated; rather, they interconnected. End-office switches in the local public exchange, which previously had connected only down to customer premises and up to a higher-level AT&T switch, began connecting to a constellation of private exchanges, mainframe computers, packet switches, and mobile terminal switches.

Computers, which also serve as network nodes, were transformed in much the same way. Users who once made a long pilgrimage (in person or through the telephone network) to a few thousand mainframes began working on tens of millions of desktop machines. Computers came equipped with a wide array of standard ports that supported interconnection with everything.

This dispersion of intelligent nodes, the multiplication of the connections between them, and the cascade of traffic handoffs that the network now supports would have been senselessly cumbersome and expensive in the days when switching was handled by plug boards and human operators. With the inexpensive electronic technology available today, no other design makes sense.

The old parallel, segregated networks of telephony and broadcast had simple Euclidean structures, with an inside, an outside, and clear divisions between them. The new networks are described by the mathematics of fractals, with nodes leading into lines, which lead into more nodes, the pattern replicating itself indefinitely down to the smallest scales. The old network made each link in the edifice utterly dependent for support on one link above and one below. Today's smart switches and terminals can hand off and receive traffic and information from all sides. Everything is cross-linked and interconnected. The old pyramid, with all its mass in the center, has become a geodesic dome, with a profusion of nodes and links unknown in the older architecture, connected around the outside.

Unbundling America

The centrifugal forces that are pulling apart the great centralized powers of the telecosm are also pulling apart everything else that is too large, bureaucratic, or centralized. As channels of communications expand, the old hegemonies shrink.

The school classroom is a technology of sorts—a medium of communication, still rooted in nineteenth-century methods and capabilities. But as Lewis J. Perelman has described in his 1992 book *School's Out*, we are fast moving into a new era, one of desktop classrooms and desktop schools. The huge, centralized university has become the greatest anachronism of all, a throwback to the days when scholars had to congregate around a few scarce libraries if they wanted to consult references or interact with intellectual peers.

Labor markets are shrinking, too. The new union has a membership of one. Teleconferencing, electronic data interchange, computerized inventory control, and groupware knit together lots of small, independent suppliers and let them do things that not long ago were centralized under a single corporate roof—and do them much more efficiently. People who really produce are in high demand, and no one much cares anymore about their race or religion, sex, social graces, or physical appearance.

Giant corporations are outsourcing and shrinking. As economics Nobelist Ronald Coase explained years ago, the internal collectivism of a corporation makes economic sense only when the cost of conducting countless little everyday transactions at arm's length with independent contractors outweighs the benefits. But every advance in new communications and computer technologies changes the equation. Car manufacturers, for example, can become efficient assemblers of parts provided by hundreds of independent suppliers. Secretaries, accountants, and designers—large numbers of people who provide an enterprise's support services—are being replaced by independent outsiders, knitted together into an efficient whole not by corporate autocracy but by the market and the electronic network. Communications technology slashes what economists call "transaction costs." As these costs decline, so does the traditional logic for keeping business inside your own cozy corporate community.

Money itself is shrinking. Gregory Millman makes the case for this in his 1995 book *The Vandals' Crown*, following up on Joel Kurtzman's 1993 analysis in *The Death of Money*. A dollar bill has no inherent value; it is just a primitive medium of communication, a record of past effort and a promise of future return. A single, master record keeper, the government treasury, with a single, centralized printing press, has absolute power to determine value. But the technologies of the tele-cosm are now privatizing money itself. Instead of greenbacks, we put our trust in a thousand different private currencies: personal checks, stock certificates, bonds, credit card slips, futures contracts, green stamps, and patronage accounts of every kind, along with yen, francs, and marks. With perfect communication, currencies of every imagin-able description can be created by the market itself, like all other goods.

Democracy is getting smaller, too. Opinion polls, call-in shows, and electronic town meetings usurp the mediating function of people like Sam Donaldson and George Will. The middleman in the dialogue of democratic government is cut out of the process, in much the same way as Sears is cut out by mail-order catalogues and 800 numbers. Governments have always derived their just powers directly from the consent of the governed, but now consent can be sought directly, quickly, and efficiently, on issues both large and small. This moves power into constantly shifting communities of shopkeepers, house-wives, Yale bulldogs, fruit-juice thinkers, nudists, sandal wearers, sex maniacs, Quakers, Nature Cure quacks, pacifists, and phesbian leminists.

Cities are spreading out. With today's tele-electronics, being on Wall Street or Madison Avenue in the flesh isn't such an advantage anymore. Anyone can have a virtual seat on the stock exchange or a video-conferenced presence in the boardroom. Architecturally speak-ing, the Internet is the exact opposite of the traditional metropolis: It is urban sprawl carried to the electronic limit, a network of networks, with Oshkoshers and New Yorkers granted equal dignity so far as the routing of bits and fortunes is concerned. The great traditional cen-ters of capital and influence are flattening out, the skyscrapers melt-ing not just into New Jersey but into Kansas.

As Walter Wriston argues in *The Twilight of Sovereignty*, the power of the telecosm is redefining the nation-state itself. To protect the land of 297 cheeses (or some such number) from the culture of Kraft Singles, the French are trying to build a Maginot Line once again, this time against photons and bytes. But entertainment is becoming as mobile as money. And any French citizen who cares to can already trade stocks, pay bills, and move cash to, from, and among American institutions at will. So far as the networks and electronic machines are concerned, it doesn't make a speck of difference whether you're sipping Perrier in Burbank or quaffing Coke in Alsace-Lorraine. Governments have to choose: A nation can enter the telecosm or it can erect walls to defend its culture, but it cannot do both. The whole point of telecommunications technology is that it transcends geography.

Even war is getting small. To begin with, the economic motives for war are disappearing. In a world where most value consists of information, labor can move instantly across frontiers. Human minds can thus escape faster than any soldier can pursue. For the most part, wars are no longer fought against people, nor even against their possessions. They are fought against what coordinates a nation—its ideas, its slogans, its propaganda, the instruments of its Thought Police.

If wars are fought anyway, telecommunications wins them fast and clean. A bomb, artillery shell, or missile is one part matter (the size of the bang) and several parts mind (where the bang occurs). In smart weapons, pounds of guidance substitute for tons of explosive. Satellite-guided, computer-controlled cruise missiles rain down with relentless precision, not on common people but on the enemy's main ministries, principal bridges, highways, central banks, electric power plants, and reserves of fuel. Then the war is over, almost as soon as it began. Only one kind of society can survive such an attack: a society with no central brain, no all-powerful Ministry in the heart of its capital city, no single place where all the wisdom of the state can be lost in an instant to a bomb addressed as precisely as a postcard.

In the telecosm, the greatest decentralization of all will involve speech itself. The new technology gives voice to the average man and woman. Bulletin boards, auditoriums, theaters, schools, stadia, squares, subway walls—electronic replacements for all the traditional public forums—can be created on demand, in the capacious light beams of the network and the airwaves of the stratosphere. The network gives the pamphleteer and soap-box orator not just a place in Speaker's Corner but the whole of Hyde Park. There is room for the Pacifist, the Communist, the Anarchist, the Jehovah's Witness, Temperance reformers, Trotskyists, Freethinkers, vegetarians, and any number of plain lunatics: All will be able to speak out over the network, all will receive a good-humored hearing from anyone who chooses to listen. Every hobby and pastime—birding, fretwork, carpentry, bees, carrier pigeons, home conjuring, philately, chess—can have its own channel, its own forum. There is room enough for flower lovers and stamp collectors, pigeon fanciers, amateur carpenters, coupon snippers, darts players, and crossword puzzle fans. The days of mindless broadcast to the mindless masses are over.

III

MAKING
CONNECTIONS

10

Pricing

The telecosm is the last refuge of Communism. Prices are still set largely by government decree. They are maintained at politically convenient levels by elaborate bureaucracies of accountants and lawyers, acting under the direction of political chiefs.

Prices set by commission follow a logic all their own. The products themselves are kept as simple and standard as military uniforms— government bureaucrats can't keep a grip on things otherwise. Prices are averaged across consumers, partly because a commission lacks resources to calibrate prices more finely and partly because uniform prices fit with populist politics. The services consumers want most are sold far below cost, just as bread was in the old Soviet Union. Cake is sold dear, to make up the shortfall.

This requires a monopoly for both bread and cake. In open markets, traders ferret out incorrect prices, buy in bulk where prices are too cheap, and undercut prices that are too high. Price averaging collapses.

Defenders of price regulation usually tell the story the other way around. The monopoly came first. Then regulators intervened to prevent gouging. If some prices are set above cost and others are set below, that just accommodates popular will. Traders and competitors are indeed barred from "skimming the cream," but so they should be. Competition of that character is inimical to the overall public good. The commission created to control monopoly must reluctantly end up protecting it.

Carriage

Telephones were added to the ICC's railroad jurisdiction in 1910. But the ICC was empowered to set aside "unjust or unreasonable" carrier rates only for railroads. It was never given comparable authority over telephony.

The 1934 Communications Act took care of that omission. The law, essentially unchanged since its enactment, sets forth detailed provisions directing common carriers to file tariffs with the FCC. The Act declares unlawful any tariffs, rates, charges, or other practices that are "unjust or unreasonable."

For five decades FCC price regulation has involved a mind-numbing process of regulatory Cuisinart. Federal regulators proceed through hundreds of stages of slicing, chopping, and dicing. Costs and revenues of regulated businesses are divided from unregulated ones. Different rates of return are applied to debt, preferred stock, and common equity. Costs are then divided among dozens of different service categories—business and residence, high-volume and low-volume, switched and unswitched, and so on. Joint and common costs incurred in providing more than one service have to be divvied up, too, even when inherently indivisible.

The most important cut of all, however, is the first one. The Communications Act divides the power to regulate carriers between federal and state authorities. Costs, revenues, profits—everything else—have to be separated accordingly. Even the seemingly local switch, phone line, telephone operator, or service technician is sliced into two pieces in the books of account, one local, the second federal.

At first this division was not seen as a vehicle for subsidizing anything in particular. Over time, however, both state and federal regulators embraced the idea that long-distance rates should help subsidize local service. This policy was formalized in the Ozark Plan of 1970.

A government with the policy of robbing Peter to pay Paul, it has been noted, can be assured of the support of Paul. There were more state regulators than federal commissioners, and together they had far more political clout. So the subsidies grew and grew. By 1980 roughly one quarter of the cost of local lines, switches, and service was being paid for by revenues from long-distance toll calls—even though these calls accounted for only 8 percent of access line usage. AT&T, the nation's main long-distance carrier, was sending about half its revenues straight back to local exchange companies—some $11 billion a year. Interstate callers paid as much as 10 cents a minute for the purely local parts of the connection—far more than those parts actually cost to provide.

The purpose of this huge cross-subsidy was to lower and average what residential consumers saw on their monthly bills as the price of local phone service. Frequent users of long-distance service paid for the nation's telephone plant far out of proportion to how much they actually used it. Subscribers who did not use toll service at all received phone service far below cost. Rural users were subsidized the most.

Broadcast

Bell's original patents were on the telephone itself; the wires in between were just a come-on for the box. The first public radio broadcasts were likewise subsidized by manufacturers of patented radios; hardware manufacturers like General Electric and Westinghouse dominated the infancy of broadcasting. Many early operators of community antenna cable systems were appliance stores that wanted to promote sales of TV sets in rural areas that didn't get many signals. In England the government still levies an annual tax on every television to subsidize the BBC. British tax collectors deploy platoons of electronic snoops to sniff out tax-evading TVs. They also tax videocassettes made in Hollywood to subsidize broadcast made in London.

When the early radio patents expired, American broadcasters needed other sources of funding. Although expelled from the industry not long after, Bell was the first to finance radio with advertising. In 1922 Bell's WEAF broadcast the first paid commercial announcement, a ten-minute monologue on behalf of a real estate company. By 1927 NBC was charging sponsors as much as $3,770 per hour on its Red network. A few years later NBC adopted a fully commercial policy.

William S. Paley, advertising manager of his family-owned Congress Cigar Company, experimented with cigar advertisements on a Philadelphia station, WCAU, and was delighted with the response. WCAU was an affiliate of a new network started by a manufacturer of gramophones, Columbia Phonograph. Paley bought the network, which was later renamed CBS. Tobacco would be a financial mainstay of broadcasting for the next four decades.

Advertisers soon learned that vaudeville-trained comedians lured larger audiences than live music, the early staple of radio. Networks leased facilities to advertising agencies, which hired the performers. In 1930 the first ratings showed that NBC's *Amos 'n' Andy* was four times more popular than any CBS show. Ratings placed broadcast on an economically sustainable course. Broadcasters didn't sell entertainment—that was free. They sold eardrums, and later eyeballs. Advertisers bought. Ratings bureaus set the price.

Without conscious deliberation, Congress made this economic structure all but mandatory in the Radio Act of 1927. The rudimentary economic arrangements that had been adopted by the infant broadcast industry became a rigid and permanent federal policy. The only correct price for broadcasting was no price—broadcasting was to remain forever free.

The Federal Radio Commission (later the FCC) was happy to enforce the policy. It blocked every initiative that threatened to shift programming from unscrambled airwaves onto any less-than-free media. Viewers were to pay for programming by buying Wheaties.

The main beneficiaries of this policy were Madison Avenue and its advertising clients. Hollywood was prevented from selling its content directly to viewers. Broadcasters were prevented from selling their delivery services directly to viewers. Both could sell only to advertisers. The FCC had suppressed outlawed competition from all the other possible buyers. Not until cable broke free were the creators of content finally permitted to sell programming directly to viewers.

Cable

The first cable systems functioned as carriers. Few local authorities bothered to regulate prices in the infant industry. And in the late 1960s the FCC ordered them not to regulate programming originated by cable operators themselves.

But as cable prospered, regulatory attitudes hardened. In 1972 the FCC directed local authorities to put in place rudimentary procedures to regulate cable rates. The Commission also took a first stab at drawing the line between basic and premium cable services. Only basic services—retransmitted broadcast signals—would be scrutinized by the price police.

For the next twenty years the trend was toward less price regulation, not more. The FCC authorized local authorities to deregulate cable completely if they chose. Most demanded the opportunity to review any proposed rate increases but didn't supervise any more closely than that. In 1974 the FCC ordered complete deregulation of all per-program or per-channel charges as well as charges for cable advertising, digital services, alarm systems, two-way, and leased channels—everything beyond a loosely defined basic tier.

The 1984 Cable Act endorsed these deregulatory initiatives. Basic service prices would remain regulated only when the cable system was not subject to "effective competition." In 1985 the FCC announced that three local broadcast signals were competition enough. The rates of almost all cable systems were immediately deregulated.

In the ensuing six years consumer complaints about cable rates and service mounted sharply. In 1992 Congress concluded that cable had become "a dominant national video medium." Few communities were served by more than one cable system, and cable rates had increased too fast. Overriding President Bush's veto, Congress set in place a sweeping new scheme of price regulation. Local franchising authorities were allowed to implement it on their own, if they proved they were serious. Otherwise the FCC would take charge. The Commission was given six months to get rate regulation rolling for eleven thousand cable systems and sixty million subscribers.

In its response, the Commission succeeded in looking vacant, affronted, and hysterical all at once, like a Regency maiden about to have the vapors.* On April 1, 1993—a well chosen date—the Commission came out with a massive new set of pricing regulations. These regulations were drastically revised a year later. Additional rulemakings were still pending a year after that. The calculations required by these rules are so complex that the FCC provides forms on electronic spreadsheets.

The FCC first declared that the handful of cable operators already subject to "effective competition" charged an average of 10 percent less than others. That average would be the new benchmark for everyone else; all other cable operators were to roll back their rates accordingly on September 1, 1992. Per-channel average prices were to be lowered to the benchmark level or cut by 10 percent, whichever was less. The average rollback would be 5.9 percent. Jubilant authors of the 1992 Act declared victory and predicted consumer savings of $1 billion a year.

But on the very day the rate cuts were supposed to occur, many cable operators raised rates, retiered channels, and jiggered their services. Prices did not fall noticeably, if at all. Quite possibly they went up, though nobody could say for sure. Cable included such wide variety of channels and service options that it was impossible to tell.

That didn't stop the Washington set. There were new cries for even stiffer regulation. The FCC reconsidered and settled on a new "effective competition" benchmark—this time 17 percent below the no-

*My debt is to the late author and zoologist Gerald Durrell.

competition average. Astonishingly, the Commission decided that all cable operators would have to cut per-channel average rates by 17 percent, even if their rates had been below average to begin with. When cable operators or consumers complained, they got case-by-case review. Thus the commission has solemnly found that $12.66 per month for basic service in Washington, D.C., was justified, while $12.22 per month for basic service in Nashville, Tennessee, was not.

None of this did consumers any good at all. This is now an established economic fact, though still vehemently denied in many quarters. The FCC's own studies confirm that cable service is quite price-elastic. Real price cuts—cuts not immediately offset by equivalent cuts in the quality of service—would produce a rapid increase in the rate at which new subscribers sign up. But there has been no such increase. All of the objective economic evidence confirms that cable companies have simply found ways to adjust downward the overall quality of service—programming, technical assistance and so on—in step with price rollbacks.

Video Unbound

The 1992 Cable Act gave heart and new employment to price regulators. The FCC's budget soared some $80 million—almost 40 percent—as the agency hired new staff to set the prices for a $20 billion industry.

But even as it spawned new employment for regulatory accountants and economists, cable had already shattered the old and far more economically inefficient paradigm of free broadcast. With cable at hand, even price-regulated cable, consumers could pay for programming directly if they wanted to. Buying Wheaties was no longer the only way.

That should have been the end of the FCC's official aversion to pay-TV. Deregulating prices is never easy, however, particularly when the effect will be new charges for service that (Wheaties aside) used to be free. The FCC therefore began deregulating broadcast prices at the flank, with direct broadcast satellite (DBS).

Satellites used for common carriage had already been largely deregulated in 1983. Direct broadcast satellites, which began operation in 1994, were price-deregulated even before they were launched. Though they compete directly against cable, DBS operators are not required to offer programming in separate basic/premium tiers, nor to set rates by reference to any competitive benchmark, nor to file any kind of tariffs at all. Landlords and others who link satellite dishes to private wiring within a single building or residential complex have been left equally free to set their own prices. Wireless cable provided over scrambled multichannel microwave is also deregulated.

When phone companies begin to offer video service, their rates will probably be deregulated, too. The 1996 Telecommunications Act leaves open the possibility that the FCC will regulate the prices of "open" video transport services offered as common carriage by phone companies, but the economic case for doing so is very weak. Local phone companies will enter the market as complete newcomers, operating in direct competition with cable, direct broadcast satellites, terrestrial wireless cable, and conventional over-the-air broadcasters.

Incumbent cable operators have abundant opportunity to evade price regulation for the few more years that it will last. The definitional lines separating basic service from premium service, and video programming from all else, are easily manipulated. Regulated companies just shuffle labels and adjust marketing packages. The 1992 act ostensibly empowers the FCC to prevent evasions of price regulation, through retiering or otherwise. The Commission has solemnly itemized some of the numerous practices that may be found to be evasive. But a broadband medium like cable is far too flexible for the cyphers in Washington. The deck is stacked overwhelmingly against the price police.

A shopping network, for example, is delighted to let any cable operator carry its round-the-clock commercials, and it will even pay for the privilege. Those payments are unregulated. Cable operators unhappy with what they are allowed to charge consumers can replace profit sinks like C-Span with people peddling ninety-nine piece tool sets and cubic zirconia rings. The FCC has also openly invited cable operators to adopt an "upgrade incentive plan": Cable operators get flexibility in pricing of new service tiers, so long as they don't raise rates for current services. And the Commission probably won't attempt to regulate the two-way, interactive cable services that represent cable's entry into telephony.

Finally, the 1996 Telecommunications Act sets in motion a process for ending rate regulation of cable entirely. All price regulation of upper-tier cable services ends March 31, 1999. Basic cable services are deregulated as soon as they face "effective competition." Smaller cable operators are deregulated at once. All cable operators are freed to give bulk discounts in competing against the SMATV services offered by apartment landlords and other institutional operators. And all cable operators are to be cut loose from price regulation entirely as soon as local phone companies begin providing competitive video services.

Voice Unbound

Voice telephony is now on a glide path to deregulation as well. In 1980 the FCC defined a new category of "non-dominant" providers of phone service whose tariffs would receive "streamlined" regulatory treatment. The Commission then tried to bar non-dominant carriers from filing tariffs altogether. A federal court ruled that deregulation of that order just didn't fit with the mandate of the 1934 Communications Act. The 1996 Telecommunications Act undid that ruling. The Commission is now permitted to "forbear" from regulating whenever it pleases.

The Commission was inching in that direction already, the 1934 Act notwithstanding. It had so radically streamlined the tariffing of non-dominant carriers that there was nothing left to the exercise. On that basis, the Commission had largely deregulated the rates of up-start long-distance carriers like MCI and Sprint and new providers of local access services like MFS and Teleport. In 1995 the Commission declared AT&T to be "non-dominant," too, and for most practical purposes deregulated that company's rates as well.

The Commission, along with thirty-five states, has also replaced rate-of-return regulation with price caps. The old approach was to permit carriers to recover their operating costs plus a return on share-holder investment. The new way is simply to cap prices on the basic residential rates that are the most politically sensitive and let carriers proceed freely from there. This is still a lot of regulation, but it is much less intrusive than it used to be. It gives regulatees, for the first time, a powerful incentive to control their costs.

Since the Bell breakup in 1984, the Commission has slashed the subsidies long-distance carriers used to pay to support local rates. In the 1980s the introduction of the federal subscriber line charge together with other line charge reforms transferred roughly $4 billion from long-distance rates to the local monthly phone bills of consumers. As prices dropped, interstate calling volumes grew dramatically. The subscriber line charge pushed up local rates sharply, but universal service was not harmed in the least. Telephone penetration is higher than ever. It turned out that what made phone service unaffordable for some consumers was not the low price of basic local service but spendthrift use of over-priced long-distance service. Rebalancing the rates made phone service more affordable all around. In 1980 the Commission also cut telephone sets, fax machines, and other forms of terminal equipment out of the regulatory picture entirely. Here, too, prices dropped and sales of phones rose sharply.

The deregulation of phone prices is still far from complete. The prices that incumbent local phone companies charge for interstate access are still regulated. And state regulators still control in-state phone rates. But the end is now in sight. Wireless phone services have been price-deregulated across the board. Cable telephony will probably not be subject to rate regulation when it arrives. It is only a matter of time now before the growth of competition forces regulators to abandon telephone rate regulation once and for all.

Losing Grip

Price regulation is becoming completely unworkable in any event. To begin with, underlying costs are impossible to nail down. Telephone companies graft video onto a regulated voice network. What makes sense for them is to charge for video at the margin; voice already pays most of the freight. Cable operators graft voice onto a regulated video market. It makes complete economic sense for them to charge only marginal cost for voice; video is already carrying the base load of costs. Broadcasters can piggyback data channels onto their existing distribution channels; that is the cheap margin there. Satellite operators are already free to attribute their costs onto voice carriage, video carriage, and direct broadcast however they please.

For every player in each of these varied industries, the line between base-load and marginal costs for providers is as elusive as the line between basic and premium services for consumers. But without a solid grip on costs, price regulation cannot remain both fair and useful for very long.

To regulate the price of a service, one must also define it precisely enough to prevent providers from evading regulation by changing the product. Price regulation of plain old telephone service was feasible because a simple voice phone call doesn't vary much in quality. Cable, by contrast, was far too complex a service to be price-regulated effectively. Is a shopping channel a substitute for a low-power TV station that broadcasts five hours a day in Urdu? Unless regulators know, they can't ensure that cable's real price doesn't rise when the quality of the service falls.

The broadband universe now unfolding comes with no "plain old" benchmark to go by. Everything is fancy and new. Bandwidth itself is infinitely variable. The mix of downlinks and uplinks (to borrow satellite jargon) can be changed in any proportion. In ordinary voice telephony the mix is roughly equal, but in dial-a-porn voice services it need not be, nor will it be in video dialtone Interactive cable and broadcast television will offer quite a different mix.

A simpleminded regulator might try charging consumers by the bit—the most elemental unit of digital information, used to encode voice, pictures, data, or anything else in a digital pipeline. But with by-the-bit billing, either television will be ridiculously expensive, because it contains so many bits, or two-way voice will be ridiculously cheap, because it contains so few. Under a bits-transmitted pricing scheme, a $15-a-month basic video charge would imply a flat-rate telephone service of one tenth of a cent per month. But not all bits are equal. Two-way voice bits, carried over a switched network, are far more valuable to consumers, and costly to providers, than one-way video bits carried over a top-down, unswitched broadcast or cable network.

When the price of content is regulated, the regulator must somehow define a standard package of content, or else leave the whole business to the cereal makers. With free TV, viewers get mass-market fare that appeals to the lowest common denominator. For now, basic cable service has simply been defined by history—its principal content being local broadcasting. Such a definition cannot survive much longer. Using broadcast television as the standard for anything at all will make no sense by the end of the 1990s.

Cucumbers and Costa Rica

With price deregulation, it hardly matters which small corner of the tent is lifted first to admit the errant nose; the camel soon follows.

Consider the seemingly modest step of cutting terminal equipment out of the regulated sphere and opening it up to full competition. One might suppose that this leaves the whole large arena of network services still safely in the regulatory grasp. Not so.

Apartment building landlords immediately install private cable networks on their own premises. These compete directly against public cable service, often for the lowest-cost, highest-revenue customers. Homeowners install their own backyard satellite dishes, too—which let them downlink the same video feeds intended to be distributed over public cable. Businesses install private branch exchanges that are, in effect, small, on-premises phone companies, typically cutting dependence on the public phone network in half.

At the margin, equipment and service are powerful substitutes. A satellite provides channels, for example; dishes receive them. Low-power satellites require big, expensive dishes, and vice versa. All radio communication involves similar trade-offs between the power of the transmitter and the sensitivity of the receiver. The antenna on a television is obviously "terminal equipment"—until it becomes a "community antenna," which at some point we relabel "cable service."

Similar trade-offs between equipment and conduit occur everywhere. Since electronic communication requires both, its real price can be regulated only if both are regulated together. If one is deregulated but not the other, the market will shift capabilities and cost toward the deregulated side.

And there has to be a deregulated side. The silicon revolution has transformed computers, cellular phones, televisions, and every other kind of terminal equipment into mass-production goods. Virtually everything can connect to the telephone network—computers, thermostats, medical monitoring equipment, even air conditioners. As broadband networks advance, virtually everything else will, too. Either we cut loose from regulation the stuff at the end of the line or we regulate the entire economy.

Similar problems arise at the other end of the line, where conduit meets content. Regulating the price of movies, newspapers, or chit-chat is both infeasible and unconstitutional. Infeasible because you can't regulate price without also regulating quality, and the quality difference between Wrestlemania and the Super Bowl is beyond the power of any commission to determine. And unconstitutional because regulating the price of speech is inimical to free speech. So content has to be price-deregulated, too.

But providers of both transport and content can often shift price and profit toward the content side of things as well. In the early days of radio, manufacturers set up broadcast stations to promote sales of receivers. Then, for a while, tobacco companies and detergent manufacturers paid for most of broadcast's freight. Today content is often sold commercial-free, with scrambling used to ensure payment at the checkout counter.

There are other alternatives. On-line services like CompuServe, home-shopping networks, credit card companies, and airline reservation services all supply free (or below-cost) information or entertainment; they make their profit on the sale of cucumbers or vacations in Costa Rica instead. *Time* magazine derives some revenue from subscriptions, some from advertising; as a come-on, it sometimes gives away a cheap telephone to new subscribers. Broadband merchants operate the same way. They sell every part of the pig, including the squeal.

Even the two most widely separated ends of the network—content, at the top, and terminal equipment, at the bottom—are economically interdependent. The British tax TV sets to subsidize programming.

But tie the television to a VCR, and the free broadcast of *Fawlty Towers* may be enjoyed any number of times, at no extra charge. In 1986 Congress considered taxing sales of audiotape and recording devices to provide compensation for home copying of sound recordings. Attempts to hold manufacturers of VCRs accountable for copyright infringement have been equally unsuccessful.

Yet in the age of digital electronic terminals, every piece of terminal equipment is potentially a copying device. The terminals turn the old rationale for regulation upside-down. Instead of a single statelike monopolist keeping output inefficiently low, a million living-room anarchists now push it inefficiently high. A provider of content, like a cable operator or satellite broadcaster, cannot operate in a broadcast mode at all unless it is allowed to control use of private receiving equipment downstream. Prices will have to be regulated end to end, too, if they are going to be regulated effectively at all.

Left to its own devices, the market collects revenues wherever it can: from the boxes at the ends of the wires, from the transport media in between, from advertising, from receipts at the electronically scrambled box office, from cucumbers, in whatever mix of profit and subsidy consumers favor at any given time. The price is loaded wherever buyers are least averse to paying it and sellers are most able to collect it. If regulators monitor only basic service, providers will boost the price of premium, and consumers will watch the boundary between them steadily shift south.

The profit mix is always changing. Cable television began as a free service, given away to promote the sale of televisions. It evolved into a carrierlike community antenna, to boost (for a fee) reception of over-the-air broadcasts. Today it supplies a stew of carriage, made-for-cable programming, and advertising, with two-way telephone capabilities coming soon. Satellites deployed to provide video carriage for cable companies also operate as direct video broadcasters for consumers who own backyard dishes. Early in the game, it may be necessary to subsidize content and transport to sell terminals. Later on, it may make sense to subsidize boxes to boost demand for services. Later still, bundling of terminal equipment and services may become necessary to sell content directly, with the box serving as decoder and cash register.

As telecom media become more capacious and versatile, services migrate effortlessly from one to another. A phone company can package and deliver Julia Roberts on a video dialtone system. A cable company puts her on cable. Ms. Roberts may also travel over a broadcast television network or over a wireless cable microwave system. Or she can be distributed nationally by direct broadcast satellite. If the price on the Pretty Woman is not uniform as she walks the streets in the electronic metropolis, she and her customers will simply congregate wherever the price police don't go.

The street corners are multiplying a thousand times faster than the police. So vastly outnumbered, so thinly spread out, so easily evaded, the constables that remain end up doing nothing useful at all. Sooner or later we recognize this. By sometime early in the next century, the constables will all be gone.

11

Universal Service

Hitler wanted a people's car. East German Communists eventually delivered the Trabant. Cheap, uniform, and affordable to all. The rear window defroster was the best feature. It kept your hands warm while you pushed.

A-chicken-in-every-pot rhetoric reached American shores, too. Unlike the Trabant, it has endured: a telephone in every parlor, a television in every living room, a cable hookup for every tube, free over-the-air television; subsidized connections to phone and cable networks; the Internet and the Web accessible to all.

Private enterprise, we are told, will always censor and limit what moves over its networks. Unsupervised by government, digital broadband will deliver the "vast wasteland" of television all over again, just vaster and more wasted. It will deliver sex, games, and shopping. It will supply only what people will pay for, not what they need. Only commissions can force the industry to promote education, productivity, international competitiveness, health care, citizen empowerment, and a more democratic democracy.

And only commissions will deliver equality, the argument continues. Society is segregating by class, the "symbolic processors" at one electronic water fountain, all others at another. Left to themselves, telephone and cable companies will wire only high-income areas. The poor are being cut loose from the future. Subsidies are essential.

Some argue that the problem is just the opposite, not have-nots but want-nots. Telecom utilities spend wastefully to meet demand that doesn't exist, then soak the ratepayers. Universal broadband will cost

$500, $2,000, $10,000 per home—too much, in any event. The have-nots can't afford it. The haves would rather not.

Still others contend that too much electronic communication is just plain bad for everyone. Broadcasting will give way to narrowcasting, which segregates audiences by class, race, religion, and wealth. "Faction—the scourge of democracy feared by its critics from James Madison to Walter Lippmann—is given the support of technology; compromise, mutualism, and empathy—indispensable to effective democratic consensus—are robbed of their national medium." The global village gives way to the Tower of Babel, "a hundred chattering mouths bereft of any common language."

Without a commission, in short, the wealth of the telecosm will impoverish us all.

Service by the Commission

But can a commission save us? Laws don't lay wires or operate switches, and aside from the occasional celebrity murder trial, law supplies little in the way of entertainment. Telecom services are delivered by private entities. One way or another, they must earn enough to cover costs and attract capital.

The law on this last point is written into the Constitution. The Takings Clause of the Fifth Amendment limits government's power to price-regulate private enterprise into giving away its assets to its customers. So far as its overall budget goes, a phone company required to provide universal service is thus no different from McDonald's. Universal service is available only insofar as society is willing to pay for it.

What makes universal phone service different from the universal hamburger is penetration and price averaging. McDonald's erects its arches only where there is enough traffic to cover its costs. Prices may be higher in the city than in a suburban mall. And lots of places get no Big Macs at all. Hamburger chains have no choice. Costs are higher in some places than others, and any attempt to overcharge suburbanites a bit to keep prices low downtown will drive business to Wendy's or Burger King—whoever is smart enough to keep prices closely in line with reality.

The only way around the problem is to outlaw the competitor. And that is what commissions have always done. With only one provider on the scene, it is perfectly possible to overcharge some customers, undercharge others, and still keep the books in overall balance. Outside a small tavern in Anchorage, Alaska, there hangs a sign that declares: "We cheat the other guy, and pass the savings on to you!" This is the commission method, too, for promoting universal service. First the commission outlaws all other saloons. Then the cheating and saving come easy.

Universal Telephony

With telephone, universal service has come to mean a network that reaches every household, even those that cannot pay for the cost of the wire.

Bell started with one great advantage—patents on the telephone itself. But while its patents lasted, Bell built its early network in large cities—and built quite slowly, compared to what happened after. When the patents expired in 1893 and 1894 independent telephone companies rushed in. Between 1894 and 1921 Bell and the independents competed fiercely.

The competitors refused to interconnect and weren't required to. So each company raced to wire as many subscribers as possible. The independents quickly established footholds in the rural areas and small towns that Bell had neglected. Before long they were establishing exchanges in the urban hubs.

Spurred by the competition, Bell built 4,500 exchanges in cities with populations under ten thousand. By 1907 commercial independents had built 10,109 exchanges—ten times the number established by Bell during eighteen years of monopoly. The independents formed associations and established regional long-distance companies. Bell also began to license independent affiliates in communities it didn't serve.

"Universal service," as the term was used by Theodore Vail in 1907, was the Bell System's answer to competition. At that point independent companies served half of the nation's telephones; 57 percent of cities were served by two providers. For Vail, universal service had nothing to do with a telephone in every household, or subsidized local service; it referred to the interconnection of these competing systems into a unified system. Vail wanted a single, nationally interconnected network. He wanted to replace disconnected competition with fully connected monopoly.

The alternative, of course, would have been connected competition—common carriers providing truly common carriage, to competitors and customers alike. Vail rejected that on the ground that it permitted Bell's smaller competitors to capture the benefits of Bell's expansion.

Telephone service was slowly monopolized, under the auspices of city councils, state legislatures, and federal authorities. The Willis-Graham Act of 1921 exempted phone company mergers from the antitrust review. By refusing to interconnect his high-capacity, high-fidelity, interexchange network to local companies that didn't affiliate with Bell, Vail crushed them. The authorities approved. Universal service required a secure monopoly.

Universal Broadcast

The 1934 Communications Act directed the FCC to deliver broadcasting to the people. From the 1930s until the 1950s, the Commission embraced AM radio as the vehicle for doing so. The Commission's preoccupation with AM radio seriously delayed its approval of FM radio and later its approval of television.

The licensing of television stations didn't accelerate until 1952, when the Commission defined twelve VHF bands and seventy UHF bands for the new medium. The FCC then declared that its top priority was to ensure coverage from at least one television station in all parts of the country.

By 1955 more than 90 percent of the population could receive at least one television station. But the government-issue abundance turned out to be rather spare. The Commission defined TV broadcast contours to promote local service. This limited the number of channels that could operate and thus sharply limited the growth of national networks.

With few outlets and little competition, broadcast slouched toward the bottom. "Of all the things I've lost," one viewer lamented, "I miss my mind the most." Broadcasting catered to the viscera, not the brain. It kept your eyes warm while you slept.

Universal Cable

When cable arrived as an alternative to broadcast, the Commission did all it could to kill it. Cable was an enemy of universal service. The FCC labored to stop cable from "siphoning" movies, sports, and advertising away from broadcasters and onto the for-pay medium. The regulatory objective was to make sure that cable service remained less appealing than broadcast.

When the FCC lost its grip on cable, subscribership soared. In the 1980s cable built out to pass virtually every home in the country. About 65 percent subscribe, and penetration continues to rise steadily. Channel capacity has grown rapidly, too. By 1993 cable was poised to overtake broadcast; it generated about $24 billion that year, compared to broadcast television's $25.8 billion.

As cable rose, regulatory perspectives changed. Cable had once been seen as a threat to universal service. Now cable would be required to supply it.

The FCC feared "hole-in-the-doughnut" deployment of cable networks—networks that served only the affluent suburbs. The Commission officially directed that "all parts of a franchise area that could reasonably be wired would be wired." Not long after, the Commission discovered that high-density urban areas were being wired faster than more thinly populated suburbs. The doughnut, it turned out, was really a peach. The anti-doughnut rule was repealed, and the FCC handed oversight of cable construction back to local authorities.

The 1984 Cable Act barred redlining of poorer areas but didn't mandate services to homes that were too remote to wire economically. Local authorities still may require such service. Much local regulation has been aimed at promoting universal service by forbidding competition. The second cable applicant is either barred outright or else required to provide as much service as the first. This makes it very expensive for a competitor to enter at all.

Some of the most hostile local regulation has been aimed at private cable operated by high-rises, hospitals, and hotels, among others, that set up their own satellite dishes and connect them to their own wires. Local authorities have frequently used a universal service mandate as the club to forbid competition of this kind. The FCC, to its credit, has taken the other side and has been backed by the courts.

The individual homeowner can receive satellite, too. A supplier of backyard dishes skims the cream one household at a time. When cable networks began using satellite extensively in the 1970s, private dishes proliferated outside hotels, bars, and homes. In 1979 the FCC fully deregulated receive-only facilities. Dish sales took off.

Universal Satellite

The advent of direct broadcast satellite is now setting off yet another redefinition of universal service and who must provide it. The backyard dishes that used to dot the countryside were big and unwieldy, because they received weak signals. Higher-power broadcasts can be picked up by much smaller dishes. The FCC began considering a new generation of satellite TV technology, DBS, in late 1980. The price of DBS dishes, now under $500, is dropping fast.

When the FCC first considered licensing DBS in the early 1980s, the National Association of Broadcasters raised the specter of siphoning once again. DBS, they said, would undermine service to minorities, rural areas, and special audiences by siphoning programming from broadcasters, fragmenting audiences, and reducing advertising support. It would rob free local television service of advertising revenues. UHF stations would be especially threatened.

The FCC, however, refused to "reject a new service solely because its entry will reduce the revenues or profits of existing licensees." DBS is unlikely to have a significant adverse impact on local broadcasters, the FCC concluded. And, in any event, DBS is itself an exceptionally universal new form of service. It provides the same signal quality across the continent, and it will offer rural households "access for the first time to a level of television service taken for granted in the rest of the nation."

Rather than suppress the new technology to protect universal service as we currently know it, the Commission insisted that DBS coverage itself must be universal. DBS operators are directed to use paired eastern and western satellites to provide nationwide coverage. The Commission drew the line at adding Alaska and Hawaii to the universal footprint.

Defending Monopoly

For a commission committed to universal service, every major advance in technology begins life as an anti-people failure. A few haves have it; many have-nots don't. At first the Commission ignores the novelty as too small to bother with. Then it denounces it as a cream-skimming conspiracy by the affluent against the rest. When the rest sign on, too, the Commission embraces the advance as a new standard for all. That begins the cycle anew, with the Commission now outlawing whatever competes against the new universal standard.

Cable, the prototypical broadband technology of the 1980s, has already passed through each of these stages. In its infancy, regulators ignored it. In its adolescence, they denounced it as the enemy of universal free television. In its maturity, they embraced it as a new standard to which no one should be denied access. Since 1934 every major advance in competition, technology, and service has had to conquer the Commission in similar fashion, at the same time as it conquered the market. Beating the Commission has usually been the hardest part.

So far as the advancement of government-issue universal service is concerned, competition is never a solution. Competition eats away at subsidies. It differentiates products and services, and it differentiates among consumers. It gives people what they will pay for, at a price that reflects the real cost of delivering the goods.

Commissions recognize intuitively that the only certain way to attain completely universal and uniform service is to outlaw change. A mature technology is easy to define and package in standard, government-issue units. An established monopolist does what it's told. It can be compelled to extend its service and average its prices in the same way as government itself can provide streets and police service on the same terms to all. The monopolist becomes a pliant tax collector and budget director. It may still have private shareholders, but its management goes public.

A Universal Service Commission therefore suppresses competition not once but twice. It bars competitors from pursuing the high-revenue, low-cost customers because cream-skimming by the market leaves no cream to be skimmed by the Commission. And it discourages competitors from pursuing the low-revenue, high-cost customers because the Commission is already delivering (thin) milk to them at a depressed price that no one else can match.

And so the pursuit of universal service always degenerates into a reactionary battle against both technology and competition. Universal service becomes the all-purpose excuse for policies that cannot be defended on any other grounds.

The last phase is a war of government against government, fought through a single, hapless, private intermediary. The agency committed to universal service anoints and defends a monopolist. The agency committed to dismantling monopolies attacks it. One arm of government promotes cross-ownership, vertical integration, bigness, and all the tax-and-spend possibilities that monopoly makes possible, because universal service is just. Another attacks the same, because competition is efficient.

Both sides are right. Collectivism is equal, universal, fair—and impoverishing. Competition is productive and efficient—and ends up unequal.

Losing Control

Or that's how it used to be. From here on out, collectivism won't be universal or fair, either, just impoverishing. Collectivizing communication isn't practical anymore. Every attempt to collectivize anyway will end up a costly failure.

Promoting the old kind of universal service was simple because the service itself was static and easy to define. The Commission counted ears (telephones) and eyeballs (televisions) and ignored most everything else. The marvel of free television is that it is free; the Commission didn't dwell much on the fact that it is mostly rubbish. The marvel of plain old telephone service is that it is ubiquitous; there is no need to carp that it is very plain indeed. Rich and poor got pretty much the same thing, little though it was, and the Commission claimed victory.

But neither "universal" nor "service" is self-defining, and the more technology offers, the harder the definitions become. Spreading famine around evenhandedly is easy; spreading abundance is not.

The arrival of cable has already sown confusion everywhere. Cable is supplied like telephone but consumed like television; it doesn't conform to either standard model of what universal service is supposed to be. A tier of basic cable was defined by federal legislation in 1992 and subjected to rate regulation, a sure sign that a service is crossing the legal line from discretionary novelty to basic essential.

Everything that lies ahead in the digital universe is more confusing still. The most demanding collectivists maintain that universal broadband service should include programming, public access, access for the disabled, education and training, and more. But the range of new possibilities quickly overwhelms the discussion.

To start with, "universal" assumes some kind of map. Universal telephone and universal cable are pursued one franchise area at a time—typically a county or municipality. But smaller territories are possible, or larger ones. Private-cable landlords offer service universally within the condominiums they own and are often denounced for doing so. Direct broadcast satellites operate on a different scale entirely. Universal service on one map covers quite a different community than universal on another.

Requiring providers to offer service to everyone in a territory, however defined, invariably favors wireless technology over wires. The cost of wire networks increases as population density decreases; rural customers cost more to serve than urban ones. Wireless technologies are much less sensitive to distance; the extreme example is direct broadcast satellite, which reaches a ranch in Wyoming at exactly the same cost as it reaches a high-rise in Westchester. A wireless provider is thus quite content to serve everyone within range of its transmitter, and at the same price. This provider also has an immaculate excuse (the absence of an FCC license) for not serving anyone else. But for a wireline provider, particularly one challenging a wireless incumbent, a universal service mandate may simply demand too much too quickly.

So far as engineering and economic considerations go, it often makes sense to serve urban consumers by wire and rural ones by wireless, with both media contending for the suburbs. Requiring both wireless and wireline providers to reach everywhere is ridiculous. In principle, a single provider might assemble the right mix of wireline and wireless technology to meet universal service obligations efficiently. But that may still be forbidden by a labyrinth of media ownership limits.

Maps only start the debate; the contents of the universal service package must be defined, too. With telephone, broadcast, and cable, the service matured before regulators stepped in to mandate service to all. The minimums—basic telephone, basic cable, and so on—were informed by market demand first. When the regulators arrived they had some assurance they were mandating something that people actually wanted. For telephone, the standard package had already crystallized as an analog copper telephone wire to every home, provided below cost, with subsidized local (but not long-distance) service. For broadcast, the package came to mean several free television channels with continuous, free programming.

But the bundle we call basic service varies widely across different media. A consumer purchasing a half hour of *I Love Lucy* can see precisely the same show on a TV broadcast, cable, or a phone company's video dialtone service. But whether *Lucy* is a matter of universal right or pay-per-view privilege depends entirely on the name attached to the service. On video dialtone, only the transport is basic; on cable, the show is, too, if it's on a basic channel, but not otherwise; on broadcast TV, the bundle is free, at least if the commercials don't induce you to patronize Gordon's Giveaway Pontiac.

The mix of basic minimums and fancy enhancements thus varies sharply from one medium to the next. Different regulators of different media have quite different conceptions of what most consumers want in the "basic" or "essential" package that everyone deserves to get. And it's simply impossible to anticipate what will become "basic" as the universe of communication doubles in size, and then doubles again. So far as this new telecosm is concerned, we are only a few minutes past the Big Bang. It's too early to think about what will be important tomorrow or beyond; it may always be too early. The explosive process of creation in this new technocosm may never stop at all.

Commissions, of course, don't have to plan for things a billion years in advance. Up to a point, their definitions of universal service can evolve incrementally. A touch-tone telephone used to be a fancy add-on; nowadays it is so basic that one can hardly get past automated answering systems without one. But a commission's central planners face a second, even more fundamental problem: setting a global telecom budget.

By cheating the other guy and passing the savings on to you, a commission can raise his price and lower yours. That flattens things out, but at what level? Cross-subsidies like this may advance some conception of fairness, but they don't establish a global budget. Should the Commission direct phone companies to invest $100 billion in new fiber-optic lines and charge everyone an extra $10 a month to pay for them? Or should it direct telephone companies to nurse aging copper lines along for a while longer and hold prices where they are?

If the Commission is doing its job right, half of all consumers would settle for somewhat less service and a lower bill, half would pay extra for more. Both camps will constantly complain—half about high price, half about low service. Dissatisfaction all around is inevitable, because commissions make collective decisions, while consumers have individual preferences.

The Universal Hamburger

For the last half century or so, government promises have always expanded. But in telecom at least, the bidding is over now. Despite a last flurry of rhetoric and political humbug in the 1996 Telecommunications Act, the pursuit of universal service by commission is now at an end. From here on out, market competition will have to do the job.

In the world of entertainment television, the transition is already almost complete. Free television is in rapid decline; all serious TV addicts—the poor even more than the rich—subscribe to cable. Pay-as-you go has delivered far more channels to far more people than Commission-mediated free broadcasting ever did. A massive, market-driven transfer of charges away from advertisers and to cable subscribers has resulted in more channels, more programming, and more service all around. The cost of living hasn't affected its popularity, nor has the cost of television deterred its audience.

In telephony, a comparable, though much larger, rebalancing of rates is under way. In the 1980s a huge transfer of charges out of long-distance service and into local rates marked a first important retreat from cross-subsidies set in place by the Commission years ago. The upshot has been higher—not lower—telephone penetration, and lower long-distance rates to boot.

The end is now in sight for Commission-mandated price averaging. Price averaging cannot coexist with competition, at least not when it costs much more to serve some customers than others. The 1996 Telecommunications Act ostensibly leaves states free to impose universal service requirements on all new entrants. The Act even invites regulators to add new services to the cluster of basic services every citizen is entitled to receive. But at the same time, most of the critical new competitive services—from cable, data networks, and wireless carriers—have been almost completely deregulated. What we have here is classic sleight of legislative hand. All the talk of universal-service mandates and commission direction is still there, in some cases louder than ever before. But all the action is in the other direction.

Competition is irreconcilable with cross-subsidy and price averaging; it deaverages costs and makes service no more or less universal than money itself. At first, competition forces a commission to collect subsidies with a lighter hand from a broader base of contributors and to target them more carefully to a narrower base of truly needy recipients. In the end, competition eliminates the commission entirely, or at least its price-setting powers. But with luck, competition by then will also have made the essentials very cheap indeed.

This is precisely what telecom competition is now doing. On television there are more channels, more programs, and, overall, more viewers than ever before. At first, cable was thought to threaten us with rich-against-poor, but instead cable has delivered far more channels to almost everyone who wants them. DBS will supply even more. In telephony, competition is outdoing the most ambitious of regulators in its willingness to sell bundled packages at averaged, distance-insensitive, or even traffic-insensitive rates.

The choice between commission and competition ultimately depends on what we want more, varied abundance or uniform scarcity. Regulation can mandate equality but cripples competition and with it innovation and productivity. Competition delivers abundance but spreads it around unequally. McDonald's and Burger King, competing head-to-head, have distributed decent hamburgers far more universally than any government cafeteria in Romania. Defenders of commissions can only respond—correctly—that the owner of McDonald's, unlike many of her customers, can dine on filet mignon. So did Nicolae Ceauçescu, however.

Experience teaches that the most universal hamburger—the Big

Mac—was supplied by the market. The best and most universal meat in Moscow today is served under golden arches, not the red flag. If the private sector begins by wiring the most profitable communities first, those communities will also underwrite the cost of developing the technology and pushing production down the cost curve. Flush toilets, cars, and most everything we take for granted today began as a luxury, not a universal staple; broadband will evolve that way, too, if market forces are unleashed.

There is, in any event, no other practical choice. Telecom technology is advancing much faster than the Commission can make policy. The private sector is prepared to spend vastly more than the public sector can underwrite. And with the convergence of services and technologies, competition is overtaking whatever commissions do. Too many alternatives have already been unleashed to be stopped now. When both technology and competition are advancing this fast, unleashing them entirely will deliver more goods to more consumers than endless commission-mediated niggling about how the new abundance should be spread around.

12

Common Carriage

The earliest common carriers were crown monopolies. This was a bad start. Over the centuries, however, common-law courts spun gold out of the original legal straw.

A private carrier hauls its own freight. A contract carrier sells service to the specific customers it chooses. A common carrier, by contrast, opts to serve all comers, at uniform rates announced in advance.

By doing business that way—by choosing not to discriminate at all among prospective passengers—common carriers shed a lot of legal responsibility. The *Oshkosh Times* must answer for libel and copyright infringement anywhere on its pages, in both news copy and the advertising alongside. If it prints the lyrics of "Happy Birthday"—which are still under copyright—it must pay the owner a royalty. By contrast, Oshkosh Telephone is not liable for copyright infringement when Clara Sweetpipe sings "Happy Birthday" to her aging mother over OshTel's lines. OshTel has little liability even to Clara herself. Because it neither knows nor controls just how desperately important any particular phone call may be, OshTel is required only to rebate Clara's monthly bill if service fails—even if the broken connection kills Clara's once-in-a-lifetime chance to sing at Carnegie Hall.

All in all, common carriage offers a sensible balance of special duties and special privileges. The duties are serious, sometimes onerous—taking on all comers can be unpleasant, most especially when some customers have the temerity also to compete. But the revenues can also be high. The networks have Larry King and Rush Limbaugh;

cellular telephony just hauls the ordinary talk of little people. Yet using the same amount of spectrum, cellular earns far more on the plain old hauling. Telephone wires likewise generate far more revenue than cable.

Why, then, do we need a commission to make sure that common carriers fulfill their public-oriented mission? We don't. Markets provide plenty of incentive. Common law developed the necessary legal framework centuries ago. And disputes about carriage can be resolved by private litigation, as they are in any market.

Carriage and Monopoly

As we saw in chapter 3, Theodore Vail built up Bell's monopoly by exploiting patents that gave it a critical edge in long-distance service. The company offered that service exclusively to its own local phone affiliates. Either independent phone companies were acquired by Bell, or they folded.

Did AT&T have the right to treat some would-be customers so uncommonly badly? How could Bell claim the rights and privileges of a common carrier while discriminating so fiercely against its largest, most desperate customers—other phone companies? The Post Roads Act of 1866, which allowed telegraph companies to run their lines freely along post roads and to fell trees for poles, had required the telegraph companies to interconnect and accept each other's traffic. The Department of Justice thought AT&T had similar duties, and it sued. In response, AT&T vice president Nathan Kingsbury committed to provide long-distance links to independent phone companies. AT&T signed a consent decree in 1914.

Other plaintiffs were litigating similar claims. Several rulings recognized a general obligation for phone companies to serve as "carriers' carriers"; several others didn't. The results were mixed, as common-law judgments invariably are early on, when judges are picking their way through complicated new issues. The early contests involved a young industry, populated by many roughly balanced contenders. Many courts were willing to wait and see what would evolve, much as courts today would probably take a wait-and-see attitude toward Microsoft, whose Windows operating system is the new, universal, carrierlike platform for spreadsheets and word processors.

But we also know that a later generation of judges would decisively reject closed networks and the refusal of one phone company to interconnect with others. They did so in the essentially common-law context of antitrust litigation. They crafted new Kingsbury

Commitments and plucked competition back up from the depths of monopoly.

That was seven decades later, however. And in between? Nothing. Decades of fertile development in the common law of phone company interconnection were replaced by decades of judicial silence. The common law was completely anesthetized.

We know precisely how. The Mann-Elkins Act of 1910 brought interstate telecommunications under the jurisdiction of the ICC. It said nothing about connections between carriers, and the ICC did nothing to require them. The Communications Act of 1934 required carriers to connect to each other only when the FCC so ordered. But the FCC never did so order.

The 1934 Communications Act loudly proclaimed common carriage, but it quietly embraced monopoly. The two objectives were—and remain—completely irreconcilable. A monopolistic common carrier can certainly serve all ordinary customers without discrimination. But so far as other carriers are concerned, it has to discriminate with lethal vengeance, for that's what preserves the monopoly. The only effective way to maintain an airtight monopoly is to boycott every encroaching competitor. And that was precisely what Congress had endorsed in the 1934 act.

The FCC would enforce that anti-common-carriage principle for the next three decades. The chloroformed courts acquiesced. Common carriage atrophied and all but died.

Carriage and Competition

The Bell monopoly grew to gargantuan proportions. Everyone could connect to its networks without discrimination—everyone, that is, except other suppliers and operators of telephones, private switches, public switches, packet-switched data networks, coaxial networks, microwave towers, cellular networks, long-distance trunks, satellite earth stations, and fiber-optic rings.

The FCC wasn't going to rise to the occasion, but it would sometimes slide over to it. The FCC finally began to support the common-carriage rights of some of these other customers in the 1960s. And with that the Bell monopoly began a slow but irreversible rise back into a world of competition.

The market for customer premises equipment was opened first. As we saw in chapter 4, Bell provided end-to-end service to its customers. That meant lip-to-lip. No Hush-A-Phone plastic cups were to snap onto the mouthpiece of any Bell telephone. In its *Carterfone* decision of 1968—a full decade after it had lost the *Hush-A-Phone* case in court—the FCC finally reversed course. And Bell's monopoly over terminal equipment disappeared.

Long-distance markets were opened up in much the same way, sixty years after the Kingsbury Commitment had shown precisely what needed to be done. In 1970 a sharply divided Commission granted MCI's long-pending application to provide private microwave service for businesses as a "specialized common carrier." With a strong shove from a federal appellate court, the FCC then began requiring Bell's local phone companies to interconnect with MCI's long-distance services.

After the Bell breakup the FCC finally put in place comprehensive equal access obligations to connections between local and long-distance carriers. Cellular phone companies won similar rights quite independently of the breakup. The jargon was new, but not the principle. It was just carriage for carriers.

From Broadcast to Carriage

Carriage by broadcasters was out-and-out illegal. The drafters of the 1927 Radio Act rejected AT&T's proposal to offer "toll broadcasting"; they feared that Bell would monopolize the airwaves in much the same way as it had monopolized wires. The Communications Act of 1934 likewise forbids the FCC from imposing common carrier obligations on broadcasters. This prohibition, too, was ostensibly needed to promote competition among broadcasters and to prevent the industry from folding into a telephonelike monopoly.

There was no good or even vaguely adequate justification for any of these rules, and they were quickly evaded. From the outset, radio broadcasters sold blocks of time to brokers, who then supplied a bundle of programming and commercial messages to fill them. Television stations rely on similar arrangements to provide specialty services, such as foreign-language programs. Network contracts often involve the sale of airtime by a local affiliate to the network in return for programming, cash, and space to insert local commercials.

But anything that drifts too close to carriage is still technically illegal. As early as 1941 the Commission indicated that while some time brokering might be tolerated, any wholesale transfer of control from a broadcast licensee to a broker was forbidden. A station could sell a bit of its time to advertisers—even to a single advertiser that sponsors a particular show on a regular basis. But it could not sell its time retail, to numerous small, individual buyers. That would make it too much like a phone company.

And yet the Commission itself knows that there's nothing wrong at all with using radio transmitters for carriage. When it licensed direct broadcast satellites, the Commission simply allowed the new operators to pick their own poison. Sell off a transponder to a private buyer? That was fine. It was equally fine for the operator to occupy a transponder itself, pumping its own video through its own channel. Or the operator could serve as a common carrier, providing transport for others. What did operators in fact choose? A bit of each, including plenty of common carriage.

Closer to earth is cellular telephony, the ultimate in time brokering. It already supplies thirty million Americans with their own private little radio station. A cellular phone company uses the spectrum of four television stations to provide connection not to four Larry Kings, but to four hundred thousand in ever major city. Granted, cellular customers don't yet get video links, but those will come, too, in a decade or so. And out of precisely the same amount of spectrum, cellular generates more jobs, more revenues, and more public welfare all around.

The wealth of cellular telephony would have emerged from the wasteland of television at least two decades earlier if the Commission had simply stepped out of the way. Even today, television stations would abandon broadcasting in droves and rush into wireless common carriage if only the Commission would let them.

The Fairness Doctrine

Broadcasters weren't allowed to broker their own time, but the Commission was certainly allowed to broker it for them. And it did.

The basic idea that would evolve into the "Fairness Doctrine" was announced by the Federal Radio Commission in 1929. The Commission was weighing the competing applications of three Chicago-area radio stations that were competing for a single license. "It would not be fair, indeed it would not be good service, to the public to allow a one-sided presentation of the political issues of a campaign," the Commission declared. "[P]ublic interest requires ample play for the free and fair competition of opposing views. . . . [T]he principle applies not only to addresses by political candidates but to all discussions of issues of importance to the public."

Thenceforth fairness ceased to be a sport for the Commission, and became a vocation. It figured centrally in every proceeding. The Commission formalized the Fairness Doctrine in 1949. Broadcasters were to cover "controversial issues of public importance" and to broadcast opposing points of view. They were to air rebuttals to their editorials. They were to write the rebuttals themselves, if no one else would. In 1959 Congress codified something along the same lines in the equal time amendments to the Communications Act. In its 1969 *Red Lion* ruling, the Supreme Court concluded that none of this offended First Amendment principle at all. The Commission reflected on the same question and decided that Congress had implicitly codified the doctrine in 1959. The doctrine was constitutional because spectrum was scarce. And it didn't chill free speech.

The question then arose: Was every message touting Pepsi to be matched by another extolling Coke? In 1967 the fairness gnomes at the FCC concluded that commercial advertising engaged the Fairness Doctrine, too. An antismoking crusader demanded time to reply from a CBS affiliate that aired cigarette ads. The Commission agreed that the station's refusal violated the Fairness Doctrine, but it expressly limited its holding to cigarettes. A federal appellate court affirmed.

A group called "Friends of the Earth" demanded time on a New York station to commend fuel-efficient cars, in response to Detroit's glorification of gas-guzzlers. With magnificent aplomb, the Commission replied that gas wasn't cigarettes. A court overruled. The Commission then exempted all commercial advertising from fairness requirements, except for "editorial advertisements" that presented a "meaningful statement which obviously addresses, and advocates a point of view on, a controversial issue of public importance." A court affirmed. This left advertising freer than anything else. Only lesser forms of speech—news coverage, political editorials, documentaries—remained subject to fairness constraints.

In 1981 the FCC threw in the towel. Fairness, the Commission now declared, was inimical to the public interest and the First Amendment, too. The old scarcity rationale for fairness had been overtaken by the new technological abundance. Congress responded by ordering the commission not to bench the fairness police pending a two-year review. The FCC benched them anyway.

In 1986 a federal appellate court addressed the doctrine yet again. A public-interest group had challenged an FCC decision not to demand fairness in teletext, the wireless predecessor to on-line services like CompuServe. Writing for the appellate court, Judge Robert Bork upheld the Commission's power to police fairness where it liked, and nowhere else. Congress had not codified the doctrine in 1959 after all. Along the way, Judge Bork shredded the scarcity logic of the Supreme Court's *Red Lion* decision.

The Fairness Doctrine returned to the same court a year later. A TV broadcaster had allegedly unbalanced the delicate equilibrium of

public discourse when it aired interest-group advertising in support of nuclear power. The court ordered the FCC to reconsider the
constitutionality of the Fairness Doctrine from scratch. In 1987 the
Commission unanimously repealed it, concluding that the doctrine
didn't serve the public interest and was unconstitutional to boot. On
appeal once again, the appellate court upheld on the first ground and
declined to reach the second. Congress overwhelmingly passed legislation reinstating the Fairness Doctrine. President Reagan vetoed it.

What is one to make of this whole sorry history? The FCC, which
required far too little common carriage of common carrier phone
companies, required far too much of uncommon uncarriers, the
broadcasters. Even while it strictly barred them from making honest
common carriers of themselves. The Commission bastardized everything. And the Supreme Court did nothing to stop it.

Carriage on Cable

Cable began life as a carrier, a "community antenna." Cable operators
plucked broadcasts from the air and piped them into households. In
1958 thirteen broadcast stations asked the FCC to define cable as a
common carrier and regulate it accordingly. The Commission declined.

Within a few years, however, the Commission decided it would regulate cable as broadcast instead. Carter Mountain, a radio common
carrier in Cody, Wyoming, wanted to use microwave to deliver local
TV broadcasts from where they originated to cable networks in several distant towns. KWRB, a TV station in one of the receiving-end
towns, objected. The Commission agreed that imports would destroy
KWRB and eliminate free service to the poor and to rural households
not served by cable. The FCC invited Carter Mountain to file a new
proposal promising that KWRB's signal would be carried on cable
alongside any imports, and not to deliver programming that would
duplicate KWRB's.

The Commission followed in 1965 with detailed must-carry rules.
It proposed to enforce them only indirectly, as conditions attached to
licenses for microwave systems used by cable operators to import distant broadcast signals. A year later the Commission extended must-
carry duties to all cable systems that retransmitted broadcast signals
of any kind.

Cable, the FCC concluded, was to perform a "valuable supplemen-
tary role without unduly damaging or impeding the growth of television broadcast service." Cable's destiny, its right and proper role

in the bureaucrat's scheme of things, was to serve as an antenna. It would provide better reception of existing over-the-air broadcasts. Cable would carry those signals, like it or not. Free television would be undermined otherwise, and the poor would be the biggest losers.

No one even paused to consider that spectrum was supposedly in scarce supply and that the must-carry rules gobbled up a large share of the new wireline capacity. By forcing cable operators to fill their channels with signals also transmitted over the air, the FCC had settled on the one policy most certain to perpetuate scarcity. The Commission had now concluded it was more important to promote free television than to promote new bandwidth. As the Commission would later acknowledge, this was all based on a "collective instinct," an intuitive, made-in-Washington guess about how cable and broadcast should fit in the marketplace. The possibility of no-holds-barred competition was rejected out of hand.

The must-carry rules survived intact for the next decade. In the 1984 Cable Act Congress explicitly declared that cable service was not common carriage. But the must-carry rules remained in place anyway. Federal appellate courts began striking them down on First Amendment grounds. Cable, these courts reasoned, was a newspaperlike publisher, which as such had the right to decide what appeared on its electronic pages.

In the 1992 Cable Act Congress resurrected must-carry yet again, packing the legislative history in an attempt to fortify the rules against constitutional challenge. The new rules are extraordinarily intricate. The statute specifies where on the dial commercial stations are to be carried. All broadcasters are given the option of invoking "retransmission consent" rights if they prefer. So far, however, broadcasters have found that they need cable more than cable needs them. As of this writing, the latest variation of must-carry is still under constitutional attack. After a trip through a three-judge trial court in Washington, D.C., through the Supreme Court, back to the three-judge court, and now on their way back to the Supreme Court, the rules still have a tenuous hold on life.

The Commission has imposed a slew of other carrierlike rules on cable operators. Cable operators must set aside some channels for "public, educational, and government" (PEG) purposes, and also some channels for outright lease to independent programmers. And oh yes, cable is still technically subject to the Fairness Doctrine, too. The Commission included cable when it promulgated the doctrine but forgot to mention cable when it repealed it. Mercifully, the Commission had announced earlier that the Fairness Doctrine did not apply to PEG and leased channels, for which cable operators do not control the content at all.

The New Common Law

The African warthog, Beryl Markham once observed, is the enduring peasant of the plains, the drab and dowdy digger in the earth. He is the uncomely but intrepid defender of family, home, and bourgeois convention. His weapons are plebeian—curved tusks that are sharp, deadly, but not beautiful, used inelegantly for rooting as well as for fighting. Much the same can be said of the common-law judge. He may cultivate the law with inelegant tools, but he persists.

In 1910 Congress thought both railroads and phones belonged under the thumb of the ICC. Just two years later, however, the Supreme Court began assembling its own body of common carrier law under the broad, common law-like sweep of the Sherman Act.

In a 1912 ruling involving a railroad terminal, the High Court announced the "essential facilities" doctrine. That same year the U.S. Justice Department prepared the suit against Bell that culminated in the 1913 Kingsbury Commitment. And then, under soporific piles of commissions, the antitrust law fell asleep. Private litigants simply did not bother to press claims that implicitly challenged what an expert federal commission had so expressly approved.

When the approval finally began to slacken, the antitrust litigators awoke. In 1969 the FCC approved MCI's application to operate a long-distance telephone system between Chicago and St. Louis. Soon after, MCI sued AT&T. The case was eventually tried in Chicago in 1980. The jury concluded that AT&T had wrongfully refused to interconnect with MCI's lines. A federal appellate court agreed. AT&T had refused in bad faith to interconnect MCI to its "essential" local switching facilities. A second major suit was filed by Southern Pacific Communications (later to become Sprint) in 1978. In this nonjury trial, a federal district judge found for AT&T. His reason? AT&T had a "reasonable basis in regulatory policy" to believe that it was not required to interconnect with MCI.

While these private cases unfolded, the Department of Justice was litigating, too. Its suit, filed in 1974, culminated in the breakup of the Bell System a decade later. It was a critical interim legal ruling that impelled AT&T to settle. FCC regulation, Judge Harold Greene decided, afforded AT&T no blanket immunity from the antitrust laws. Local phone monopolies were lawful, but they were also "essential facilities" for long-distance carriers. AT&T therefore had "an obligation to furnish equal or substantially equal access to its [long-distance] competitors." And it hadn't. On the strength of this midtrial pronouncement, AT&T surrendered.

The single most important provision of the consent decree was the one directing Bell's local phone companies to provide equal access to other long-distance carriers and providers of information services. The decree contained no comparable provision for providers or users of customer premises equipment, but Judge Greene announced a similar requirement for them some years later.

And so, with the addition of two new words to the legal lexicon, an entire new jurisprudence of common carriage began to evolve. The government, AT&T, the Bell Companies, and independent players hammered out new equal access mandates for pay phones, billing services, calling cards, electronic signaling services, and collect calls. The decree had neglected to mention equal access for wireless carriers, but this too was shoehorned in later on.

As discussed in chapter 8, the bureaucratization of the decree was far from satisfactory. The Department of Justice and Judge Greene slowly metamorphosed into a shadow FCC, with legions of economists and technical experts on call. Nevertheless, the decree, and its implementation of equal access mandates in the first few years after divestiture, resurrected common carrier principle from the deep coma in which decades of commission law had put it. And it was the resurrection of common carriage principle, now under the rubric of antitrust, that began the irreversible de-monopolization of the entire industry.

Unbundling by Commission

The commission that spent decades protecting the end-to-end anti-carriage hegemony of the integrated phone network will spend the next five years undoing the handiwork of its own past. Market forces would do the job better, and probably almost as fast. But the political pressure to get on with things has created a slew of federal and state mandates, which the FCC and its state counterparts have now been charged with implementing.

Regulators have been directed not only to enforce common carriage but also to define every station at which the telecom train must stop and start. If market forces had been left alone for the last half century, none of this would now be necessary. But they weren't, so perhaps it is.

Having assembled tightly integrated monopolies, incumbent phone companies begin with powerful advantages over newcomers—the ability to offer end-to-end, one-stop shopping to all comers immediately. Competitors have to build up piece by piece, a process that can take years. The only way they can offer comparable service while they build is to resell the services of the incumbents in the interim. In due course, competition will force incumbents to break down their integrated services into smaller pieces, but a certain amount of well-placed regulatory dynamite can certainly accelerate things.

By this point the process is familiar enough—it is the logical extension of all the common-carriage-for-carriers principles developed in the 1970s and 1980s, some by the FCC itself, some by the antitrust courts. Rules are already in place for terminal equipment, inside wiring, wireless phone service, long-distance networks, and competitive access providers. The FCC's Open Network Architecture proceeding of the late 1980s attempted to ensure that independent providers of Internet-like services had access to key components of basic local phone service. By 1996 states across the country—Illinois, California, New York, Ohio, and others—were drafting more-aggressive unbundling mandates. The 1996 Telecommunications Act makes unbundling the key thing local carriers must give in exchange for freedom to enter long-distance markets.

Local phone companies will spend the next five years negotiating with state and federal regulators to complete far-reaching unbundling and interconnection arrangements. Physical facilities will be unbundled, as will be virtual ones such as telephone number databases, signaling channels, operator services, electronic order processing facilities, and so forth.

Much of the unbundling will be economically arbitrary, and much of it will be wasteful. Market forces ordinarily decide just how many checkout lines a supermarket opens up; regulators trying to prescribe the equivalent for a phone company are almost certain to settle on too few or too many. Traditional antitrust law requires unbundling only to the extent that the provider can control price and output of two plainly discrete products. But in their new rush to promote the competition that not long ago they suppressed, regulators have a more ambitious agenda. The unbundling of local phone company networks has become an article of regulatory faith. How much gets unbundled, and at what pace, will depend relatively little on economic logic. It will depend largely on effective advocacy and lobbying in regulatory and political circles.

It will, in short, be as bad as commission prescription ever is. The one saving grace is that today's Commission initiatives, inept though they will inevitably be, may accelerate the correction of yesterday's. Sometimes two wrongs do make a right, or at the very least a lesser wrong, and that is probably true here. This, after all, is the same Commission that forty years ago told Hush-A-Phone it would be prosecuted if it sold a cup to snap on to a Bell handset. Local networks would never have been sewn up so tightly, with so few points of interconnection, but for Commission policies of the past that demanded one-stop shopping, one-size-fits-all service, and averaged prices for all. The business arrangements that were created as a result were a disservice to consumers yesterday and impede the rapid transition to competition today. When government itself erects an enormous statue of Lenin on otherwise valuable real estate, a case or two of government explosive at the base may in fact do some good. What government helped cement together, government must now help blow apart.

One can only hope that the work is done quickly and that the government will have the wisdom to get out right after the detonation, leaving it to the market to reassemble the pieces.

Carriage by Consent

A simple fact is now clear: Competition flourishes wherever competitors are assured the same rights of carriage as any other customer. Competition used to be officially impossible in markets for phones, faxes, and private switches, as it was in markets for long-distance and for wireless telephony. As soon as competitors won rights to interconnect with landline networks, competition thrived.

All the theories about natural monopoly and the inherent efficiencies of exclusive franchises collapse when common carrier rules guarantee carrier-to-carrier interconnection. Those rules make competition not only possible but also inevitable.

Weighing its history as a whole, the FCC has not promoted common carriage; it has suppressed it. In telephony, it proclaimed common carrier law, but it protected monopoly. It labored uselessly to maintain walls between carriers and other enterprises. And then it labored unconstitutionally to impose pseudo-common carrier laws on broadcasters.

Antitrust courts performed better, and the essential facilities doctrine has served reasonably well. But this mountain of new law need not be piled on the intellectual back of the Sherman Act by a single judge, in a single courtroom. There is an older, more venerable, more robust common law to turn to: the law of common carriage itself. It is reinforced on its flanks by libel and copyright laws, which impose real penalties for straying too far off the common carrier reservation. With the media now at hand, common carrier law should be given back its traditional label and enforced by those who invented it, the common-law courts.

There is no other workable choice. A robust, adaptable, evolving law of common carriage is essential to all orderly development in the telecosm. No one-stop lawmaker, no congressional committee, no federal commission, can do the job. The common-law courts can. They will rebuild the law channel by channel, port by port, interface by interface, the way common-law courts have always built things, enforcing rights to interconnect here, punishing uncommon discrimination, and affirming the legal immunities that truly nondiscriminatory carriage legitimately deserves.

And with the common law of common carriage put back on a secure footing, pricing and universal service will be of no further concern. Competition will take care of both.

13

Reassembling the Pieces

People have long been admonished not to put all their eggs in one basket. But as Mark Twain observed, that is a fool's advice, for it only scatters one's investment and attention. The wise man says: "Put all your eggs in one basket—and watch that basket!"

The old monopolies certainly offered one-basket management. They made life very simple. They sold standard, overbundled parcels—one size to fit all—at one price. Competition is more complex. It disassembles bundled service, average prices, and monopolists themselves.

Consumers accustomed to the old ways hate it. They long for the old simplicity. This isn't just laziness or a perverse rejection of free markets. For routine staples, most consumers prefer to let others take care of the details.

And so that is precisely what competition returns to in the end. The most valuable service a firm can provide in today's fractious telecosm is skillful reassembly of the pieces. All the new alliances and mergers, so loudly decried by the prophets of market doom, are aimed at reassembling bundles of goods and services that can be sold in the baskets that consumers want.

One System, One Network

The 1984 divestiture decree separated telephone equipment from local service, and local service from long-distance service. The post-1996 competitors will bring them all back together.

Equipment is already routinely recombined with service in many markets. Cellular companies give away phones; cable companies supply converters; modem manufacturers bundle in start-up subscriptions to on-line services. Phone companies will be fully back in the same game soon enough.

They are reuniting geographically as well. Long-distance carriers like AT&T and MCI are already free to build their networks down to the consumer. They are doing so as fast as they can. By 1998 local phone companies will win permission to build long-distance facilities, or affiliate with existing long-distance carriers, or resell their services. They will do so at once.

The divisions between local and long-distance service have already all but disappeared in data communications. Internet connections cost the same whether they are used to move data across the street or around the globe. Divisions between local and long-distance wireless service are fading, too. GTE and Sprint have been bundling local cellular service with long-distance service for some years. By the turn of the century all wireless carriers will sell one-brand, one-bill, one-stop integrated wireless service.

With voice and data, wire and wireless, the new, reintegrated phone companies won't offer their customers equal access to other vendors. No principle of common carriage requires that they should, so long as they sell what they sell to anyone who wants to buy it, other vendors included. The whole marketing pitch will center on just the opposite: the simplicity and reliability of shopping from a single, name-brand provider, with nothing to pick but the name.

AT&T will exploit its strong brand identity as aggressively as anyone, and it will prosper by doing so. A significant fraction of consumers will buy their phone service—all of it, end to end—from AT&T, just as they did in 1980.

Many others won't. That will be the difference.

Broadcast and Cable

Wireline networks have already far surpassed the airwaves for distributing video programming. And they can much more easily accommodate the voracious transmission requirements of high-definition television. Over sixty million homes are already cabled. As cable becomes as ubiquitous as telephone wire, television signals in the air will make about as much sense as flying elephants. These spectrum-devouring leviathans can be transmitted more clearly and abundantly underground. With new spectrum-management technologies, discussed in chapter 6, the same spectrum can now be used much more profitably for services like wireless telephony.

Large cable companies like TCI are arranging to carry broadcast network programming to communities that can't get it otherwise. While they still fear alienating their broadcast affiliates, the networks are gradually preparing for the transition.

There is going to be a messy falling-out between companies whose main asset is entertainment and those whose principal business is distributing it. The national television networks will emerge healthy enough when they finally give in and stampede toward cable. Local broadcasters are going to have to scramble. Their most valuable asset is a government ticket to a slice of spectrum. But the ticket is stamped "broadcast," the one thing that cablecasters do far better by wire. The terror of local broadcasters is that their government ticket will just gradually erode in value until someone in Washington finally ends the misery by handing it over to someone else, perhaps a cellular phone company.

The misery, and much reactionary opposition, could be ended much more gently. The FCC first banned cable/broadcast cross-ownership in 1970; Congress codified the ban in 1984. But the 1996 Telecommunications Act eliminates the statutory ban and directs the FCC to revise its rules.

When the law finally steps out of their way, broadcasters and cable operators will surely combine. Antitrust officials will never let them continue operating duplicate video transport facilities in the same market, but the new entities wouldn't do that. The programming half of local broadcasting, along with the network affiliations, will migrate to cable. The freed-up spectrum will then be used for wireless telephony. This transition is all but inevitable, if only because so much spectrum is now so profligately wasted in delivering video by air to sixty million households that already get the same signals on cable. Cable's competition will come not from conventional broadcasting but from direct broadcast satellite and new forms of wireless cable.

Established broadcasters will choke at these thoughts, but then, people often choke at both competition and change. The fastest and smoothest way to make this happen is to let local cable and local broadcasters get together, move the video underground, and let the spectrum be used for more-valuable, mobile services.

Voice, Video, and Data

All the old, township-dividing labels—telephone and cellular, broadcast and cable, carrier and broadcaster—will soon be obsolete. The new, competitive technologies of the telecosm are too fluid and powerful to be locked into the old regulatory categories of common carriage and broadcast.

This is the most important lesson we have learned from cable. Cable is too capacious. It does not fit any neat, bureaucratically convenient pigeonholes. It retransmits over-the-air broadcasts, and when it does, it is essentially a carrier. It provides leased lines or public access channels, and those are even more carrierlike. It transmits cablecasting—that's publishing. It provides two-way phone service—that's carriage again.

It is no longer useful to think of broadband pipes as ordinary wires. They are bundles of virtual channels, carrying clusters of constantly evolving services. Cable channels operated for pure carriage, without discrimination, are one legitimate business. Cable channels operated for pure cablecasting are another. Cable channels operated for phone service are yet another. And the way a channel is peddled and used can, of course, change with time.

All the other broadband technologies now unfolding are chameleons, too. Both radio and television broadcasters also use parts of their spectrum to provide carriage. Many paging services piggyback their signals on FM subcarrier frequencies; when a Seattle resident travels to Miami, her office tracks down the beeper in her pocket with the assistance of FM radio stations around the country. Paging—a locator service—is bought and sold as common carriage, but it depends on broadcasting to locate travelers.

Satellite technology straddles the old regulatory divisions as well. Satellite operators are mostly carriers, except for the four million homeowners who own a large enough antenna; for them, satellites are direct broadcasters. Higher-powered satellites can reach much smaller antennas. By scrambling signals, and then selling decoders, broadcasters redefine themselves as for-pay narrowcasters. Cellular telephony or television can privatize broadcast spectrum even more.

Landline phone companies move in the opposite direction. Video dialtone services do for video what 976 services did for voice, effectively transforming the telephone network into a "broadcast" medium, capable of delivering the Super Bowl to millions of households. A dial-a-porn service is far more like a topless radio station than like a Sunday afternoon phone call to Aunt Gwendolyn in Missoula. Broadcasters, in short, are mastering the art of keeping the broad while narrowing the cast. Telephone companies are keeping their switched, addressable capabilities while widening their bandwidth and their reach.

With the advent of digital technology, the old divisions between voice, video, and data services are disappearing once and for all. A full-bore digital broadband network will empower everyone to cast broadly or narrowly at will. The on-line world already does so: Anyone can create a bulletin board, and anyone can post musings on it, whether wise, foolish, tasteful, crass, or crude, to be read by the world. With digital broadband technology, the text-based bulletin boards will support voice and video. Broadband carriers will have room to carry anything anywhere, and on their networks anyone can be an instant broadcaster. Tomorrow's broadcasters will have the power to narrow and address their signals at will, and on their networks anyone can be an instant carrier.

A few die-hard providers may decide to keep their businesses strictly on one side of the old definitional line or the other, or they may be forced to do so by reactionary regulators. For the most part, however, the clean, familiar legal divisions between carriers and broadcasters will be impossible to maintain. In the broadband telecosm, carriers and casters will compete head-to-head in a single, unbounded arena.

The End of Price Regulation

From the consumer's perspective, prices for the newly rebundled services will appear to have been fully deregulated by the year 2000. Consumers will be offered a dizzying array of bundled voice, video, and data services, supplied over both wireline and wireless media, at an equally dizzying array of prices. The composition of the bundles will change often, as will their prices. Business consumers, and all profitable residential consumers, will have ceased relying on regulators and public tariffs to prescribe simple, standardized packages and uniform prices. They will shop by name brand, price, and packaging, much as they already shop for wireless, operator, on-line, and long-distance services. Some improvident consumers will get gouged. Most will take their new responsibilities seriously and will shop intelligently.

The prices that providers may charge for bundled packages of services will have been largely deregulated—as they already are, for example, in wireless markets. Regulators will still define and price-regulate a few packages of basic voice services, and possibly (though probably not) basic cable. But nothing more. All the important sales will be made beyond the reach and contemplation of the price police.

The End of Standards

Large networks have always confounded market skeptics. How can so many things connect together without a central authority to set standards? A telephone line must operate at a voltage, current, and frequency compatible with telephone sets and fax machines. Set-top boxes operated by a small cable operator in Alabama must be capable of decoding digital signals coded in Hollywood and uplinked to a satellite in New Jersey. High definition television requires a government-prescribed standard at first so that TV broadcasters and set manufacturers will work toward a common end. Skeptics say that connections won't happen unless some central authority is there to define the interfaces—an FCC, say.

Yet all sorts of connections do happen on their own. A Duracell battery fits comfortably into a Toshiba laptop computer. A Motorola modem connects to an Apple. So does a Hewlett-Packard printer. No Federal Computer Commission ever prescribed those interfaces. The interfaces simply evolved in the market, like the separate products themselves.

Markets do take time to build new interfaces, just as they take time to build integrated circuits. A national authority can establish a standard far faster. That's how it used to work: the king simply announced one day that the unit of measure would be the length of his foot. The old Bell System set uniform standards that way, too. When one company with one lab and one chief executive controls an entire industry, standards come easily.

But they don't come well. Not all standards are equal. Bad standards impede interconnection quite as much as good ones facilitate it. Without market forces in play, there's no pressure to select better standards over worse ones. Central commissions can establish bad standards even faster than they can establish good ones.

Up to a point, competition is the relentless enemy of standardization. The most ambitious competitor's objective is to establish a brand-new standard, which defeated rivals will be forced to copy down the line. Leaders compete by differentiating themselves; followers compete on price alone.

And in an industry where voice, data, and video are all converging onto the same channels, radically different standards are bound to collide. The old standards were all forged in the hermetic, commission-segregated townships; small wonder that they're vastly different. The notion that a central commission must now be preserved to forge new ones is perverse indeed. Monopoly delivers standards the same way it delivers averaged prices and universal service—by suppressing competition and innovation. Competition delivers real standards more slowly but far more robustly.

The Power of One

With telecommunications, as with eggs, there is nothing wrong with having just one basket. The mistake is to have just one hen, guarded by just one fox, even a fox that calls itself a commission. That was Congress's mistake in 1927, when it nationalized all the airwaves. It was Lenin's ten years earlier, when he nationalized everything. That is the one mistake competition will not re-create. The environment is too fractious, growth too fast, innovation too destabilizing, the marketing possibilities too numerous. The market will grow far faster than would-be monopolists could ever dream of merging.

IV

THE MARKETPLACE
OF IDEAS

14

Free Speech

The problem of censorship has been solved. Digital space is so vast that every view, no matter how vile, finds a ready outlet. There is room enough for every form of diseased intelligence. No commission can oversee even the tiniest fraction of the telecosm anymore.

The problem now is free speech itself. The telecosm contains extortion, fraud, libel, debauchery, and on-line clubs of individuals who molest children. Pushed to pathological limits, free speech ruins reputations, corrupts youth, incites violence, and coarsens the populace.

So we need censorship more than ever before. The challenge is to find censorship that works.

The Censors Move In

In 1885 a court in Ohio upheld a local phone company's decision to terminate service to a subscriber who had uttered a naughty word on the line. The subscriber had said to an operator, "If you cannot get the party I want, you can shut up your damned old telephone." The company's contract stipulated that its lines weren't to be used for any "profane, indecent or rude language." One judge dissented from the court's ruling. Damned was not profane, he felt, and in any event the subscriber was entitled to a hearing before termination.

When they arrived some decades later, the common-carrier regulators should of course have sided with profanity. The core principle of common carriage, the most ancient and important principle of all, is nondiscrimination. Business, gossip, seduction, and pillow talk should all travel on precisely equal terms down all lines.

Instead Congress drew the line at pillows. The 1934 Communications Act prohibited knowingly "permitting a telephone under [one's] control" to be used to make "any comment, request, suggestion or proposal which is obscene, lewd, lascivious, filthy, or indecent." This echoed laws written in the 1860s, in which Congress had banned immoral, indecent, fraudulent, and obscene materials from the mails.

No one took much notice until the 1980s. Then phone companies began offering a new category of high-toll dial-up lines, prefaced by the digits 976 or 900. Porno-logues rushed in. One early dial-a-porn service in New York City received six million calls a month. When the Reagan FCC decided that no law barred dial-a-porn, Congress immediately passed one that did. When a federal appellate court struck down the indecency part of that law as unconstitutional, Congress passed another.

By 1996 dirty pictures from the Internet had replaced dirty talk as the main center of concern. One section of the 1996 Telecommunications Act makes it a federal crime to convey dirty pictures to minors. It doesn't matter who initiates the call. Bulletin board operators must demand credit card payment or interpose some other adults-only filter.

The broadcast censors started even earlier. The 1927 Radio Act denied the FCC any power to censor broadcasts but simultaneously proscribed obscene, indecent, or profane language on the air. In due course the FCC listed fourteen kinds of unacceptable material. In the 1960s the Commission would declare war on "topless radio"—sexually oriented talk shows that had been launched by a few small, mostly urban stations. Radio's chest was soon safely covered again. One station, however, would still be fined $2,000 for having broadcast a how-to discussion of oral sex.

That same year a radio station broadcast George Carlin's "Filthy Words," a monologue including the seven words never to be uttered on radio or television. In response, the FCC banned all programming that described "in terms patently offensive as measured by contemporary community standards" any "sexual or excretory activities and organs, at times of the day where there is reasonable risk that children may be in the audience." Congress demanded a ban round the clock. Indecency laws, regulations, lawsuits, and constitutional rulings flew thick and fast.

Indecency wasn't the Commission's only concern. The 1927 Radio Act had given the FCC general power to monitor the "good character" of licensees. For every licensed broadcaster, good name became the immediate jewel of its soul. If you lost that, you ended up poor indeed.

The new Federal Radio Commission immediately announced that each licensee should offer "a well rounded program, in which entertainment . . . religion, education and instruction, important public events, discussions of public questions, weather, market reports, and news and matters of interest to all members of the family find a place." Thereafter the commission would promulgate an intricate array of content guidelines for all broadcasters to follow.

The FCC concocted the Fairness Doctrine, discussed in chapter 12, to temper what broadcasters said on talk shows, news reports, and advertising, on the subject of gas-guzzling cars, tobacco, and nuclear power. Liquor commercials were strongly discouraged; the commission (unlike Dorothy Parker) preferred a frontal lobotomy to a bottle in front of me. The Commission would go on to regulate advertising of lotteries, horse races, and cigarettes, as well as the total amount of airtime devoted to advertising of any kind. It banned program-length "infomercials."

Children have always been a special concern. The Children's Television Act of 1990 required regulation of advertising aimed at children. In 1993 the FCC delayed renewing the licenses of seven TV stations until they proved they were fully meeting their responsibility to educate the nation's youth. As of this writing, the FCC is poised to promulgate yet another set of KidVid broadcasting rules. Yet despite decades of Commission attention to their needs, a single fact remains beyond serious dispute: Television educates best when the set is unplugged. All the FCC's different pronouncements on the subject should have been accompanied by a cone-shaped hat, a star-studded cloak, and the sounding of a Chinese gong.

Meanwhile, cable operators were getting their tickets from local boards. The boards regulated cable content through the franchising process, mainly by specifying in detail which channels franchisees were required to deliver. The 1984 Cable Act curtailed that power a bit. Earlier, however, the FCC itself had tried to bar advertising from cable entirely, to protect broadcasters' revenues. The Commission also barred cable indecency.

Cable operators are reluctant carriers, too. They are required to lease or give away free channels to independent video programmers and to the general public to use in the manner of *Wayne's World*. In 1972 the FCC ordered cable to keep indecency off the giveaway channels as well. After a federal appellate court said that was unconstitutional, viewers in Columbus, Ohio, were presented with a woman describing how she wanted to administer an electric shock to a man's genitals. Cable viewers in Kalamazoo stumbled upon X-rated scenes of oral and homosexual sex. Orange County got *Out Late with Ricky D*, a nude talk show featuring porn stars. All unscrambled, all free, as required by federal law. The cable operators didn't like it, but they had been told to submit.

Congress then directed the FCC to ban such transmissions from public access channels and authorized cable operators themselves to keep it off leased channels. The 1996 Telecommunications Act authorized more of the same.

Scarcity, Ubiquity, and the Constitution

In rulings from the 1800s to the 1920s, the Supreme Court had upheld the government's right to ban lottery promotions and socialist magazines from the mails and to condition use of the mails however else it pleased. It wasn't until 1945 that the Court struck down the postmaster general's attempt to deny second-class mailing privileges to the depraved pages of *Esquire* magazine.

Two years earlier, however, in the monumentally misguided opinion by Justice Felix Frankfurter, the Court had upheld broad FCC oversight of the airwaves. A federal licensing commission is needed to ration the shortage of spectrum, Frankfurter reasoned. Once rationing by commission is accepted, it's reasonable to supervise content, fairness, and advancement of the public interest as well. From the 1930s on, courts had upheld general content prescriptions for broadcasters on similar grounds. This same scarcity logic persuaded the Supreme Court to uphold the Fairness Doctrine, unanimously, in 1969.

The "scarcity" case for censorship never amounted to anything more than a pseudo-scientific rationale for suspending the First Amendment. The electronic media, both wired and wireless, offer vastly more abundance than wood pulp and have done so since the day they were invented. A television conveys more data in a minute than an entire newspaper. Today many towns have only a single newspaper. But virtually every American can pick up 150 channels of television from direct broadcast satellite and transmit voice, data, pictures, and (before long) full-motion video over telephone lines to 140 million other phones in the United States alone.

In half a century of jurisprudence the Supreme Court has never paused to consider where all the supposed scarcity came from. Unspecified laws of physics were to blame, the Court implied. But there are no such laws. The scarcity was created by Congress when it nationalized the airwaves in 1927 and handed them over to a federal bureaucracy for management. Private property rights in the spectrum would have solved the supposed problem.

And with or without private property, engineers were going to keep on building more and more transmitters, with more and more capacity. Scarcity wasn't going to last. Sooner or later the courts would be forced to pull up this Oratorical Pegasus short, and choose another mount.

In 1978 the Supreme Court decided that when it came to rationalizing censorship of the airwaves, abundance would serve just as well. At issue this time was the midafternoon broadcast of George Carlin's seven "Filthy Words." These were indecent, not obscene—a hairsplitting but legally critical difference. Obscenity may constitutionally be barred from print media; mere indecency may not. The commission, however, had banned both. The High Court approved. Unlike magazines, say, the broadcast medium is "uniquely pervasive" and "uniquely accessible to children."

Cable put an end to both scarcity and ubiquity. Wires weren't scarce, but they weren't free, either. They didn't link up to your television uninvited. Nevertheless, several early court rulings baldly analogized cable to broadcast and upheld cable censorship accordingly.

Legal perspectives on cable slowly improved. "[I]f an individual voluntarily opens his door and allows a pig into his parlor, he is in less of a position to squeal," one court pointed out in 1985. When the Supreme Court finally addressed cable's constitutional status in 1994, however, the case ended in a tangle of concurrences and dissents that resolved little. All the Justices agreed that "economic scarcity" does not bring cable under the broadcast precedent. But a thin, five-Justice majority reasoned that cable does nonetheless have "unique physical characteristics," particularly its de facto monopoly over local wireline delivery of video.

Whether the High Court can do any better with telephones remains to be seen. A 1989 ruling struck down a dial-a-porn ban. As of this writing, the Supreme Court is poised to review the Internet indecency provisions of the 1996 Telecommunications Act.

Again the court has consistently failed even to consider where all the problematic ubiquity came from. It is the law of common carriage that requires phone companies to carry everyone's traffic on equal terms. In upholding must-carry regulation of cable, the Supreme Court failed even to note that cable monopolies had been isolated from competition by the same gang of regulators who wanted to regulate cable content. And in one ruling after the next, the Court utterly failed to consider how radio and television had come to be so "uniquely pervasive" and "accessible." It was Congress that had required broadcasting to be ubiquitous and free. It was the FCC that had forbidden scrambling, suppressed lock boxes, and crippled for-pay broadcasting. The authorities themselves had forced broadcasters to make all their wares equally accessible to adults and children. That fact completely escaped the Court's notice.

Time and again the Court has blamed the laws of physics and engineering instead. But these laws are beyond the Court's jurisdiction and don't say what the Court thinks they say. Over-the-air broadcasting can be scrambled and sold on a for-pay basis, as it is with direct broadcast satellite. Cable can be funded by commercials and infomercials, rather than subscription fees, as it is with shopping channels. Set-top boxes and televisions are just different stews of tubes, transistors, and wires; both decode, demodulate, or unscramble transmissions that our eyes and ears can't otherwise detect. Any medium can be electronically locked or unlocked at pretty much any point in the chain of transmission. Left to themselves, engineers and markets solve the problem of ubiquity, just as they solve the problem of scarcity. It is the commission—the would-be censor—that creates the problems that justify its own existence.

Ubiquity, Scarcity, and the Audience's Consent

If you had everything, where would you keep it? While courts have labored to drape constitutional logic on the language of ubiquity and scarcity, technology has completely transformed the practical meaning of those words.

Ubiquity used to be a peculiar aspect of broadcasting: only a few, high-powered wireless transmitters reached everywhere. But today anyone can cast broadly, at least at Internet speeds. Goosed-up telephones make transmitters as ubiquitous as receivers.

Ubiquity now transcends national borders. Satellites have continent-wide footprints. Dial-a-porn operators have already relocated offshore. The *Forbes* columns I've posted on my own Internet home page elicit reactions from Slovakia. Every country with telephones can breed Internet pigs, and most do. In this kind of environment, a national Indecency Act may inconvenience a few large U.S. concerns, but it will not measurably slow the flow of electronic lascivity, filth, indecency, or excretion on U.S. wires. To censor Internet filth at its origins, we would have to enlist the Joint Chiefs of Staff, who could start by invading Sweden and Holland.

At the same time, however, technology now gives individuals at the receiving end effective power to re-create scarcity as they see fit. The V-chip, for example, is to be installed in televisions, to serve much the same purpose as Hollywood's "voluntary" rating system for movies. The cable industry has agreed to rate programs for violence and has declared its support for something like the V-chip on a voluntary basis to enable parents to block coded programs. The 1996 Telecommunications Act calls upon the industry to establish a "Television Rating Code" and to transmit ratings along with programming. TV manufacturers will build chips into sets that allow viewers to reject in advance all programs of any particular category.

While broadcasters grumble about free speech, the V-chip scheme entails nothing more than routine product labeling. And it will ultimately broaden the range of choice, not narrow it. Cable premium channels are already far more diverse and daring than broadcast television precisely because the channels are labeled and scrambled, and Blockbuster video is more varied still. Given suitable V-chips, broadcasters should be able to broadcast anything that can air in a movie theater.

More generally, cataracts of information are useless without powerful switches, tuners, scramblers, and lock boxes to determine precisely what goes where. Broadband technology need not be broadcast. In fact, it's more like the opposite. The higher the bandwidth, the narrower the cast. Senders and receivers alike have more power than ever to narrow the range of the connections established.

The V-chip is just a first, primitive example of what can be done. Much finer degrees of automated self-censorship are possible. Technology can supply electronic eye shades, earplugs, and brown paper bags quite as efficiently as it can deliver pornography or violence. The problem of the unwilling viewer, the inadvertently exposed child, is fast receding.

And that has profound legal implications. Courts have always tolerated some degree of "time, place, and manner" regulation of speech. Whatever the content, one simply cannot have sound trucks in residential neighborhoods at midnight, and X-rated movie theaters cannot be permitted beside primary schools. For similar reasons, First Amendment principle has always turned, in part, on how an audience is likely to react. "Fighting words" provoke fights, pornography is said to encourage sexual assault, graphic violence may inspire copycat crimes, loud trucks at midnight interrupt sleep. For legal purposes, obscenity is defined by specific reference to "contemporary community standards." Falsely shouting "Fire!" in a crowded theater is not a constitutional right mainly because of the crowd.* Your constitutional rights to bellow falsehoods are much broader when the theater is empty.

Until recently these standards have all been at war with telecom technology. Tame fun for men on Polk Street in San Francisco may seem unspeakably depraved to parents on Main Street in Oshkosh. But the whole point of telecommunications is to unite residents of both. To impose local norms on media that are inherently unlocal is to cripple the media themselves. In 1990 an Alabama grand jury indicted Home Dish Satellite Network under a state anti-obscenity statute. Home Dish's satellite carriers, first U.S. Satellite, and later GTE, then refused to carry the service to avoid going to trial themselves, forcing Home Dish to discontinue its Exxxtasy channel. With enough sufficiently different local norms brought into play, the network will be permitted to transmit nothing but mush.

But the more power individuals have to choose their electronic guests, the less justification there is for general rules aimed at protecting everyone from bad company. Indecency on public radio is obviously different from indecency on a telephone dial-up service. The Supreme Court itself has acknowledged as much. Indeed, obscenity—as defined by the Supreme Court—cannot really exist at all in well-ordered cyberspace: Community standards within any group of speakers and listeners can be completely uniform and harmonious, even if uniformly depraved or violent by standards outside that network community. People don't inadvertently tune in to alt.sex.pedophilia while driving to a Sunday picnic with Aunt Gwendolyn. Somebody who logs onto the appropriate Internet forum and types "Show Panties" can hardly be heard to complain about the shock to his sensibilities that follows.

The concept of deviance thus loses its meaning when communities of the like-minded are formed entirely by consent. Freedom of association is so complete in cyberspace that traditional limits on freedom of speech are no longer needed.

What judges haven't yet fully grasped, however, is just how advanced that freedom of association has become. Turnstiles, gates, and

---

*"The most stringent protection of free speech would not protect a man in falsely shouting fire in a theatre and causing a panic. . . . The question in every case is whether the words used are used in such circumstances and are of such a nature as to create a clear and present danger that they will bring about the substantive evils that Congress has a right to prevent." Schenck v. United States, 249 U.S. 47, 52 (1919).

locks are possible everywhere. They will be installed quickly enough once commissions stop outlawing the locksmiths.

The real problem for broadcasters is FCC policy that requires them to broadcast everything in the clear, and for free. Set aside those requirements, and lockboxes can readily be added by the broadcaster itself, one community at a time, so that bestiality (say) will be peddled to viewers in the 10011 zip code but blocked to all viewers in the 39000. A cable company today can't legally sell you a kids-only package of channels, with Disney, say, and not the standard prurience peddled by the broadcast networks. A phone company that chooses on its own initiative to cut off service to a dial-a-porn operator commits both a state and a federal crime.

Instead of trying to appoint new public censors, Congress and judges must liberate private ones. Give absolute legal immunity to any good-faith, voluntary, private initiative by any carrier, broadcaster, or provider of content to limit sex and violence or access to it by wire or radio. The 1996 Telecommunications Act takes a few modest steps in this direction. These provisions will inevitably be attacked as new attempts to censor. But private censorship is just the freedom of the editorial room—the essence of free speech itself. America knows how to operate under laws like those. Phone companies in Ohio grasped the basic idea in 1885.

Common Law

Free association and private consent will take care of a lot, but still not everything. Libel is harmful not because it is unwelcome to the receiver of the intelligence but because it defames a third party. Pornography and violence may be equally welcome in some parlors; the harm comes when the psychopath goes out hunting afterward. In 1974 NBC aired the movie *Born Innocent*, which graphically portrayed a particularly brutal gang rape of a girl by means of a plumber's helper. A real child was the victim of a copycat crime four days later.

The problems are real; commission-centered solutions aren't. No modern incarnation of the Star Chamber can possibly begin to address them. The technology won't allow it, and all the problems revolve around specific facts of specific cases. It is the common law that must become, once again, the main line of defense against destructive forms of speech. New legal norms and procedures must be developed anew in the common law, by private litigants pressing private claims before judges and juries, not commissioners.

The common law of defamation dates back to England before the

Norman Conquest. The original remedy was a public apology followed by punishment—cutting off the defamer's tongue, for example. By 1535 the basics of the common law of defamation were in place, intended to promote legal remedies over alternatives like dueling. "[I]f an impudent writer attacks your reputation, break his head," Benjamin Franklin wrote later. But defamation suits were a reasonable alternative, he conceded, if "it should be thought that this proposal of mine may disturb the public peace."

The private law of defamation enshrines no grand principle of freedom of speech or press. Quite the contrary: The common law of defamation, along with its sibling, copyright, gives an individual clear rights to limit what appears about him in the public press. A rich array of related common-law torts have been developed more recently: harassment (including telephone harassment), invasion of privacy, misappropriation of the right of publicity, intentional infliction of emotional distress, disparagement, and discrimination in a commercial context.

Consider, for example, the law concerning "tarnishment," which places limits on just how freely you can portray somebody else's trademark in an unwholesome or unsavory context. A lawsuit filed by Hormel, the Minnesota-based manufacturer of Spam, attacked the *Muppet Treasure Island* movie, which featured a noxious wild boar named Spa'am. The boar wears a headdress that includes a human skull and a necklace of smaller pig heads; Hormel complained that the movie had "intentionally portrayed the Spa'am character to be evil in porcine form." The movie's producers responded that there wasn't any good name to tarnish. A newspaper had already described an annual contest among cooks where the dishes must include Spam. One entry—"Spampers"—had featured a mother, her three-month old baby girl, a diaper pail, and a Spam "paté."

Muppets and Spam may not seem serious, but the underlying legal issues are. Conflicts like these arise all the time; they have to be resolved, and there is no single, simple principle like free speech to resolve them summarily. Private suits under these theories aren't censorship, for the simple reason that the rights in question are privately enforced. Enforcement is simply a matter of striking some reasonable balance between one private citizen's freedom and another's.

In a landmark decision in 1964 the Supreme Court declared that even libel suits are subject to First Amendment limits. That case, however, involved a suit brought by a public official in Montgomery, Alabama, who had allegedly been libeled by a civil rights ad carried in the *New York Times*. In limiting the right of public officials to attack speech through libel law, the Supreme Court made the right call. Henry the Eighth demonstrated years ago that even a courtroom can become a forum for commissionlike defense of the government in some circumstances. Unfortunately, the Supreme Court declared that it was neutering common-law libel suits brought by any public figure, not just government officials. The Court began to backtrack a few years later by narrowing the definition of "public figure." It should finish the job. Government officials should not be able to bring libel suits on the basis of any criticism related to the exercise of their public powers. Private citizens have no public powers, so their strictly private rights need not be curtailed by First Amendment doctrine.

This is not to say that every private plaintiff who sues should win. The facts bearing on cause and effect in cases like these are usually thin at best and are often nothing but rank speculation. In the suit following the real-life gang rape inspired by *Born Innocent*, NBC prevailed. Producers of a movie about gangs weren't held liable to a plaintiff who was shot by another viewer after leaving a theater. A plaintiff who sued the three major networks alleging that years of violent television had caused him to kill his elderly neighbor lost on the ground that the causal nexus was too speculative. But a radio station was held liable for having its disc jockey travel about town in a red automobile broadcasting his location to listeners and offering a cash prize to the first listener to reach him; two teenagers vying for the money forced a third driver into a fatal accident. While every claim must be approached skeptically, serious claims must be given serious hearings. Such hearings offend no principles of free speech so long as they are enforced on a case-by-case basis by private litigants and cautious courts, giving careful attention to solid facts.

Unfortunately, courts continue to inject constitutional norms into these private controversies, much as they have in the libel cases. The court in the neighbor-murder case declared that the violent TV programming enjoys First Amendment immunity, even from private tort suits. Walt Disney Productions likewise prevailed on a First Amendment defense against a suit stemming from a child's imitation of a stunt shown on the *Mickey Mouse Club* show. NBC successfully invoked the First Amendment in its defense in the *Born Innocent* case. The Supreme Court of Rhode Island rejected, on similar grounds, claims involving a child who died while imitating a hanging stunt he saw on the *Tonight Show*. But these rulings all started from the wrong legal premise. Private tort suits are a quite different beast from public prosecutions. National commissions that enforce criminal laws in court put free speech in true jeopardy. Private individuals who press private claims don't. How else could we have a functioning law of copyright?

Many First Amendment purists recoil at the thought that we should make it easier to bring tort suits against speech of any kind. But federal commissions like the FCC provide far more reason to recoil. One way or another, the telecosm needs a robust rule of law to address private speech that leads directly to serious, concrete, private harm. As for the choice between commission law, which is both indiscriminate and ineffectual, and common law, which can be both discriminating and effective, it should be easy. Common-law courts will always retain the flexibility to harmonize tort rights and First Amendment values case by case. The sooner we reaffirm a healthy tort law in this sphere, the faster we will be able to get on with the business of dismantling the institution that truly offends First Amendment principle, the Commission itself.

A Return to the Past

The Scandalum Magnatum of 1275 commanded that none "be so hardy to cite or publish any false news or tales whereby discord or occasion of discord or slander may grow between the King and his people or the great men of the realm." John Twyn was executed in 1663 for printing "a seditious, poisonous, and scandalous" book suggesting that the king should be accountable to his subjects. When Henry the Eighth took the throne in 1509, he faced the grave new peril of the printing press. He set up the Star Chamber, which promptly invented a new crime, seditious libel.

Blackstone would later describe seditious libel as a common-law doctrine, indistinguishable from ordinary defamation But Blackstone was wrong. The Star Chamber was an administrative tribunal. It operated without juries; its members served at the king's pleasure and concocted oppressive new criminal laws to protect the crown. Seditious-libel laws were enforced from the top down, through prosecutions by the state. Common-law courts developed private defamation law from the bottom up, to resolve private disputes between private citizens.

Faced with the same pair of choices in our century, between a federal censorship commission, on the one hand, and a legal regime of private civil right, on the other, we too made the wrong choice. It is time now to relearn the lessons of history. The administrative tribunal is the worst of all possible censors. Private right, privately enforced, is the best.

Getting the Commission out of the censorship business is a matter of good legal house-keeping and proper sanitation, no more. The Commission no longer seriously threatens free speech; so far as free speech goes, the Commission is now just an offensive joke. The telecosm today carries the proclamations of generals before battle, the speeches of führers and prime ministers, the solidarity songs of public schools and left-wing political parties, national anthems, temperance tracts, papal encyclicals, and sermons against gambling and contraception. And it carries the chorus of raspberries from all the millions of common men to whom these high sentiments make no appeal. Whether the Commission lives or dies, the age-old problem of censorship has been solved.

The problem now is free speech itself and the right of each citizen to enjoy some shelter from assaults that masquerade as discourse. It is a problem for common-law courts, not commissions. No larger, more powerful, or more centralized institution can do the job.

15

Speech for Sale

Free speech is easy now. It's commerce that's hard. Private property implies a right to exclude. Today's networks supply limitless power to include.

Property rights in words, sounds, and pictures have traditionally centered on how they are conveyed. Copyright law originated in the technology of copying—the printing press. The Stationer's Company, a guild of London bookbinders, booksellers, calligraphers, and illuminators, was founded by royal decree in 1556. By registering the title of his "copie" with the Company, a stationer acquired the right to publish the work or assign it to others. In 1710 the English Parliament codified the Statute of Anne, "[a]n act for the encouragement of learning by vesting the copies of printed books in the authors or purchasers of such copies, during the times therein mentioned."

The framers of the U.S. Constitution denied Congress any public power over speech or the press. But first, in Article I, Section 8, they affirmed the importance of private censorship that inheres in copyright. The first federal copyright act, covering books, maps, and charts, was passed in 1790. In due course copyright was extended to printed words, music, the fine arts, photographs, movies, sound recordings, architecture, computer software, and then any other "original works of authorship fixed in any tangible medium of expression, now known or later developed." The owner of a copyright is granted exclusive rights to reproduce the work in any tangible form, to distribute copies to the public, and to perform or display it.

Copyright and Common Law

But copyright still presents a fundamental economic conundrum. Information is a public good—it can be consumed many times over without being diminished. Once Madonna has sung, the tape would ideally be sold for the cost of the plastic alone, the marginal cost of producing an additional copy. But Madonna is a material girl: If the law allowed anyone to sell her golden voice for the price of plastic, she might not sing at all. Some might consider that a public benefit, but many others would consider it a loss.

The law therefore deliberately maintains some measure of scarcity to encourage production, recognizing all the while that scarcity inhibits consumption. Courts strike the balance case by case. Sometimes Congress codifies their decisions; occasionally it overturns them. Most of the time it just lets them be.

The performance right, for example, is of great importance to owners of copyrights in musical compositions. At first only public performance was protected. Once bought and paid for, a book or sheet of music could be privately enjoyed again and again; no one was going to collect for each successive performance by and for an audience of one. But where does public performance begin? In a salon? A sports stadium? A local radio station? And how about parodies, like 2 Live Crew singing "Ugly Woman"? Or lengthy quotations from President Ford's memoirs, published by a magazine as "news"? May a radio announcer read on the air the front page of a local newspaper—with full disclosure of what she's reading? May a TV station air a movie clip as part of a movie review? A clip of another station's sports broadcast? No legislative committee can begin to codify an answer for every possible variation on controversies like these. So courts do the work, one case at a time.

Most of these controversies are analyzed under the legal rubric of "fair use." The doctrine was first articulated in 1841 by Circuit Justice Joseph Story as an adaptation from the English common law. Congress eventually codified it in 1976. The Supreme Court's first occasion to interpret that effort came in 1984. Universal Studios sued Sony, the manufacturer of the first mass-market VCR, for contributory infringement of Universal's movie copyrights. Sony was peddling instruments of burglary, the argument ran. Five Justices of the Supreme Court disagreed. Home recording of TV broadcasts is a fair use, a bare majority of the Court concluded.

The Court had written its most important decision about unfair use much earlier, in 1918. The case didn't even technically involve copyright law; it hinged instead on a common-law tort, "misappropriation of intellectual property." Barred by British censors from sending war cables to the United States, Randolph Hearst's International News Service was copying war news as it appeared from the Associated Press wire in the Eastern papers. AP neglected to copyright its stories. But it owned them anyway, the Supreme Court ruled. The Court brushed aside International News's argument that the public had some amorphous right to know. Even if AP lacked the general right to forbid reproduction of its uncopyrighted reports, it still had a legal right to protect itself against their use, for profit, by a direct competitor.

For many years thereafter the *International News* decision was simply ignored. Judge Clark's 1940 observation in an exchange with Judge Learned Hand was typical: "[T]his case is entirely indistinguishable from *International News Service v. A.P.* . . . and we might as well admit it. But we have conquered the *News* case before; it can be done again." *International News* survived nevertheless. It would subsequently be invoked to enjoin the unauthorized broadcasting of professional baseball games and a radio station's decision to paraphrase a local newspaper rather than subscribe to a wire service. Until Congress enacted the Sound Recording Act of 1971, *International News* provided the legal framework state courts needed to stop record piracy.

With the courts doing all the real crafting of the law of intellectual property, is Congress needed at all? Rights to own ordinary kinds of personal property and land evolved without much help from commission or legislature. Intellectual property rights have, too. For the future, there is no other practical choice. Commissions and legislative committees can no longer keep up with the chaotic pace of change in the technology of copying.

Carriers and Broadcasters

Copyright infringement is a civil wrong, a tort. Tort liability usually extends to anyone who helped commit the wrong. Yet the phone company is never liable. Why not? Courts long ago crafted a passive-carrier exemption from copyright liability; Congress codified it in 1976. This makes obvious sense. Your phone company doesn't know that you're transmitting a digital copy of Madonna's "Material Girl" over the phone line. You don't want it to know.

Broadcasters are different. In 1925 the copyright owner of "Dreamy Melody" sued a radio broadcaster for playing his song over the air. A federal appellate court agreed that broadcast is a "public performance." Congress eventually codified but also limited that decision, prescribing set fees for broadcasters to pay record companies. Madonna, in other words, no longer has an exclusive performance right in her recorded songs. Television broadcasters, by contrast, have no comparable rights to "perform" movies that they don't own. They have to buy movies at whatever price the market commands.

Things get more complicated downstream. In 1931 the Supreme Court concluded that a hotel had unlawfully "performed" copyrighted music by piping it from a single master radio receiver to all rooms in the hotel. The decision seemed to turn on the fact that the broadcast itself was unauthorized; in a footnote, the Supreme Court suggested that the result would have been different if the radio station had been broadcasting with permission. Apparently you could steal from honest broadcasters but not from thieves.

That case was, in turn, virtually overruled by the Supreme Court in 1975. A fried-chicken emporium used four mounted speakers in its dining rooms to play broadcasts from a local radio station. No infringement, the Court ruled. In 1976 legislation, Congress agreed that small commercial establishments may play standard radios or TVs for their customers without infringing. Landlords and hotel-keepers may likewise operate master antennas to distribute local signals at no charge within their buildings.

What about a satellite dish sold for home use but installed by a sports bar to attract consumers of beer and pretzels? Or Satellite Master Antenna TV (SMATV), where the antenna mounted on top of a high-rise apartment building pipes down satellite channels? In 1985 the National Football League and the St. Louis Cardinals sued a local watering hole for showing home games that had been blacked out locally. The bar had gone too far, a federal judge ruled.

But the main copyright problem for broadcasters has been, quite simply, an obsolete conception of what broadcasting is all about. The only business model Congress contemplated when it passed the 1927 Radio Act was free broadcasting. For the next half century the FCC suppressed scrambling of any kind. For a time even cable TV was suppressed on similar grounds: Shielding programs in pay-to-view wires was unacceptable.

Cable

Cable was a puzzle. Was it like telephone—a mere carrier of broadcast signals? Or was it like broadcast—an integrated form of electronic publishing?

The obvious copyright question arrived at the Supreme Court in

1968, in *Fortnightly v. United Artists Television*. Several cable operators were retransmitting the signals of five broadcast stations to whom United Artists had granted exclusive licenses. There was no copyright infringement, the cable operators insisted; they were just making broadcasts broader. The Supreme Court agreed. A cable system did "no more than enhance the viewer's capacity to receive the broadcaster's signals." By equating cable operators with viewers, the Court handed them a license to steal.

It was a horrendously bad call. "Enhancing reception" is the function of every printing press, transmitter, recorder, and copying machine. It is one thing to use a pair of binoculars to enhance your reception of a baseball game from an apartment overlooking Wrigley Field. It is quite another to replace the binoculars with the Goodyear blimp and broadcast the World Series to the nation. The *Fortnightly* majority made no attempt to draw any such distinction.

The economic implications got worse when cable operators began importing distant signals. A national network like CBS might not care if Oshkosh viewers watch Sunday football as broadcast by a station in Oshkosh or one in Okefenokee. But those two affiliates care a lot. Gordon's Giveaway Pontiac in Oshkosh won't pay extra to have its commercials aired in Okefenokee, whereas Make-a-Deal Denny in Okefenokee will pay less when its own local station loses viewers to the Oshkosh broadcast.

When the matter came back to the Supreme Court in 1974, the Court completed the devastation. *Fortnightly* had dealt only with binocular-sized community antennas; *Teleprompter Corp. v. CBS* involved the blimp—five cable companies that were using microwave to import distant broadcast signals. The Supreme Court simply reaffirmed *Fortnightly*.

With these two rulings, the Supreme Court effectively abolished the copyrights of broadcasters, at least vis-à-vis cable. The worst of it was that the Court's conclusion had been anchored not in common law but in the logic of the 1934 telecom legislation and in the language of the federal copyright statute. Common-law courts can correct their errors fairly easily; they simply take another look and reject their earlier reasoning. It's much less easy to get a second reading of a statute; legislative interpretations tend therefore to be much more rigid. It is unlikely that the Supreme Court would even have agreed to decide *Fortnightly* and *Teleprompter* when it did if those two cases had been based on emerging common-law doctrine rather than on two major federal statutes. Having taken and decided both cases on statutory grounds, the Court had shut down the process of legal evolution in the courts. It was now up to other branches of government to change the rules, if they cared to.

Copyright by Commission

The FCC tried first. While insisting that "the issue of fairness to copyright owners" was not one it could resolve, the Commission set about reassembling the equivalent of the copyright protections that the Supreme Court had repudiated. In the wake of *Fortnightly*, the Commission proposed to replace its old distant-signal rules with a new regime of retransmission consent. There would be sharp limits on cable's right to import distant signals without the consent of the original broadcaster.

For six years the commission fiddled, adjusted, and revised these rules. Finally it acknowledged that its retransmission consent regime "simply will not wash" and announced its intention to "break new ground." It abandoned retransmission consent and resurrected its distant-signal rules, reaffirmed anti-leapfrogging rules, and added other rules covering cable imports of syndicated, non-network programming. Almost before the ink had dried on each new pronouncement, the FCC began to amend and backtrack. The tangle just grew and grew.

Congress finally reacted. What it should have done was simply overturn *Fortnightly* and *Teleprompter* and leave it to market forces to work out relations between broadcast and cable. In 1992 that was what Congress would finally do. In 1976, however, Congress decided to move a huge slab of copyright out of the market and into a new commission.

In the Copyright Act of 1976 Congress agreed that cable companies should pay for the programming they retransmit. But program-by-program or signal-by-signal negotiations over royalties—market forces, in other words—were just too cumbersome. The Act therefore handed cable companies the right to intercept certain TV signals from outside a local viewing area and to retransmit them upon payment of Commission-prescribed prices.

The commission in question was a new FCC, with the middle C now standing for "Copyright." It was named the Copyright Royalty Tribunal. Though its mission was never described quite so candidly, the Tribunal was in effect empowered to purchase all broadcast programming at government-announced prices and then resell it—for far less than it would have commanded on the open market—to cable operators.

The 1976 Act set initial royalty fee schedules and authorized the new Tribunal to make adjustments as deemed appropriate. Every cable operator, regardless of the signals it carries, pays a small baseline percentage of gross receipts from subscribers. Each then pays a bit more based on the number and type of distant signals retransmitted. No charges are assessed for the retransmission of local signals, nor for the retransmission of network programming, on the assumption that advertisers will pay more for broader local transmission, and copyright owners anticipate broad distribution from the outset in contracting with the networks.

Receipts are distributed to the owners of copyrighted non-network programming. Congress did not specify any precise formula for distribution. Division of each year's copyright royalties takes three to five years and involves a quagmire of impenetrable procedure. The first distribution formula, for 1978, granted 75 percent of receipts to program and movie syndicators, 12 percent to sports organizations, and only 3.25 percent to television stations. Courts wearily approved this allocation in 1982. The 1979 proceeding, which resulted in a similar distribution, was again contested; the reviewing court again upheld the award. A copyright owner's royalties for a given year, much less for a given program or market, defy prediction. For sixteen years this abominable process swept aside all semblance of property and contract in what is now a $30 billion market for cable-delivered video programming.

Congress finally altered course in 1992. The Tribunal remained in place, but the 1992 Cable Act gave broadcasters the power to veto retransmission absent contractual agreement. The retransmission consent provision gives broadcasters themselves (though not the owners of programming copyrights) a new property right in their "signal," distinct from copyright in the programming itself. Consent may be priced at whatever the market will bear.

In the first round of negotiation, completed in 1993, the market would not bear much. Gambling correctly on the assumption that the networks needed cable more than cable needed the networks, cable operators simply refused to offer any cash at all. The major networks traded retransmission consent for free carriage of cable channels that they owned. But this will change abruptly once serious competitive alternatives for cable are up and running. Then local broadcasters' content will suddenly become a valuable commodity, and alternative local video carriers will bid aggressively to get it.

Signal Piracy and Copy-Tap

What would have happened if the Supreme Court had decided *Fortnightly* and *Teleprompter* the other way? As it happens, we know the answer. We learned it when the cable companies became broadcasters themselves—satellite broadcasters.

This time, however, the legislators and commissioners stayed out. They created no presumption that cablecasts were to be freely available to all takers. Left to their own devices, courts wove a new, generally sensible jurisprudence of common-law copyright out of an obscure provision of the 1934 Communications Act.

The 1934 Act contains an anti-wiretap clause. This originally had nothing to do with copyright; the 1934 Congress intended to prohibit the interception and publication of wire and radio transmissions, especially police or fire department dispatches. Picking up broadcast signals intended "for the use of the general public" was expressly permitted.

In the 1960s, however, the FCC grudgingly allowed some stations to begin broadcasting subscription radio and television services. Hackers quickly learned how to intercept and decode the scrambled signals. The subscription operators then sued the manufacturers of decoders.

The 1934 Act permitted interception of any broadcast "for the use of the general public." And at that time the Commission and the courts still labeled subscription television a broadcast service. In 1979 the FCC announced that pay-TV operators were protected anyway. Most courts eventually agreed. The key to determining whether an operator was entitled to wiretap protection, they concluded, turned on the operator's intent. Scrambled signals are obviously not intended for receipt by anyone who shops at Radio Shack. The manufacturers of decoders weren't actually intercepting signals themselves, but the wiretap provision also covers those who "assist in receiving." The statute requires that unauthorized reception be followed by "publication or divulgence"; courts got around that by declaring that the decoder manufacturer "divulges" or "publishes" whatever the device is ultimately used to intercept.

From the perspective of sound judging, this was all shameless fabrication. The wiretap clause includes criminal sanctions, and in ordinary circumstances criminal statutes are never stretched and manipulated as they were here. But that legalistic detail aside, the rulings were very sound indeed. Courts had simply invoked an obscure, vaguely related, loosely phrased provision of the 1934 Act to begin building a new common law against signal piracy—in effect, a new common law of copyright. Call it "copy-tap" law.

Its strange parentage notwithstanding, copy-tap law has proved robust. People who manufactured boxes for signal piracy got sued; copyright owners got protection. Copy-tap extended protection to signals intercepted for personal use as well as commercial use. In that regard, and in others, it is much broader than ordinary copyright. In 1984, and again in 1988, Congress endorsed these legal developments. It raised the civil and criminal penalties for intercepting scrambled (or otherwise privatized) video programming. And it gave private parties expanded authority to sue.

Courts and Congress extended copy-tap protection to satellite broadcasters as well. A relay satellite is just a TV station on a very tall mast. If terrestrial broadcasts could be pirated with impunity, by all logic satellite broadcasts could be, too. But Congress had not, of course, imagined satellite broadcasting in 1934, and the Commission had never forced satellite broadcasters into the free-television model of operation.

This accident of technological history made it easy to categorize satellite as something quite different. In 1978 the Commission declared that "unauthorized" interceptions of satellite signals were prohibited by the wiretap laws. Courts agreed when content owners like the NFL sued sports bars. Congress then codified what the courts had begun to develop. The law authorizes interception of "satellite cable programming" for private viewing—but the right evaporates the moment the satellite broadcaster either scrambles the signal or merely establishes a system for selling it. Most major cable networks promptly did both, and that was the end of the matter. Cablecasters that distributed their programming by satellite were now fully protected under the copy-tap laws. So were the landline cable networks. Courts extended copy-tap protections to cable, and Congress followed suit in 1984.

And so, from Ted Turner in Atlanta up to the satellites, back down to earth, and along the length of terrestrial cable networks, cablecasters and cable operators got far more protection than the broadcasters on whose pirated signals cable had nursed in its infancy. Until 1992 broadcasters were protected only by the Copyright Royalty Tribunal, which was no protection at all.

With less interference from Congress and the Commission, common-law courts would have assembled a solid body of copy-tap law much earlier, to protect not just cable and satellite but plain old broadcasting, too. There is something quite obviously wrong about grabbing someone else's creation and selling it as your own. Courts knew this all along. The precedent was there, as old as Randolph Hearst and the International News Service. It was the crude, overbearing model of free-to-all broadcasting codified in the 1934 Act and rigidly enforced by the FCC that deterred the courts from building on that precedent much earlier.

They are catching up now. Some courts apply *International News* only to cases where one competitor palms off another's work as his own. But signal theft doesn't usually involve that—the pirated HBO signal is still identified as HBO. Other courts have been more liberal. One 1982 ruling, for example, addressed American Television's purchase of exclusive rights to display HBO programming in Denver. The company used a wireless cable microwave service to distribute the signals to a subscriber's home, which it equipped with a special antenna and converter. Another company sold pirate antennas and converters. Applying *International News* and related precedent, a Colorado court concluded that the elements of unfair competition and misappropriation had been established.

But however the law is labeled—wiretap or misappropriation—the process is what counts. What we are witnessing is the creation of a new common law of copyright, conjured out of the depths of Supreme Court precedent from 1918 and an obscure anti-wiretap clause codified in 1934.

Scrambling

Putting aside its bizarre statutory foundations, copy-tap law shows precisely how law should evolve through a common-law process as markets and technology change. Piracy meant nothing to early broadcasters—they wanted as many listeners and viewers as possible. It meant a lot to for-pay broadcasters and cablecasters. Scrambling technology gave them their start; courts then crafted a new, essentially common-law jurisprudence to meet the new needs.

The legal advances were essential, but technology will do most of the important protecting down the line. Clint Eastwood collects his rent through ticket sales at the movie theater; freeloading is suppressed by concrete, which shields the screen from public view. The old broadcasters never had that capability. Anyone who wanted to tune in could.

Scrambling now offers the electronic equivalent of the box office and theater walls. On switched telephone lines, it is easy to set up a dial-a-joke service (the equivalent of pay-per-listen radio) or a dial-up video service . . . or the Web, which is all of the above. The same can be done on the air. As Princess Diana ("Squidgy") discovered to her sorrow, a cellular telephone is a broadcast device, like a radio station. It nevertheless provides individual service at metered rates, like a movie theater. Sophisticated coding algorithms that scramble what is sent can readily be combined today with terminal equipment smart enough not only to decode but also to report faithfully on just what has been decoded, in much the same manner as a postage meter. The set-top boxes at the end of the cable television line perform similar functions.

Technology offers great simplification for copyright law. It makes intentions unambiguously clear: a scrambled signal is intended for a limited audience only. Good scrambling is hard to beat, and every advance in microprocessor technology makes scrambling better. Copy-tap law can then focus on fairly concrete things, like illegal decoders, which are relatively easy to outlaw or seize.

This brings copyright law full circle. The law originally focused on the medium—the paper, the "copie" itself. But in the new telecosm, media are infinitely changeable. Human eyes and ears are not, however. An electronic interface—a software-based reader, viewer, descrambler, or decoder—is still needed. That is the tangible key on which the courts can come to focus once again.

In the stumbling, groping way so characteristic of the common law, that is precisely what courts are now doing. The process is inelegant; like the making of sausage, the manufacture of common law is always inelegant. But it is working, pretty much as it should, and far better than any commission-centered alternatives.

16

Privacy

From a technical perspective, privacy is now secure, or can be for anyone who cares to secure it. The remaining threats to privacy are public ignorance, which will eventually be dispelled, and government obstruction, which won't.

Tapping a wire is no use if the message intercepted is in unbreakable code. Unbreakable coding engines, based on sophisticated mathematical algorithms, can now easily be built into chips or software at modest cost. As microprocessors grow more powerful, the gap between code makers and code breakers keeps widening.

Networks themselves are developing in ways that make tapping far more difficult. Existing wireless networks use analog technology that is not at all secure. But in the next few years cellular systems will be converted to digital technology, which is far harder to tap. Both spread-spectrum and packet-switching technologies disassemble messages and transmit them over different frequencies and different lines. They are reassembled only at the receiving end. Wiretaps are then useless unless they are placed very close to the point of origination or final receipt. This sharply limits the number of points where snooping can even begin. Beyond that, every would-be snooper has to search for messages of interest within cataracts of other, useless information. In the ever-growing electronic crowds, there is more privacy than ever.

The technical fact is this: Any individual who really wants to privatize his electronic communications has means readily at hand to do so—coding algorithms too powerful for even the National Security

Agency to crack. If people still routinely surrender their privacy anyway, it is either because they have nothing they care to conceal or because they simply don't understand that privacy is possible.

The more difficult practical problem is escaping the conversation of others. There are, first, intruders like comedian George Carlin. His on-the-air discussion of the seven "Filthy Words" is usually analyzed in terms of "free speech," but for the father listening to the radio with his young son, it really comes down to privacy in a car. The radio can indeed be switched off, but Carlin still fouls the air while you lunge for the dial.

Carlin intrudes on privacy almost anonymously, through general rudeness. Narrowcast incursions are more common and more troubling. The new enemies of privacy make calls instead—private calls to sell, harass, poll, or proselytize. The development of automatic dialing technology has enabled solicitors of any description to make thousands of calls per day at very low cost. Disgruntled lovers and con men use the telephone to hound and harass. The telephone, as Ambrose Bierce foresaw, has become an "invention of the devil which abrogates some of the advantages of making a disagreeable person keep his distance."

But technology-based defenses against tele-solicitation and tele-harassment are evolving rapidly, too. Caller ID service displays the telephone number of an incoming call before the phone is answered. The service can easily be combined with equipment that will allow almost any degree of advanced electronic screening. Businesses love this; it lets their computers instantly direct calls to appropriate agents. Pop-screen software pulls up electronic records the moment the phone is answered.

The Commission in the Chips

Congress and the FCC know about the underlying problems. The rules they've codified to address them pay lip service to the ideal of privacy. But they often suppress the technology that secures it.

If seven dirty words are too many to broadcast to car radios, how about five on basic cable? Or three on pay-per-view? The level of olfactory offense, and the degree to which it is confined, can be adjusted indefinitely. And there are, of course, some people who actually like being exposed to foul air, much as nudists enjoy nudity.

So the FCC has diligently tried to strike some general balance between free speech, on the one hand, and privacy, on the other. This is the same FCC, of course, that forbids the scrambling of over-the-air broadcasts—the technology that confines the delivery of rude signals to coarse sensibilities. Having outlawed real scrambling in 1927, Congress made Scrambling Lite mandatory in 1996. As discussed in chapter 14, the 1996 Telecommunications Act demands a V-chip in every television, to empower families to tune out pigs like Carlin entirely.

Commissions have tried to address the telephone equivalent of Carlin, too—the harassing phone call. Nearly every state has enacted a criminal statute forbidding telephone harassment in the form of obscene, anonymous, repeated, or nonconsensual calls. The Federal Telephone Harassment Statute, enacted in 1968, likewise imposes criminal liability on interstate use of the telephone to make "obscene, lewd, lascivious, filthy, or indecent" phone calls or to make anonymous calls "with intent to annoy, threaten, or harass," or "repeatedly or continuously to ring, with intent to harass."

But all these laws suffer from the same practical defect. Criminal prosecutions are a serious business. From the perspective of at least one citizen—the defendant—the prosecution itself is the ultimate threat to privacy, there being little privacy in court or in prison. Under constitutional doctrines of vagueness and "overbreadth," even a caller whose conduct lacks any legitimate justification may escape conviction because the criminal statute is too imprecise or sweeps too far into other conduct that would be protected. Criminalizing any but the most deliberate and unconscionable invasions of privacy is thus rarely the answer.

Commission attempts to curtail ordinary solicitations, whether charitable or commercial, are even more impractical and even less effective. Some states prohibit calls made at "inconvenient" or late hours, or calls that significantly prevent the recipient from using his or her own phone. In 1991 Congress enacted a bill that bars automatically dialed or prerecorded telephone calls. The FCC is directed to grant exemptions business by business, product by product, service by service, so that consumers may continue receiving calls of a type "the consumer would not ordinarily object to receiving." Survey research is to be exempted, unless combined with a sales pitch. Local solicitations by small businesses and newspapers are to be exempted depending on the "extent and effectiveness" of local "better business" community standards And the FCC may also exempt some (but probably not all) calls from companies the consumer has previously done business with. In crafting such minute adjustments of speech and privacy rights, the FCC is implored to remain "consistent with the free speech protections embodied in the First Amendment of the Constitution." The Commission will undoubtedly try. But no general rules of this kind will ever survive constitutional challenge.

So the main defense against Carlins on the phone is to hang up. Or better still, not to answer. Caller ID is the V-chip for telephones—both tell you what to expect before you connect. But Caller ID itself raises further questions. The service obviously enhances privacy some of the time, but not always. Many people making routine calls to utility companies, department stores, and other commercial establishments may not want their numbers swallowed into a computer database; Caller ID may promote more unwanted solicitation on the rebound than it deters at the outset.

A few state lawmakers have therefore outlawed Caller ID. Some invoked state criminal statutes already on the books that prohibit wiretapping and eavesdropping or that forbid phone companies to reveal information about callers without their consent. The Pennsylvania Supreme Court concluded that Caller ID had been outlawed by the state's wiretapping act. Most commissions, however, have supported the service. The FCC has mandated the passage of interstate Caller ID as well.

But even if ordinary Caller ID does, on balance, add more to the privacy of people who receive calls than it subtracts from the privacy of people who make them, the balance might easily change when the technology is pushed a bit further. The first generation Caller ID disclosed only a number. Then came names; addresses could be added easily enough. In due course an upstart new phone company might begin offering a capsule credit history, too—a record, say, of how faithfully the phone bill has been paid in the last twelve months. Are commissions to review the service every time phone companies add a byte of new data to the signal?

V-chips and Caller ID let us close the door to George Carlin. The Clipper Chip is intended to open it again, to the FBI. The plan is to require installation of a Clipper Chip in electronic encryption hardware, or at least make installation the accepted norm. The government will define an approved encryption system, which will be built into a standard chip installed in all telephones, modems, fax machines, and so forth. Ordinary people won't be able to penetrate the inner workings of the chip, but federal agencies will still hold the secret keys, which they will release to enforcement agents when permitted by a court. Every two years the Department of Commerce will conduct hearings to ensure that "deficiencies or abuses" in the system are corrected.

The Department of Commerce has gone ahead and made the Clipper Chip the standard encryptor to be installed in government electronics routinely purchased for unclassified communications. But the Clipper initiative has not progressed much further. Nor is it likely to. It has been loudly condemned by almost everyone outside the federal government itself, both domestically and abroad.

While it failed to enlist the manufacturers of telephones in its anti-privacy campaign, Congress did get the phone companies themselves. Large new digital switches move torrents of data through huge pipes. Trying to listen in on just one call is like trying to drink a Coke through a straw—a Coke spilled into the Niagara River just upstream of the falls. In 1994 Congress passed the Digital Telephony Act, directing phone companies to deploy technology that facilitates wiretapping by the police.

Retail Privacy

Even when it sincerely tries to protect privacy, Congress keeps overlooking new possibilities for snooping. The wiretap clause in the 1934 Communications Act states that "[n]o person not being authorized by the sender shall intercept any radio communication and divulge or publish [its] existence, contents, substance, purport, effect, or meaning." As we saw in the last chapter, judges have recently transformed this obscure wiretap clause into a new common law of intellectual property.

Congress set out to update the anti-wiretapping law in 1968, with a new Wiretap Act. The revision was supposed to "protect [] the privacy of wire and oral communications" while providing and specifying "circumstances and conditions under which the interception of wire and oral communications may be authorized." But the new act was limited to wire and oral communications; microwave transmissions and fiber-optic systems did not seem to be covered at all. Nor did the act cover cordless or cellular telephones, whose transmissions can easily be intercepted. Nor communications transported by anyone but common carriers. A department store security officer thus escaped conviction for intercepting employee telephone calls on the store's in-house phone system.

Congress then enacted the Electronic Communications Privacy Act of 1986. That law purported to protect all "electronic communications." But cordless phones still weren't covered. Yet another federal law enacted in 1992 directed the FCC to outlaw radio scanners capable of intercepting cellular phones. But all cellular phones are scanners, and therefore may be easily converted into listening devices.

That Congress now finds it necessary to write a new federal wiretap law every few years is a sure sign that federal lawmakers can't keep up with the technology, even when they earnestly want to favor privacy. And as Clipper demonstrates, sometimes they don't.

Government attempts to promote privacy inevitably collide with free speech principles, too. Every rule that promotes privacy will, in some way, suppress communication. Privacy and communication are, after all, two sides of the same coin, a right to speak versus a right not to be spoken about. Caller ID, which clearly creates some measure of new privacy, arguably runs afoul of wiretap laws, which purport to protect privacy as well. General laws against telephone solicitation and harassment present similar conundrums. When a private individual slams down a phone in disgust, that's freedom. When a commission tries to choreograph the same, it isn't.

A final and fundamental problem concerns the nature of privacy itself. Every unhappy family is unhappy in its own way; most intrusions on our privacy are equally particular and personal. It's almost a matter of definition—the contours of private space are themselves private matters.

Broad-brush, general laws, and especially criminal laws, are too crude. The hard cases invariably involve a delicate balance of privacy versus free speech, or one person's privacy versus another's. The balance is difficult enough to strike when a specific, concrete case arrives in court. Trying to strike it wholesale, beforehand, in a commission or legislature, never produces a satisfactory solution.

Search and Seizure

"The right of the people to be secure in their persons, houses, papers, and effects, against unreasonable searches and seizures, shall not be violated," the Fourth Amendment declares. But the framers of that amendment did not establish a Federal Privacy Commission to enforce it. The greatest enemy of privacy, they recognized, is government itself, most particularly the executive branch, where federal commissions reside.

So enforcement was left to the courts. The next clause of the amendment, which effectively defines the word *reasonable*, declares that "no warrants shall issue, but upon probable cause, supported by oath or affirmation." Warrants are judicial instruments, issued by judges or magistrates. Courts stay in charge after the search by excluding from the courtroom evidence seized without the appropriate judicial say-so beforehand.

For better or worse, everything America made of the Fourth Amendment thereafter was made through a common-law-like process in the courts. One decision built on the next, and over time a concrete structure of law was erected. The building didn't go up overnight, especially not in the telecosm. The courts did not perform with distinction. They just performed better than one might ever have hoped of any of the possible alternatives.

In 1928 the Supreme Court decided that the Fourth Amendment protects only physical entry; intercepting messages on telephone wires was not a "search" or "seizure" at all. Justice Brandeis wrote a foreboding dissent. In 1942 the Court ruled that electronic eavesdropping into a phone booth was not of any Fourth Amendment concern, either. For the first century after the invention of the telegraph, the federal government could thus tap wires pretty much as it pleased.

In 1967 the Supreme Court finally concluded that the Fourth Amendment protects "people, not places;" it shelters any "reasonable expectation of privacy." Since 1967 three rulings from the Court have suggested that privacy rights may also extend to disclosures from government files and databases—the publicity side of privacy. In each case the Court ultimately concluded that legitimate government interests permitted what was being done. Still, the very fact that these arguments were given serious hearings is heartening. In court, where it was supposed to be enforced, the Fourth Amendment is alive and well. It stands as the citizen's main line of defense against intrusions on privacy by the government.

Common Law

In today's telecosm, however, assaults on privacy are at least equally likely to come from the private sector. No supermarket's cash-register-cum-computer will ever rival the spy satellites of the CIA. But there are far more cash registers than satellites, and they are backed, overall, by far more computing power to monitor and trace. After a bomb blew up a federal building in Oklahoma City, the FBI sent out an appeal for the tapes from all private video security cameras operated by landlords, security desks, and automatic teller machines.

As we have seen, congressional and commission attempts to broker privacy conflicts among private actors have not worked well. The technology changes too fast, and in any event, privacy has to be defined on a case-by-case basis. The common law must do the job, or the job won't get done. Happily, a new legal framework is gradually settling into place.

Through the end of the nineteenth century, virtually no court had ever recognized a right to individual privacy as such. One of the chief catalysts of the privacy right may have been the consternation felt by a turn-of-the-century Harvard law professor's wife when her social activities were splashed across the pages of the Boston tabloids. The professor, Samuel D. Warren, and his (at the time) little-known colleague Louis D. Brandeis published an article in the *Harvard Law Review* advocating recognition of a civil tort action for damages for invasion of privacy. The idea caught on. By the end of the 1970s only one state—Rhode Island—had still failed to recognize such a tort.

Common-law courts have recognized claims for the intrusion half of privacy in a number of different contexts. These, roughly speaking, maintain the Fourth Amendment protections where the amendment itself does not apply—when the search is conducted by private parties rather than government officials.

Whenever the state tries to make something criminal, a civil tort remedy will often be inferred from that, too. Thus the criminal anti-harassment statutes, which have been difficult to enforce as criminal matters, have much more promise for the civil norms that may evolve out of them. Other cases have covered searches of bags in a store, eavesdropping, wiretapping, peeping, and telephone harassment. A woman photographed with her dress unexpectedly blown up in a fun house—an unwitting Marilyn Monroe—was permitted to sue. Ralph Nader won a judgment against General Motors after the company tried counterintelligence in response to the imminent publication of *Unsafe at Any Speed.* Another plaintiff was allowed to sue on the claim that the CIA had been covertly opening first-class mail sent between American citizens and individuals in the Soviet Union.

Common-law courts have likewise developed a line of precedent to protect against unreasonable publicity, however the underlying information was obtained. After a rough start, for example, courts have affirmed that an individual owns his name and his likeness. For better or worse, your mug is your trademark, and you can protect it against infringement.

The seminal case was decided in New York in 1902; it involved a woman's picture used to advertise flour. The court denied her any recovery, partly on the grounds that recognizing such a right would unduly restrict free speech. There was a storm of public disapproval, and the New York legislature enacted a statute that defined this sort of thing as both a misdemeanor and a tort. In 1983 a portable toilet company was accordingly required by Johnny Carson himself to stop marketing its "Here's Johnny" product, advertised as "The World's

Foremost Commodian." A broadcaster paid for having filmed a human cannonball's entire act, over his objection, and having aired it on the local news; the Ohio Supreme Court concluded that the First Amendment protected the broadcast, but the U.S. Supreme Court disagreed. By seizing the whole show, the broadcaster had substantially threatened the entire economic value of the performance; the First Amendment supplies no absolute right to do things like that.

Another line of common-law precedent covers public disclosure of private facts calculated to shock, offend, or embarrass. The father of a murdered rape victim, for example, sued a TV station that had broadcast the victim's name. The Georgia Supreme Court rejected the argument that the First Amendment protected this sort of disclosure. The U.S. Supreme Court reversed, because the victim's name had been disclosed in public records in connection with the prosecution of the murderer.

Related cases have recognized rights of action for publicity that places an individual "in a false light," even if not quite defamatory. A family that was held hostage for nineteen hours by three escaped convicts won a $30,000 verdict against *Life* magazine, which published an article about a Broadway thriller that was said to reenact the family's ordeal. The story gave the impression that the play was an accurate account of the experience of the Hill family. The New York Court of Appeals upheld the verdict; the U.S. Supreme Court reversed, on free speech grounds.

As the back-and-forth character of these cases reveals, privacy claims must always be balanced against other rights, including rights of free speech. And the absence of consent—express or implied—is key. All in all, common-law courts have performed tolerably well when it comes to affirming rights of privacy and providing reasonable means to vindicate them, in balance with countervailing freedoms to watch, listen, and speak. No single ruling has the same impact as a national pronouncement from the FCC, but in this sphere, that's all the better. A tort suit for invasion of privacy involves no public prosecutor and only very limited "state action." It therefore presents far less of a threat to other important interests, particularly free speech, that require protection, too.

As all these cases illustrate, privacy rights are almost impossible to define intelligently unless they are defined case-by-case. Rights have to be hammered out service by service, technology by technology, and the hammering will continue for as long as technology evolves. The Fourth Amendment itself had to be rediscovered to deal with telecom technology, and the process of rediscovery will continue as long as the technology of communication continues to improve. Other privacy rights will remain robust only if they are grounded in authority that is equally flexible and adaptable. Broad-brush statutes that delineate rights and duties in general terms may do some good, but for the most part, they get in the way more than they help.

What is needed here is a robust common law that is articulated when people feel aggrieved enough to sue, and not before. Common law can adapt far faster than Congress can legislate or commissions can make rules. When Congress finds itself attempting to rewrite federal privacy law every few years and trying to design chips, from "Clipper" to "V," to make interception easier or harder, it is safe to conclude that privacy law would be better law if manufactured elsewhere.

Privatizing Privacy

The largest lesson here is that good privacy rulings are small. They must be tailored to fit specific cases and controversies, not the entire telecosm. Working out good privacy rules for issues as different as wiretapping and Caller ID is no job for Congress or a commission.

Broad-brush principles and rules are easy enough to articulate, but useless or worse thereafter. A broadly drafted anti-wiretapping law may at first provide useful protection against wiretapping. Then it may be creatively construed to provide desirable protection against signal piracy. But in the end it may outlaw Caller ID, which raises fundamentally different issues, in a quite different context, where there are competing privacy interests at both ends of the line.

Perhaps commissions can be of some help in protecting against private snooping. But the possibilities vary too much and the technologies change too quickly for any commission to keep up. A retreat to the decentralized, adaptable, evolutionary womb of the common law is the only workable alternative.

And no federal commission has ever really protected the citizen's privacy from the government itself. Commissions are the government; try as they may, they inevitably end up more part of the problem than part of the solution. Real protections against government snooping come from the courts, where privacy law is invented one technological variation at a time, as common law proper or under the common-law-like jurisprudence of the Fourth Amendment.

17

A People's Constitution

The rhetorical case for dismantling the FCC often begins with the Star Chamber and the First Amendment. Telecommunication is speech. Electronic technology is just a faster printing press, just another star in what Marshall McLuhan called "the Gutenberg Galaxy." The First Amendment covers Gutenberg. It covers Marconi and Bell, too.

So far, however, I have mentioned the Constitution only in passing—because the Constitution has failed. And because in any event, the common law matters more.

State Action

The real constitutional debate ended in 1927, when Congress declared a state of scarcity and nationalized all the airwaves. A few years later Congress declared phone lines to be scarce, too, this time for economic reasons. The lawmakers who announced these facts did not trouble themselves with the Constitution; they created facts instead. No court was going to knock down the only administrative structure that made broadcasting technically possible or phone lines economically viable. No constitutional quibbling was going to stand in the way of immutable scientific reality. None did.

With the FCC itself through the eye of the constitutional needle, the rest was detail. The Commission could constitutionally license electronic presses, since scarcity left no other alternative. The Commission could constitutionally regulate its licensees, because a privileged trustee of government property could, of course, be asked to manage the estate as the owner directed. The telecosm was now public, like the Grand Canyon. The new Park Service would regulate all vendors of trinkets and postcards. And it would make the premises safe for children, perverts, or sociopaths who might tumble in if Park Rangers did not maintain the fences.

No one paused to consider just how far this logic might reach. Newspapers use public spaces, too, for trucks and newsracks. Most papers are monopolies as well; few towns have more than one. Happily for newspapers, the Printing Press Commission had been tried in England in 1509, and repudiated on American shores in 1791. But the framers of the Constitution had neglected to mention photons.

So the FCC slipped quietly into place. As the years passed, its constitutional status grew secure. Today few serious lawyers would even dare to suggest that the Commission might be unconstitutional, Title to Title, top to bottom. The big constitutional claim died of neglect in its infancy and has never been seen again.

We have been occupied instead by all the little constitutional issues that swarm out of the Commission like maggots. In 1943 the Supreme Court had to decide whether the FCC could constitutionally regulate network broadcasting. In 1969 the Court had to pass on the constitutionality of the FCC's Fairness Doctrine. In 1984 a federal appellate court had to pass on the constitutionality of licensing DBS. Half a dozen different courts addressed the constitutionality of rules that barred video programming by phone companies. In 1994 the Supreme Court had to rule on whether Congress could constitutionally require cable operators to carry broadcast signals. Virtually every major licensing decision by the Commission has been attacked on constitutional grounds; those that have not yet will be. Any ruling by the Commission that has any major impact on the structure of the telecosm is constitutionally suspect.

This infestation of constitutional vermin was inevitable. The Constitution limits government's powers, not the people's—state action, not private conduct. A private publisher may set prices, deliver service, provide carriage, and censor content all it likes. It may search, seize, discriminate, and exclude, so long as it does so in a strictly private context. But all of these become constitutional issues when performed to please a commission.

And yet the Commission's rules have mostly been upheld. The reason is almost too discouraging to record. It is like the punch line to the old joke. All we're negotiating now is the price.

The challenge going forward is not to fine-tune the Commission or distinguish good commission law from bad. It is to get beyond the Commission—and thus beyond the Constitution—entirely.

Deconstructing the Telecosm

Get rid of the Commission, and the constitutional debates go away, too. But so does the Commission's power to anesthetize the antitrust laws. Those laws, all in all, protect competition far better than a commission-tolerant Constitution.

As we have seen, much of the Commission's work, for most of its life, has had the effect of protecting monopoly and promoting scarcity. The Commission separated carriers from content, programmers from transmission facilities, telephone wires from cable, and wires from spectrum. By erecting walls willy-nilly, the Commission saved us from the unlikely threat of one huge monopoly. And it saved us, too, from the far more likely prospect of robust competition.

Why didn't the First Amendment's presumption in favor of a free "marketplace of ideas" get enforced? If the First Amendment means anything, it surely means that a federal agency may not establish and shelter a small group of elite speakers to the exclusion of everyone else. As interpreted by the courts, however, the constitutional standard is flaccid when applied to content-neutral economic laws. The Supreme Court set out the standard in a 1968 case called *United States v. O'Brien*. Laws of this kind pass muster if they serve an "important or substantial" governmental interest unrelated to the suppression of speech, and if they burden expression no more "than is essential" to further that government interest.

These words are weak in the best of times; they are worthless for constraining a large, expert federal agency like the FCC. The Commission is not staffed with fools. Some "important" interest can always be cooked up; it's always possible to postulate some loss of universal service, some threat of monopoly tomorrow, to justify the FCC's own monopoly-protecting walls today.

The antitrust laws take a quite different tack. They pivot on yesterday's schemes to fix prices or carve up territories and on today's market realities. They absolutely forbid all private deals not to compete. If a phone and cable company privately agree not to poach on each other's turf, the deal makers go to jail. Carving up markets is lawful only when the FCC does it. The Constitution has provided no protection against economic conspiracy by commission. The antitrust laws have provided real protection against conspiracy by private agreement. So long as matters are kept outside the Commission, competition will thrive.

This, then, is the people's constitution for the economics of the telecosm. Not regulation by commission, not even a commission regulated itself by *O'Brien*. The people's constitution is antitrust law, developed in the courts under the short, broad mandate of the Sherman Act. The right role—the only constitutionally legitimate role—for Congress and its agencies is to establish property rights, dezone bandwidth, open entry, and then let the market be. Antitrust laws will take care of the rest.

Making Connections

In 1776 Pennsylvania's Constitution declared that printing presses should be common carriers. The presses, it said, were to "be free to every person who undertakes to examine the proceedings of the legislature, or any part of government." The intensely partisan colonial newspapers were thus directed to open their columns to opposing viewpoints and carry all contending opinions, much like the mails. According to contemporary left-wing theory, the First Amendment not only permits but requires much the same today.

In 1939 the Supreme Court itself gave a passing nod of approval to something along these lines. The streets and parks, Justice Roberts observed, "have immemorially been held in trust for the use of the public and, time out of mind, have been used for purposes of assembly, communicating thoughts between citizens, and discussing public questions." This stray comment has evolved into something called "public forum doctrine." What it dimly suggests is a body of common-carriage law emerging from the shadows and penumbras of the First Amendment.

Today's streets and parks are in the airwaves, which the federal government has nationalized, or in glass and wire, which run under public streets controlled mostly by local authorities. Is the government obliged, then, to maintain a Public Forum commission to see to it that diverse voices may vent their views over these inescapably public media?

Public-forum doctrine is a stopgap, a last line of defense after government has taken control of all the real estate and there is nowhere left to speak but on public land. Trying to pluck common-carriage obligations out of the obscure depths of the First Amendment, however, does more harm than good. The First Amendment itself implies negative rights, too—rights not to salute, not to pledge, not to embrace government propaganda, not to publish replies, not to insert proclamations in bills, not to disclose membership lists, not to display political slogans on license plates, and not to pay unwillingly for the political speech of others. Rights like these can't be squared with mandates that require cable companies to open their networks to pornographers or that require TV stations to air commercials denouncing commerce.

Price regulation and universal service are constitutionally indefensible, too. No Federal Newspaper Commission would be permitted to regulate the price of the *Washington Post* or demand that it be sold at uniform prices on every corner of the city. Any requirement of price-averaged, universal service puts the provider and all its customers in a single economic pot. Your phone bills subsidize or are subsidized by escort services, handgun dealers, and dial-a-porn operators. The telephone company must put up with the whole lot. Neither association nor speech is anywhere close to free when economic cohabitation of this order is required by five commissioners in Washington.

Even more plainly unconstitutional are carrierlike duties imposed by commission to promote fairness in the marketplace of ideas. The FCC enforced the Fairness Doctrine against radio and TV broadcasters for years. The Supreme Court upheld the rule in 1969, in a case pitting Lyndon Johnson's FCC against a radio station's defense of Barry Goldwater. In 1974, by contrast, the Supreme Court struck down a Florida law that required any newspaper attacking the record of a political candidate to offer an opportunity to reply. "A newspaper is more than a passive receptacle or conduit for news, comment, and advertising," the Court reasoned. To its shame, the Court failed even to mention, still less distinguish, its Fairness Doctrine precedent.

Any Public Forum Commission would also collide with the Takings Clause of the Fifth Amendment. Public-forum doctrine affirms the public's right to speak out on government property; takings law affirms the private owner's right to maintain peace and quiet on his own. Private property includes bandwidth, compression algorithms, and databases, all of which reside in glass or silicon. When government seizes such things, it is seizing property, no matter how worthy its ultimate motives. Micro-takings are no different than macro ones. No one doubts that the Fourth Amendment's search-and-seizure clause applies in the telecosm. The Fifth Amendment's Takings Clause should, too.

So do all common carriers operate under a body of law that is simply unconstitutional? Yes, so far as common-carrier law is imposed unilaterally by Commission edict. But traditional common-carrier principles don't originate in Commission mandates. Individual carriers freely elect common-carrier status in exchange for limits on their own liability. The common carriers of the common law assume common-carrier status voluntarily. There is nothing unconstitutional about that.

This, then, is the people's constitution for connection to the telecosm. No Pricing Tribunal, Public Forum Commission, or Fairness Doctrine; just the common law of common carriage, engaged by choice, not by compulsion.

The Marketplace of Ideas

So much for economic matters. Beyond lie the great issues of the information age: free speech and its complements, property and privacy. Ironically, the Constitution is all but irrelevant here. The First Amendment is, of course, of some general interest. But so is Article I, section 8, of the Constitution, which empowers Congress to enact a copyright law. And so too is the Fourth Amendment, which addresses searches, seizures, and, by implication, privacy.

The whole purpose of the second and third rights is to limit the first. In the reign of Queen Mary copyright law was an instrument of censorship. The old Soviet government sought to manipulate international copyright law to suppress books worldwide. The whole point and purpose of copyright is to limit free speech. Privacy rights limit it, too. Electronic privacy is the right not to be put unwillingly at the wrong end of someone else's telecommunicating machine. Every right to speak collides with some reciprocal right not to listen, not to be heard, not to see or be seen, not to surrender one's own words, thoughts, privacy, or solitude.

Commissions try, of course, to sort out conflicts like these. They give a bit of free speech here, for political protest, a bit of copyright there, for cablecasters, and a little privacy at the next turn, for people who might otherwise be harassed by telemarketers.

With the crude, indiscriminate media of over-the-air broadcast—electronic sound trucks, so to speak—collectivizing choices like these seemed inevitable. Collectivizing the media collectivized the message. But the precise media of narrowcasting offer far better private substitutes. By arming individuals, technology makes it possible to disarm government. The key to truly free speech—mutual consent—

can be vindicated without government interference or assistance. Indeed, it cannot be vindicated any other way.

Technology is at hand to protect the negative dimensions of free speech, copyright, and privacy. Caller ID, backed by computer screening, offers a new level of privacy and control from the assault by telephone. The V-chip will empower parents to limit what their children watch, and it will soon be succeeded by more-powerful chips that permit precisely calibrated private censorship. Communities of speakers and listeners then become completely consensual. The logic for management by commission disappears.

A robust law of copyright promotes speech in much the same way. Copyright is what gives people a real, tangible, financial stake in speech itself. And it is that stake, not the dry words in the Constitution, that supplies the most durable protection of a free press. Despite its disreputable origins three centuries ago, copyright was the "uniquely legitimate offspring of censorship."

There remains speech that inspires psychotics, or motivates sociopaths, or defames reputations. But here too the main lines of defense can be private, not public. Liability suits can deter communication that incites violence—and such suits can properly take aim at conduct, not speech itself. Private libel suits ensure fairness and honesty much better than a fairness doctrine.

The final objection to brokering these rights in a Commission is the most fundamental. Collectivizing individual rights eviscerates them. The whole point of copyright is to privatize what is otherwise too public. Move copyright out of Steven Spielberg's hands and into a Copyright Royalty Commission's, and Spielberg's rights are sharply devalued. Move privacy itself out of private hands, and a commission will simply end up splitting the difference between people who prefer more solitude and people who prefer less. The very process of transferring rights like these from private to public hands defeats them. The rights exist only so long as they are exercised one individual at a time, not by a Commission on behalf of all.

This, then, is the people's constitution for the marketplace of ideas: private property and private choice, privately exercised in open markets. And private right, privately enforced, in common-law courts.

Common Law for the Telecosm

We end where we began, with two profoundly different engines for the making of law. One is top-down: it is law by edict and national commission. The other is bottom-up: law built by adjudication in common-law courts. One kind of law occupies thousands of pages in the U.S. Code and the Federal Register. The other evolves as a pure product of common law, or under short, general mandates like the Bill of Rights or the Sherman Act.

In the telecosm, as elsewhere, commission law leads society down the road to serfdom. However good the original intentions, central planning always ends up maintaining the privilege and power of the planners themselves. From markets and the common law, by contrast, there emerges spontaneous order that is rational, efficient, and intelligent. Though never planned, never even fully articulated, common-law rules adapt and evolve by common consent, like the rules of grammar. Society organized by commission is inherently limited by what the minds of the planners can grasp. Common law, in the aggregate, is far wiser. England, the land of the Magna Carta, never did get a written constitution. But it got the common law, and with it the most stable, decent, and consensual legal order on the planet.

Small-scale and privately-centered common law is the only kind of law that sits comfortably with our traditions of individual freedom and private liberty. The first word of the First Amendment is "Congress," and the phrase that follows is "shall make no law." In the arena of communication, federal government is the principal suspect, the least-trusted branch. The bias is against the big, not the small; against state action, not private undertaking; against the commission, not the private citizen.

Nothing grander than common law is even practical anymore. The telecosm is too large, too heterogeneous, too turbulent, too creatively chaotic to be governed wholesale, from the top down. This is, of course, unsettling. The stability of management from the top is much more reassuring. But only because a commission's greatest power is to maintain the status quo. The telecosm's promise is to transform it.

Left to common law, the telecosm will become again a place of vast freedom and abundance. There will be room enough for every sight and sound, every thought and expression that any human mind will ever wish to convey. It will be a place where young minds can wander in adventurous, irresponsible, ungenteel ways. It will contain not innocence but a sort of native gaiety, a buoyant, carefree feeling, filled with confidence in the future and an unquenchable sense of freedom and opportunity.

Notes

Chapter 1

3   **runs some one hundred pages:** Telecommunications Act of 1996, Pub. L. No. 104-104, 110 Stat. 56 (1996). *See* Peter W. Huber, Michael Kellogg, and John Thorne, The Telecommunications Act of 1996 (1996).

5   **$200 million budget:** FCC, Fiscal Year 1996 Budget Estimates 6 (Feb. 1995). The Clinton administration proposed a budget for fiscal year 1996 of $224 million, a 62 percent increase over 1994 levels. FCC, Fiscal Year 1996 Budget Estimates 6 (Feb. 1995).

Chapter 2

15   **goulash of concerts, news, and novels:** Jergen Wouters, Washington Technology, Vol. 10, No. 2 at 18 (1995).

Ninety-four percent of households have telephones: U.S. Dep't of Commerce, Statistical Abstract of the United States 1995 at 574 (Sept. 1995).

seven television broadcast channels: Warren Publishing, Television and Cable Factbook at A-1, C-60 (1996).

97 percent of television households: NCTA, Cable Television Developments at 1 (Spring 1996).

an average of fifty-three video channels: The Force Behind the Fireworks, Broadcasting & Cable, June 17, 1996 at 26.

some 4.5 million subscribers: Untitled article, Communications Daily, June 25, 1996 at 7.

16   **revenues of $56 billion a year:** NCTA, Cable Television Developments 8-9 (Spring 1996); Second Annual Report, In the Matter of Annual Assessment of the Status of Competition in the Market for the Delivery of Video Programming, 11 F.C.C. Rcd 2060, 2114 (1995). Advertising revenues for broadcasting are extrapolated from figures for the first half of 1995.

16   **only about twenty-five minutes a day:** Industry Analysis Div., FCC,
       Trends in Telephone Service at 35 (May 1996). Usage is for all calls and for
       1994, the last year for which figures are available.
       generates about $103 billion a year: USTA, Phone Facts 1995 at 3.
       generates another $45 billion: Gross revenues are in fact about $69.8 bil-
       lion, but $24.6 billion of that is paid to local carriers and so is also counted
       as part of their revenues. FCC, Statistics of Communications Common
       Carriers, 1995/1996 Edition at Tables 1.4, 6.2 (1996).

17   **Entrepreneurs then set up microwave towers:** NCTA, A Brief History
       of Cable at 1 (1991).
       FCC has backed cable's right: *See, e.g.,* Memorandum Opinion, De-
       claratory Ruling and Order, Cox Cable Communications, Inc., Commline,
       Inc., and Cox DTS, Inc., 102 F.C.C.2d 110 (1985).
       mid-1970s and the early 1990s: Emmanuel Desurvire, Lightwave Com-
       munications: The Fifth Generation, Scientific American, Jan. 1992 at 116.

18   **two to ten times the power of a conventional bird:** *See* P. L. Meredith
       and F. O. Schroeder, Privately-Owned Commercial Telecommunications
       Satellites: Licensing and Regulation by the Federal Communications
       Commission, 27 Cal. W. L. Rev. 111 (1990).
       Microwave frequencies are now used by pay-TV: Notice of Proposed
       Rulemaking, Rulemaking to Amend Part 1 and Part 21 of the Commis-
       sion's Rules to Redesignate the 27.5–29.5 GHz Frequency Band and to Es-
       tablish Rules and Policies for Local Multipoint Distribution Service, 8
       F.C.C. Rec. 557 (1993).

19   **FCC approved commercial implementation of CellularVision:** Notice
       of Proposed Rulemaking, Rulemaking to Amend Part 1 and Part 21 of the
       Commission's Rules to Redesignate the 27.5–29.5 GHz Frequency Band
       and to Establish Rules and Policies for Local Multipoint Distribution Ser-
       vice, 8 F.C.C. Rec. 557, 565–566 (1993).

20   **promote competition in long-distance phone service:** Second Report
       and Order, Establishment of Domestic Communications-Satellite Facili-
       ties by Non-governmental Entities, 35 F.C.C.2d 844 (1972).

22   **wire will go by air, and vice versa:** *See* Nicholas Negroponte, Products
       and Services for Computer Networks, Scientific American, Sept. 1991 at
       106.
       Poetry and the Microphone: George Orwell, Poetry and the Micro-
       phone, *in* The Penguin Essays of George Orwell at 245, 250 (1984).

23   **technologies of freedom:** Ithiel de Sola Pool, Technologies of Freedom
       at 26–27 (1983).

Chapter 3

24   **the Ministry would tower:** George Orwell, Nineteen Eighty-Four at 5–6
       (1977).

25   **would be considered indispensable:** *See* Robert W. Garnet, The Tele-
       phone Enterprise: The Evolution of the Bell System's Horizontal Struc-
       ture, 1876–1909 at 12 (1985).
       merged with Bell or folded: *See* Glen O. Robinson, The Federal Com-
       munications Act: An Essay on Origins and Regulatory Purpose, reprinted

in A Legislative History of the Communications Act of 1934 at 7 (Paglin ed. 1989).

26   **backed the idea enthusiastically:** *See* John Steele Gordon, Postalization: It Meant That the Government Should Run the Telephone System. And There's a Reason the Word Is Forgotten, American Heritage, Oct. 1994 at 16–18.

covers only that part which is profitable: Statement of Theodore Vail, Bell Chairman, quoted in G. Brock, The Telecommunications Industry: The Dynamics of Market Structure at 158–159 (1981).

Mann-Elkins Act of 1910: Commerce Court (Mann-Elkins) Act of 1910, ch. 309, 36 Stat. 539 (1910).

27   **unjust discrimination or undue preference:** Essential Communications v. AT&T, 610 F.2d 1114, 1118 (3d Cir. 1979) (citing Mann-Elkins Act §§7, 12, ch. 309, 36 Stat. 539 (1910)).

landmark 1930 decision: Smith v. Ill. Bell Tel. Co., 282 U.S. 133 (1930).

ICC presided over only four telephone company rate proceedings: *See* Glen O. Robinson, The Federal Communications Act: An Essay on Origins and Regulatory Purpose, reprinted in A Legislative History of the Communications Act of 1934 at 7 (Paglin ed. 1989).

ICC was authorized to approve: Willis-Graham Act of 1921, ch. 20, 42 Stat. 27 (1921). This Act overturned the Kingsbury Commitment and permitted consolidations subject to ICC approval, conferring antitrust immunity on those approved.

it approved almost all of them: *See* Glen O. Robinson, The Federal Communications Act: An Essay on Origins and Regulatory Purpose, reprinted in A Legislative History of the Communications Act of 1934 at 8 (Paglin ed. 1989).

effective federal counterweight to AT&T: *See, e.g.,* Hearings H.R. 8301 Before the House Committee on Interstate and Foreign Commerce, 73rd Cong., 2d Sess., at 134–135 (1934), reprinted in A Legislative History of the Communications Act of 1934 (Paglin ed. 1989) (statement of John E. Benton).

President Roosevelt asked Congress: S. Doc. No. 144, 73rd Cong., 2d Sess. (1934).

Both houses passed legislation: *See* 77 Cong. Rec. 10968 (June 9, 1934) (House); 77 Cong. Rec. 10912 (June 9, 1934) (Senate).

into law on June 18: *See* 77 Cong. Rec. 12451 (1934).

a factor of importance: Quoted in Ithiel de Sola Pool, Technologies of Freedom at 31 (1983).

28   **condition of radio communication:** R. H. Coase, The Federal Communications Commission, 2 J. L. & Econ. 1, 2 (1959).

one hand must control it: R. H. Coase, The Federal Communications Commission, 2 J. L. & Econ. 1, 3 (1959).

Wireless Ship Act: Wireless Ship Act of June 24, 1910, ch. 379, 1, 36 Stat. 629 (1910).

"etheric bedlam" of numerous unregulated stations: S. Rep. No. 659, 61st Cong., 2d Sess. at 4 (1910).

authority to register broadcasters: Radio Act of 1912, 37 Stat. 302 (1912). The duty of licensing a wavelength was mandatory upon the secretary—he had discretion only in selecting a wavelength that, in his judgment, would result in the least possible interference.

28   **certain segments of spectrum:** Hoover v. Intercity Radio, 286 F. 1003, 1004, 1006 (App. D.C. 1923).

29   **claims with the Department of Commerce:** *See* Thomas W. Hazlett, The Rationality of U.S. Regulation of the Broadcast Spectrum, 33 J. L. & Econ. 133 (1990).

and hours of operation: United States v. Zenith Radio Corp., 12 F.2d 614 (N.D. Ill. 1926).

Hoover sought clarification: *See* Andrew F. Inglis, Behind the Tube: A History of Broadcasting Technology and Business at 79 (1990).

decide these things for themselves: *See* R. H. Coase, The Federal Communications Commission, 2 J. L. & Econ. 1, 5 (1959).

court delineated rudimentary property rights: Tribune Co. v. Oak Leaves Broadcasting Station (Cir. Ct., Cook County, Ill. 1926), *reprinted in* 68 Cong. Rec. 216 (1926).

veering toward collapse: National Broadcasting Co., Inc. v. United States, 319 U.S. 190 211–214 (1943).

30   **ownership right in the ether:** *See* New York Times, July 21,1926, at 18.

Radio Act of 1927: Radio Act of 1927, Pub. L. No. 632, 44 Stat. 1162 (1927).

newly created Federal Radio Commission: The Interstate Commerce Commission retained authority over common-carrier use of radio spectrum.

transmitters, and regulate networks: Radio Act of 1927, Pub. L. No. 632, 44 Stat. 1162 §4(a)-(i), (k) (1927).

public interest, convenience or necessity: Radio Act of 1927, Pub. L. No. 632, 44 Stat. 1162 §§9, 11 (1927).

do whatever it pleased: In 1932, the Supreme Court ruled that the FRC had broad discretion to distribute frequencies among stations, even to terminate the license of an existing station in favor of another applicant in defiance of its own quotas. The Court insisted that the public interest criteria "is not to be interpreted as setting up a standard so indefinite as to confer an unlimited power," and that stations "are not to be the victims of official favoritism," but imposed no practical limit on the FRC. Nelson Bros. Bond & Mortgage Co., 289 U.S. 266, 285 (1932).

shut down marginal competitors: *See* Andrew F. Inglis, Behind the Tube: A History of Broadcasting Technology and Business at 79–80 (1990).

sharply curtailed new entry: *See* Thomas W. Hazlett, The Rationality of U.S. Regulation of the Broadcast Spectrum, 33 J. L. & Econ. 133, 154 (1990).

Radio Act was folded intact: *See* Jonathan W. Emord, The First Amendment Invalidity of FCC Content Regulations, 6 Notre Dame J. L. Ethics & Pub. Pol'y 93, 185 (1992).

31   **Title II set out the Commission's authority:** The Act itself defines a "common carrier" as "any person engaged as a common carrier for hire, in interstate or foreign communication by wire or radio." 47 U.S.C.A. §153(h). The meaning of the term was already well established as common law in 1934. *See, e.g.,* United States v. Calif., 297 U.S. 175, 182 (1936).

31   **regulated under both Titles II and III:** *See* National Ass'n of Regulatory Util. Comm'rs v. FCC, 525 F.2d 630 (D.C. Cir. 1975); 47 U.S.C.A. §332.
      newfangled radio stations: *See* Report and Order, Establishment of Domestic Communications-Satellite Facilities, 22 F.C.C.2d 86, Appendix C (1970).
      Communications Satellite Act of 1962: Communications Satellite Act of 1962, Pub. L. No. 624 §102, 76 Stat. 419 (1962) (*codified as amended at* 47 U.S.C.A. §§701–757 (1988)).
      broadcasters asked the FCC: In 1958 thirteen broadcast stations concluded that the 288 infant cable systems operating in thirty-six states threatened television's economic security. They asked the FCC to define cable as a common carrier and regulate it accordingly. Memorandum Opinion and Order, Frontier Broadcasting Co. v. Collier, 24 F.C.C. 251, 253–254, 256 (1958).
      Commission agreed to fill it: Carter Mountain Transmission Corp. v. FCC, 32 F.C.C. 459 (1962).

32   **bold new assertion of power:** United States v. Southwestern Cable Co., 392 U.S. 157, 172–174 (1968).
      swept away virtually all: United States v. Midwest Video Corp., 406 U.S. 649 (1972).
      tried to order larger cable systems: National Ass'n of Regulatory Util. Comm'rs v. FCC, 533 F.2d 601 (D.C. Cir. 1976).
      like telephone: FCC v. Midwest Video Corp., 440 U.S. 689, 709 (1979).
      1984 Cable Act: Cable Communications Policy Act of 1984, Pub. L. No. 549, 98 Stat. 2779 (1984) (*codified at* 47 U.S.C.A. §§521–613).
      over President Bush's veto: The Cable Television Consumer Protection and Competition Act of 1992, Pub. L. No. 385, 102d Cong., 1st Sess., 106 Stat. 1460 (1992) (amending Title VI of the Communications Act of 1934, and codified at 47 U.S.C.A. §521 et seq.).

33   **rationalize some of the lines:** Telecommunications Act of 1996, Pub. L. No. 104-104, 110 Stat. 56 (1996). *See* Peter W. Huber, Michael Kellogg, and John Thorne, The Telecommunications Act of 1996 (1996).

Chapter 4

35   **own them all himself:** *See* Frederick S. Siebert, Freedom of the Press in England, 1476–1776 (1965).
      abominable licensing practice: John Brewer, Party Ideology and Popular Politics at the Accession of George III at 149 (1976); 4 William Blackstone, Commentaries on the Laws of England at 151–152 (1765–1769).
      December 15, 1791: *See* Jonathan W. Emord, Freedom, Technology, and the First Amendment at 85 (1991).
      blocked virtually all government: *See generally* Laurence H. Tribe, American Constitutional Law §12–36 (2d ed. 1988); R. Rotunda, J. Nowak, and J. Young, Treatise on Constitutional Law: Substance and Procedure §20.16 (3d ed. 1986).

36   **Both Phones:** *See* Defendants' Third Statement of Contentions and Proof, vol. I at 139, 140–143, United States v. AT&T, No. 74-1698 (D.D.C. Mar. 10, 1980).
      an unregulated monopoly: Quoted in John Steele Gordon, Postalization:

It Meant That the Government Should Run the Telephone System. And There's a Reason the Word Is Forgotten, American Heritage, Oct. 1994 at 16–18.

36   **raises costs for all:** *See* W. Baumol, O. Eckstein, and A. Kahn, Competition and Monopoly in Telecommunications Services at 5, Bell System Exhibit No. 46, FCC Dkt. No. 19129, Phase II. William Sharkey defines natural monopoly as a condition that obtains "in a particular market if and only if a single firm can produce the desired output at lower cost than any combination of two or more firms." W. Sharkey, The Theory of Natural Monopoly at 54 (1982).

      shut down competition: *See* Johnson County Home Telephone Co., 8 Mo. P.S.C.R. 637, 643-644, 1 PUR 650 (1919). See also Defendants' Third Statement of Contentions and Proof, vol. I at 143–144, 146–147, United States v. AT&T, No. 74-1698 (D.D.C. Mar. 10, 1980).

      public convenience and necessity: 47 U.S.C.A. §214(a); 47 C.F.R. §63.01.

      created by its owners: *See* Dean Burch, Common Carrier Communications by Wire and Radio: A Retrospective, 37 Fed. Com. L. J. 85 (1985) (*quoting* S. Rep. No. 781, 73d Cong., 2d Sess. 2 (1934)).

      wastes of duplication: MacKay Radio & Tel. Co. v. FCC, 97 F.2d 641, 643 (D.C. Cir. 1938).

      required private users to abandon: *See* Allocation of Frequencies to the Various Classes of Non-Government Services inthe Radio Spectrum from 10 Kilocycles to 30,000,000 Kilocycles, 39 F.C.C. 298, 300 (1948); AT&T, Charges and Regulations for Television Transmission Services and Facilities, 42 F.C.C. 1, 22–24 (1949).

      steadfastly barred competition: *See, e.g.,* MacKay Radio and Tel. Co., 2 F.C.C. 592 (1936).

      refused to require Bell: Establishment of Physical Connections and Through Routes and Charges Applicable Thereto, 17 F.C.C. 152 (1952).

      only to ultimate customers: Memorandum Opinion and Order, American Telephone and Telegraph Company, et al., Restrictions on Interconnection of Private Line Services, 60 F.C.C.2d 939, 940 (1976).

37   **operators of private networks could not:** *See* Resale and Sharing of Private Line Communications Services: AT&T Restriction and FCC Regulation, 61 Va. L. Rev. 679 (1975).

      communications favor[ing] competition: MacKay Radio and Tel. Co., 15 F.C.C. 690, 699 (1951).

      given too little attention: RCA Communications, Inc. v. FCC, 346 U.S. 86, 86, 93, 95 (1953).

      would be a great advantage: Deposition of Theodore N. Vail, Western Union Tel. Co. v. AT&T, Exh. C, "Evidence for the Defendant," Boston, 1909, *reprinted in* Defendants' Third Statement of Contentions and Proof, vol. I at 122, United States v. AT&T, No. 74-1698 (D.D.C. Mar. 10, 1980).

38   **"incidental to" transmission:** 47 U.S.C.A. §153(b)-(c).

      noise in crowded offices: *See* Hush-A-Phone Corp. v. United States, 20 F.C.C. 391 (1955).

      gravely weighing the matter: *See* Michael K. Kellogg, John Thorne, and Peter W. Huber, Federal Telecommunications Law §§10.1–10.5 (1992).

38   **telephone company personnel:** Jordaphone, 18 F.C.C. 644, 647 (1954).
threw out that ruling: Hush-A-Phone Corp. v. United States, 238 F.2d 266, 269 (D.C. Cir. 1956).
mainframes over the phone lines: *See* Gene Dippel and William C. House, Information Systems: Data Processing and Evaluation at 67–68 (1969); Note, The FCC Computer Inquiry: Interfaces of Competitive and Regulated Markets, 71 Mich. L. Rev. 172, 173–174 (1972).
facilities and services: Final Decision and Order, Regulatory Pricing Problems Presented by the Interdependence of Computer and Communication Facilities, 28 F.C.C.2d 267, 269 (1970).
new industry out of the wild: *See* Order, Regulatory and Policy Problems Presented by the Interdependence of Computer and Communications Services and Facilities, 40 F.C.C.2d 293 (1973) (Computer I).

39   **raised a new challenge:** While its Computer I inquiry was pending, the FCC decided a case involving an early information service for members of the stock exchange. Memorandum Opinion and Order, Western Union Telegraph Co. Tariff F.C.C. No. 251 Applicable to Sicom Service, 11 F.C.C.2d 1 (1967).
intermingled with basic telephony: *See* Michael K. Kellogg, John Thorne, and Peter W. Huber, Federal Telecommunications Law §§11.1–11.2 (1992).
between telephone and computer: *See* Final Decision and Order, Regulatory Pricing Problems Presented by the Interdependence of Computer and Communication Facilities, 28 F.C.C.2d 267, 269 (1970).
first Computer Inquiry: *See* Order, Regulatory and Policy Problems Presented by the Interdependence of Computer and Communications Services and Facilities, 40 F.C.C.2d 293 (1973) (Computer I).
Computer Inquiry II: *See* Memorandum Opinion and Order on Further Reconsideration, Amendment of Section 64.702 of the Commission's Rules and Regulations (Second Computer Inquiry), 88 F.C.C.2d 512 (1981).
proposed two new definitions: Final Decision, Amendment of Section 64.702 of the Commission's Rules and Regulations, 77 F.C.C.2d 384, 420–421 (1980).
FCC's regulatory radar: Memorandum Opinion and Order, Frontier Broadcasting Co. v. Collier, 24 F.C.C. 251 (1958).
"interstate" after all: Second Report and Order, Amendment of Subpart L, Part 91, to Adopt Rules and Regulations to Govern the Grant of Authorizations in the Business Radio Service for Microwave Stations to Relay Television Signals to Community Antenna Systems, 2 F.C.C.2d 725 (1966).
needed FCC licenses: *See* Decision, General Telephone Co. of California, 13 F.C.C.2d 448 (1968).
ban universal and permanent: Final Report and Order, Applications of Telephone Companies for Section 214 Certificates for Channel Facilities Furnished to Affiliated Community Antenna Television Systems, 21 F.C.C.2d 307, 325 (1970).
not video programming: Only rural telephone companies were exempted from the blanket prohibition.
stayed out of the new market: Final Report and Order, Applications of

Telephone Companies for Section 214 Certificates for Channel Facilities Furnished to Affiliated Community Antenna Television Systems, 21 F.C.C.2d 307, 326 (1970).

40 **new Cable Act:** 47 U.S.C.A. §533(b); 47 C.F.R. §63.54(a)-(b) (1970).

41 **Radio Act of 1927:** Radio Act of 1927, Pub. L. No. 632, 44 Stat. 1162 (1927).

"comparative hearings": 47 U.S.C.A. §309(a).

no "property rights": Radio Act of 1927, Pub. L. No. 632, 44 Stat. 1162 §1 (1927); *cf.* 47 U.S.C.A. §§301, 304, 309(h)(1).

three, five, or seven years: 47 U.S.C.A. §307(c).

without Commission approval: Radio Act of 1927, Pub. L. No. 632, 44 Stat. 1162 §12 (1927).

Commission saw fit: 47 U.S.C.A. §312(a).

prevent "etheric bedlam": National Broadcasting Co., Inc. v. United States, 319 U.S. 190, 213 (1943).

principally for ships: *See* E. Doering, Federal Control of Broadcasting Versus Freedom of the Air at 4 (1939).

42 **NBC soon came to dominate:** Fifteen years later NBC was finally forced to divest itself of one of its two national networks; this became the American Broadcasting Company (ABC). *See* National Broadcasting Co., Inc. v. United States, 319 U.S. 190 (1943).

flatly forbade any operation: *See* Ithiel de Sola Pool, Technologies of Freedom at 136–138 (1983).

might be tolerated: Some block programming, for example, was allowed because it "contributed variety and imagination to broadcasting." Memorandum Opinion and Order, Licensee Responsibility to Exercise Adequate Control Over Foreign Language Programs, 39 F.C.C.2d 1037 (1973).

could not surrender control: Metropolitan Broadcasting Corp., 8 F.C.C. 557 (1941).

43 **Bengali, Japanese, and Russian:** Cosmopolitan Broadcasting Corp. v. F.C.C., 581 F.2d 917 (D.C. Cir. 1978) (*citing* WHBI, Exhibit #6, Supplemental Joint Appendix at 31–58).

refused to renew: Application of Cosmopolitan Broadcasting Corporation for Renewal of Main, Auxiliary and SCA Licenses for WHBI (FM), 59 F.C.C.2d 558 (1976).

small, individual buyers: Memorandum Opinion and Order, Application of Cosmopolitan Broadcasting Corporation for Renewal of Main, Auxiliary and SCA Licenses for WHBI (FM) 61 F.C.C.2d 257, 257–258 (1976).

in fair proportion: Application of Great Lakes Broadcasting Co. (FRC Docket No. 4900), 3 FRC Ann. Rep. 32 (1929).

Blue Book: FCC, Public Service Responsibility of Broadcast Licensees (1946).

issued in 1960: Report and Statement of Policy Re: Commission en banc Programming Inquiry, 44 F.C.C. 2303 (1960).

desires of the community: *See generally* Charles D. Ferris, Frank W. Lloyd, and Thomas J. Casey, Cable Television Law §2.06 n. 21 (1993). A federal appellate court upheld this new directive against constitutional challenge. Suburban Broadcasters v. FCC, 302 F.2d 191 (D.C. Cir. 1962).

officially frowned on: Lee Roy McCourry, 2 Rad. Reg. 2d (P & F) 895, 907 (1964).

44 **suggested 10 percent:** Order, Amendment of Part O of the Commission's Rules, 43 F.C.C.2d 638 (1973).

  question any license: Order, Amendment to Section 0.281 of the Commission's Rules, 59 F.C.C.2d 491 (1976).

  not dictating tastes: Citizens Committee to Preserve the Voice of Arts in Atlanta v. FCC, 436 F.2d 263, 272 n. 7 (D.C. Cir. 1970).

  appellate court overruled: Citizens Committee to Save WEFM v. FCC, 506 F.2d 246, 268 (D.C. Cir. 1973).

  needs of children: *See* John Thorne, Peter W. Huber and Michael K. Kellogg, Federal Broadband Law §11.5.1 (1995).

  Children's Television Act of 1990: H.R. 1677, 101st Cong., 2d Sess., Pub. L. No. 437 (1990). In all renewal proceedings the FCC is directed to consider whether a licensee has served "the educational and informational needs of children through the licensee's overall programming, including programming specifically designed to serve such needs." 47 U.S.C.A. §303(a)(2).

  solemnly defined key terms: Report and Order, Policies and Rules Concerning Children's Television Programming, 6 F.C.C. Rec. 2111, 2114 (1991), *recon.*, 6 F.C.C. Rec. 5093, 5098–5099 (1991).

  portrays family values: Notice of Inquiry, Policies and Rules Concerning Children's Television Programming, 8 F.C.C. Rec. 1841, 1842 (1993). The FCC delayed renewing the licenses of seven stations until they provided better evidence that they met their responsibility to educate the nation's youth. Notice of Inquiry, Policies and Rules Concerning Children's Television Programming, 8 F.C.C. Rec. 1841 (1993).

45 **divided the country:** Radio Act of 1927, Pub. L. No. 632, 44 Stat. 1162 §2 (1927), repealed June 1936, 49 Stat 1475 (1936).

  Amendments enacted: Davis Amendment, amending 45 Stat. 373 §5 (March 28, 1928).

  were to be distributed: 47 U.S.C.A. §307(b).

  In 1933 the Supreme Court: Federal Radio Commission v. Nelson Bros. Bond & Mortgage Co. (Station WIBO), 289 U.S. 266, 273 (1933).

  addressing local issues: *See* Mike M. Vukelvich, 22 F.C.C. 891 (1957); FCC, Public Service Responsibility of Broadcast Licensees 18 (1946).

  not Oshkosh Cable: The 1996 Act permits a 10 percent stake. Telecommunications Act of 1996, Pub. L. No. 104-104, §302(a), 110 Stat. 56 (1996) (to be codified at 47 U.S.C. 652(a)).

  same goes for owning two: *See* 47 C.F.R. §73.3555(a)-(c).

46 **positively encouraged alliances:** *See* Second Report and Order, Amendment of Sections 73.34, 73.240, and 73.636 of the Commission's Rules Relating to Multiple Ownership of Standard, FM, and Television Broadcast Stations, 50 F.C.C.2d 1046, 1054 (1975).

  radio with UHF or VHF TV: Second Report and Order, Amendment of Section 73.3555 of the Commission's Rules, the Broadcast Multiple Ownership Rules, 4 F.C.C. Rcd 1741 (1989).

  Oshkosh Cable may not affiliate: *See* Memorandum Opinion and Order, Amendment of Part 74, Subpart K, of the Commission's Rules and Regulations Relative to Community Antenna Television Systems, 58 F.C.C.2d 596 (1976). The ban was then codified in the 1984 Cable Act. *See* 47

U.S.C.A. §533(a). The Fifth Circuit upheld it over a constitutional challenge. Marsh Media, Ltd. v. FCC, 798 F.2d 772 (5th Cir. 1986).

46   **may not own a terrestrial:** *See* Second Report and Order, Amendment of Parts 21, 43, 74, 78 and 94 of the Commission's Rules Governing Use of Frequencies in the 2.1 and 2.5 GHz Bands, 6 F.C.C. Rec. 6792 (1991). The 1992 Cable Act codified the prohibitions. *See* 47 U.S.C.A. §533(a)(2). The FCC has sought comments as to whether the 1992 Cable Act's cross-ownership prohibition on MMDS should be interpreted as applying to LMDS as well. As of this writing, the Commission had tentatively decided not to write any such cross-ownership limit on its own initiative. Notice of Proposed Rulemaking, Order, Tentative Decision and Order on Reconsideration, Rulemaking To Amend Part 1 and Part 21 of the Commission's Rules To Redesignate the 27.5–29.5 GHz Frequency Band, 8 F.C.C.R. 557 (1993).

may not affiliate with the Oshkosh Daily News: *See* Memorandum Opinion and Order, Rules Relating to Multiple Ownership of Standard, FM, and Television Stations, 53 F.C.C.2d 589 (1975). The ban is codified at 47 C.F.R. §73.3555(d).

Oshkosh Cable, by contrast, is permitted: The 1984 Cable Act authorized the FCC to promulgate cross-ownership rules involving cable and other mass media that serve the same community. *See* 47 U.S.C.A. §533(c). The FCC, however, has declined to do so. Memorandum Opinion and Order, Cable Television and the Extension of Waiver and Discontinuance of Service by Carriers, 49 Fed. Reg. 48,949, ¶3 (1984).

but not with NBC: *See* Second Report and Order, Amendment of Part 74, Subpart K, of the Commission's Rules and Regulations Relative to Community Antenna Television Systems, 23 F.C.C.2d 816 (1970); 47 C.F.R. §76.501. Neither the 1984 Cable Act nor the 1992 Cable Act codified the FCC's national network/cable cross-ownership ban. Section 613(a) of the 1984 Act (codified at 47 U.S.C.A. §533(a)(1)) made it unlawful for cable operators to own or control television broadcast stations in communities served by such cable systems. The 1992 Cable Act made it unlawful for cable operators to offer MMDS or SMATV services in areas served by their cable systems. *See* 47 U.S.C.A. §533(a)(2).

was the rule until 1996: *See* Telecommunications Act of 1996 §202(f)(1). The Commission shall revise section 76.501 of its regulations (47 C.F.R. §76.501) to permit a person or entity to own or control a network of broadcasting stations and a cable system.

forced NBC to spin off: *See* NBC v. United States, 319 U.S. 190 (1943).

six FM radio stations: Amendment of Sections 3.35, 3.240, and 3.636 of the Rules and Regulations Relating to Multiple Ownership of AM, FM and Television Broadcast Stations, 100 F.C.C.2d 17, 21 (1984).

three television stations: The limit was raised to five in 1944. Rules Governing Broadcast Services Other than Standard Broadcast, 9 Fed. Reg. 5442 (1944). The maximum number was set at only three stations "on the unedifying rationale that the more limited television channels make three such stations the limit for the main television band." Amendment of Sections 3.35, 3.240, and 3.636 of the Rules and Regulations Relating to Multiple Ownership of AM, FM and Television Broadcast Stations, 100 F.C.C.2d 17, 21–22 (1984).

46   **seven AM radio stations:** *See* Memorandum Opinion and Order, Amendment of Sections 3.35, 3.240, and 3.636 of the Rules and Regulations Relating to Multiple Ownership of AM, FM and Television Broadcast Stations, 100 F.C.C.2d 74 (1985), currently codified at 47 C.F.R. §73.3555(d).
      Commission repudiated: Report and Order, Amendment of Sections 3.35, 3.240, and 3.636 of the Rules and Regulations Relating to Multiple Ownership of AM, FM and Television Broadcast Stations, 100 F.C.C.2d 17, 19, 54-55 (1984).
      contains intricate limits: Telecommunications Act of 1996 §202(b)(1). But only in the smallest markets is the limit stated in conventional market share terms—there the upper limit is half the stations. Id. at §202(b)(1)(D).

47   **25 percent of households:** Memorandum Opinion and Order, Amendment of Section 73.3555 of the Commission's Rules Relating to Multiple Ownership of AM, FM and Television Broadcast Stations, 100 F.C.C.2d 74, 90-91 (1985).
      Today's rules allow: 47 C.F.R. §73.3555(e). If the stations are minority-owned, the maximum limits are extended to twenty-three AM stations, twenty-three FM stations, and fourteen television stations (with an aggregate national audience reach of no more than 30 percent).
      1992 Cable Act: Cable Television Consumer Protection and Competition Act of 1992, Pub. L. No. 385, 106 Stat. 1487 §11 (codified at 47 U.S.C.A. §533(f)(1)(A)).
      more than 30 percent of U.S. households: Report and Order, Implementation of Sections 11 and 13 of the Cable Television Consumer Protection and Competition Act of 1992, 8 F.C.C. Rec. 8565, 8567 (1993). The Commission will permit, however, a single entity to own additional cable systems, up to 35 percent of homes passed nationwide, provided such systems are minority-controlled. See Daniels Cablevision v. United States, 835 F. Supp. 1 (D.D.C. 1993).
      ten or fewer commercial radio stations: As written, the rule states: "[I]n a radio market with 14 or fewer commercial radio stations, a party may own, operate, or control up to 5 commercial radio stations, not more than 3 of which are in the same service (AM or FM), except that a party may not own, operate, or control more than 50 percent of the stations in such market." The five-station limit is thus replaced by the 50 percent limit in markets served by ten or fewer stations. Telecommunications Act of 1996 §202(b)(1)(D).
      more than forty-four stations: "(A) [I]n a radio market with 45 or more commercial radio stations a party may own, operate, or control up to 8 commercial radio stations, not more than 5 of which are in the same service (AM or FM)." Telecommunications Act of 1996 §202(b)(1)(A).

48   **losses continue to mount:** *See* The WEFA Group, Economic Impact of Deregulating U.S. Communications Industries at 89 (1995).

Chapter 5

51   **"community antenna":** *See* M. Hamburg, All About Cable §1.02 (rev. ed. 1985).

52   **regulate cable after all:** For a full discussion of cable regulation, *see* John

Thorne, Peter W. Huber, and Michael K. Kellogg, Federal Broadband
Law §5.5 et seq. (1995).

52   **for its community:** A local government's power to franchise cable television operations is rooted in the state constitution or in state statutes delegating such power to the local government. Some states pass their own cable regulations and rules governing franchising. *See* Daniel L. Brenner and
Monroe E. Price, Cable Television and Other Nonbroadcast Video
§§3.01, 3.02 (1993).

management plan in 1984: The FCC was to "establish franchise procedures and standards" and establish "orderly" franchise renewal procedures.
47 U.S.C.A. §521(2), (5).

profits to themselves: This is analogous to spectrum auctions. *See*
Richard A. Posner, Cable Television: The Problem of Local Monopoly,
Mem. RM-6309-FF (Rand Corp. May 1970).

favored by local worthies: *See* M. A. Zupan, The Efficacy of Franchise
Bidding Schemes in the Case of CATV: Some Systematic Evidence, 32 J.
L. & Econ. 401 (1989).

5 to 10 percent of cable's gross revenues: Cable Television Report and
Order, Amendment of Part 74, Subpart K, of the Commission's Rules and
Regulations Relative to Community Antenna Television Systems, 36
F.C.C.2d 143, 219 (1972). The FCC approved fees under the 3 percent
limit automatically, presuming that these were generally necessary to de-
fray regulatory costs. *Id.* at 209–210.

TV sets for city officials: Clarification of the Cable Television Rules and
Notice of Proposed Rulemaking and Inquiry, Amendment of Part 76 of the
Commission's Rules and Regulations Relative to the Advisability of Federal Preemption of Cable Television Technical Standards or the Imposition of a Moratorium on Non-Federal Standards, 46 F.C.C.2d 175, 205
(1974).

stock to political insiders: *See* John A. Barnes, Why Cable Costs Too
Much: How Local Politicians and Cable Companies Conspire to Make
Cable TV Overpriced, 21 Washington Monthly 12 (1989).

Community groups were bought off: *See* "Rent-a-Citizen" Controversy, Washington Post, Sept. 28, 1980 at L3.

regulating noncash deals: Clarification of the Cable Television Rules
and Notice of Proposed Rulemaking and Inquiry, Amendment of Part 76
of the Commission's Rules and Regulations Relative to the Advisability of
Federal Preemption of Cable Television Technical Standards or the Imposition of a Moratorium on Non-Federal Standards, 46 F.C.C.2d 175,
205 (1974). The FCC promised it would continue to monitor exorbitant
local demands case by case. *See, e.g.,* Memorandum Opinion and Order,
Complete Channel TV, Inc., 34 Rad. Reg. 2d (P & F) 1372 (1975).

5 percent cap in 1984: 47 U.S.C.A. §542(b).

no attempt to restrict: *See* H.R. Rep. No. 934, 98th Cong., 2d Sess. 19,
65, reprinted in 1984 U.S.C.C.A.N. 4655.

simultaneously stripped the FCC: 47 U.S.C.A. §§542(i).

53   **common way to thwart:** Some states have passed laws to prevent
cream-skimming by a second cable operator. *See, e.g.,* Calif. Gov't Code
§53066.3(d) (West 1995).

53   **Posner accepted this reasoning:** Omega Satellite Products Co. v. City of Indianapolis, 694 F.2d 119, 126 (7th Cir. 1982).

Private dishes began popping up: HBO made its first broadcast by satellite on September 30, 1975, when it aired the "Thrilla in Manila," the heavyweight title fight between Muhammad Ali and Joe Frazier. Soon after this broadcast, H. Taylor Howard, a Stanford electrical engineering professor, constructed the first home earth station. Howard offered to pay HBO for the free programming he began receiving, but the company failed to respond to his offer. David Owen, Satellite Television, Atlantic Monthly, June 1984 at 47.

FCC gradually curtailed: Memorandum Opinion, Declaratory Ruling and Order, Orth-O-Vision, Inc., 69 F.C.C.2d 657 (1978). The Commission knocked down state and local regulation of satellite master antenna TV undertaken "simply because it's a competitive threat to cable television." Memorandum Opinion, Declaratory Ruling and Order, Earth Satellite Communications, Inc., 95 F.C.C.2d 1223, 1233 (1983).

chipping away at zoning: Report and Order, Preemption of Local Zoning or Other Regulation of Receive-Only Satellite Earth Stations, 59 Rad. Reg. 2d (P & F) 1073 (1986).

55   **Cable could retransmit broadcast:** Fortnightly Corp. v. United Artist Television, Inc., 392 U.S. 390 (1968).

56   **As early as 1952:** National Ass'n of Theatre Owners (NATO) v. FCC, 420 F.2d 194, 195–196 (D.C. Cir. 1969).

authorized one tiny trial: *See* National Ass'n of Theatre Owners (NATO) v. FCC, 420 F.2d 194, 196 (D.C. Cir. 1969). The court upheld the FCC's authority to license the trial station in Connecticut. Committee Against Pay TV v. FCC, 301 F.2d 835 (D.C. Cir. 1962).

station was to be subject: First Report, Amendment of Part 3 of the Commission's Rules and Regulations (Radio Broadcast Services) to Provide for Subscription Television Service, 23 F.C.C. 532 (1957).

equally crippling restrictions: Fourth Report and Order, Amendment of Part 3 of the Commission's Rules and Regulations (Radio Broadcast Services) to Provide for Subscription Television Service, 15 F.C.C.2d 466, 473 n. 20, 483–488, 495, 518 (1968).

expectation of free service: A new carrier service for subscription TV— multipoint distribution service (MDS)—emerged in 1970 as another potential competitor to free television. The FCC crippled that too by imposing layers of stifling carrier obligations. In 1987 the FCC adopted rules that permit licensees the option of non-common carrier status. *See* Report and Order, Revisions to Part 21 of the Commission's Rules Regarding the Multipoint Distribution Service, 2 F.C.C. Rec. 4251, 4252 (1987).

development is manifest: Black Hill Video Corp. v. FCC, 399 F.2d 65, 69 (8th Cir. 1968). A decade later, to its credit, the Eighth Circuit repudiated this arrant nonsense. Midwest Video Corp. v. FCC, 571 F.2d 1025 (8th Cir. 1978); *but see* Central Telecommunications, Inc. v. TCI Cablevision, Inc., 800 F.2d 711 (8th Cir. 1986).

extended its anti-siphoning: Memorandum Opinion and Order, Amendment of Part 74, Subpart K, of the Commission's Rules and Regulations Relative to Community Antenna Television Systems, 23 F.C.C.2d 825 (1970).

56 **Cablecasters were strictly forbidden:** Memorandum Opinion and Order, Amendment of Part 74, Subpart K, of the Commission's Rules and Regulations Relative to Community Antenna Television Systems, 23 F.C.C.2d 825 (1970). The FCC also limited the number of hours of pay cable operation that could be devoted to sports and feature films to 90 percent of total pay operations. 47 C.F.R. §§73.643, 76.225 (1975).

To crown it all: An exception was allowed for advertisements for other pay cable programs. 47 C.F.R. §76.225 (1975).

57 **FCC categorically forbade:** Second Report and Order, Amendment of Part 74, Subpart K, of the Commission's Rules and Regulations Relative to Community Antenna Television Systems; 23 F.C.C.2d 816 (1970).

codified by Congress in 1984: 47 U.S.C.A. §533(a).

Supreme Court upheld cable's right: Teleprompter Corp. v. Columbia Broadcasting Sys., Inc., 415 U.S. 394 (1974).

58 **specter of "etheric bedlam":** National Broadcasting Co. v.United States, 319 U.S. 190 (1943).

courts simply analogized: *See, e.g.,* Black Hills Video Corp. v. FCC, 399 F.2d 65 (8th Cir. 1968). As late as 1981, one federal appellate court ruled that cable's natural-monopoly economics were a form of scarcity that justified more regulation than newspapers, but not as much as broadcast. Community Communication Co., Inc. v. City of Boulder, 660 F.2d 1370 (10th Cir. 1981).

arrived before an appellate court: Home Box Office (HBO) v. FCC, 567 F.2d 9, 21 n. 20, 13, 24, 37, 39, 49, 45 n. 80 (D.C. Cir. 1977).

59 **but that was broadcast:** *See* National Ass'n of Theatre Owners (NATO) v. FCC, 420 F.2d 194, 207–208 (D.C. Cir. 1969).

could justify the rules: *Cf.* Miami Herald Publishing Co. v. Tornillo, 418 U.S. 241, 247–256 (1974).

rules had to go: Order, Amendment of Part 76, Subpart G, of the Commission's Rules and Regulations Pertaining to the Cablecasting of Programs for Which a Per-Program or Per-Channel Charge Is Made, 67 F.C.C.2d 252 (1977).

simple economic fact: *See* Florence Setzer and Jonathan Levy, Broadcast Television in a MultiChannel Marketplace, OPP Working Paper No. 26, 6 F.C.C. Rec. 3996, 4004–4008 (1991).

Doritos-crunching audience: *See generally* Jora R. Minasian, Television Pricing and the Theory of Public Goods, 7 J. L. & Econ. 71 (1964); Paul A. Samuelson, Public Goods and Subscription TV: Correction of the Record, 7 J. L. & Econ. 81 (1964).

outbid in-the-clear ("free") broadcasters: *See* Florence Setzer and Jonathan Levy, Broadcast Television in a MultiChannel Marketplace, OPP Working Paper No. 26, 6 F.C.C. Rec. 3996, 4004–4008 (1991).

Regulation-minded politicians: *See, e.g.,* Football Prices Set, Opponents Hit Sports Migration to Pay Per View, Charging Sports Monopolies, Communications Daily, July 7, 1992 at 5.

As recently as 1984: *See* Robert A. Garrett and Philip R. Hochberg, Sports Broadcasting and the Law, 59 Ind. L. J. 155, 184–185 (1984). The FCC had informally declared that such restrictions were inconsistent with federal policies and therefore unenforceable. Letter to Ian D. Volner, from

Chief, FCC Mass Media Bureau (Jan. 25, 1984), *cited in* Robert A. Garrett and Philip R. Hochberg, Sports Broadcasting and The Law, 59 Ind. L. J. 155, 184–185 (1984).

59   **empowering local authorities:** *See* Cable Conferees Work Out Differences, Retain Senate Retransmission Consent, Daily Reportfor Executives, Regulation, Economics and Law, 1992 DER 176 d25 (BNA 1992) (Sept. 10, 1992).

"investigate and analyze": The Cable Television Consumer Protection and Competition Act of 1992, Pub. L. No. 385 §26, 106 Stat. 1502 (1992), directs the Commission to "conduct an ongoing study on the carriage of local, regional, and national sports programming by broadcast stations, cable programming networks, and pay-per-view services" and to issue reports to Congress on or before July 1, 1993, and July 1, 1994. 47 U.S.C.A. §521.

duly announced in 1993: *See* Interim Report, Implementation of Section 26 of the Cable Television and Consumer Protection and Competition Act of 1992, Inquiry into Sports Programming Migration, 8 F.C.C. Rec. 4875, 4891 (1993).

60   **preferred to have left closed:** *See generally* Ira C. Stein, Cable Television §5.18 (1985); James C. Goodale, All About Cable §4.03[2] (1988).

watershed case was brought: Preferred Communications, Inc. v. City of Los Angeles, 754 F.2d 1396, 1406, 1332–1333 (9th Cir. 1985).

pass First Amendment muster: *See also* Century Federal, Inc. v. City of Palo Alto 648 F. Supp. 1465, 1476–1478 (N.D. Cal. 1986); Pacific West v. City of Sacramento, 672 F. Supp. 1322, 1331–1339 (E.D. Cal. 1987). *But see* Nor-West Cable Communications Partnership v. City of St. Paul, 802 F.2d 642 (8th Cir. 1986).

Satellite Master Antenna alternatives: *See, e.g.,* Memorandum Opinion, Declaratory Ruling and Order, Earth Satellite Communication, Inc., Petition for Expedited Special Relief and Declaratory Ruling, 95 F.C.C.2d 1223, 1235 (1983).

operators challenged the order: New York State Comm'n on Cable Television v. FCC, 749 F.2d 804, 810 n. 7 (D.C. Cir. 1984).

obligations, in order to encourage competition: News, Action in Docket Case, FCC Issues Report to Congress on the State of Cable TV, 1990 FCC LEXIS 4061 at *35–36 (1990).

"unreasonably" exclusive franchises: 47 U.S.C.A. §541(a)(1). The 1984 Cable Act authorized municipalities to grant "one or more" franchises, which local authorities had interpreted as allowing them to grant one exclusive franchise.

suffice to make it constitutional: *See* Cox Cable Communications, Inc. v. United States, 992 F.2d 1178 (11th Cir. 1993).

61   **working in collaboration:** Interestingly, the telephone portion of the cable–telephone company combination drovepenetration growth for the video side. In the first year that cable companies offered telephone service, they saw their cable subscribership increase by more than 53 percent. In less than three years the number of subscribers to cable television more than tripled, to nearly 475,000. Dixon, Goodwin & Co., Technology Assessment—UK CATV/Telephony 2–3 (Aug. 1993).

61   **implicitly barred cable:** The FCC had not construed things that way. In the Commission's view, cable companies are not barred from acquiring interests in new entrants that provide competing telephone service. The Commission has ruled, for example, that in their own service areas, cable operators could also provide competitive access services, cellular radio services, other wireless telephone services, and long-distance telephone services.

Chapter 6

63   **a mirror in the sky:** *See* Arthur C. Clarke, How the World Was One at 124 (1992). For a good overview of satellite telecommunication systems, *see* Stan Prentiss, Satellite Communications (2nd ed. 1987).
        regenerated and sent back down: *See* Milton L. Smith III, The Orbit/Spectrum Resource and the Technology of Satellite Telecommunications: An Overview, Rutgers Computer Tech. & L. J. 285, 294 (1987).
        first national "superstation": *See* Don R. Le Duc, Cable Television and the FCC at 777 (1973).

64   **"open skies" policy:** Report and Order, Establishment of Domestic Communications-Satellite Facilities by Nongovernmental Entities, 22 F.C.C.2d 86 (1970).
        theater owners had gone to court: National Ass'n of Theatre Owners (NATO) v. FCC, 420 F.2d 194, 198, 204–205 (D.C. Cir. 1969).
        handily rejected all three: *See also* Sable Communications of California, Inc. v. FCC, 492 U.S. 115, 133 (1989); Jackson v. Metropolitan Edison Co., 419 U.S. 345 (1974).
        In 1982 broadcasters raised: Memorandum Opinion and Order, Application of Satellite Television Corporation for Authority to Construct an Experimental Direct Broadcast Satellite System, 91 F.C.C.2d 953 (1982).
        no legal right to exist: National Ass'n of Broadcasters v. FCC, 740 F.2d 1190 (D.C. Cir. 1984).

65   **licenses were to be distributed:** 47 U.S.C.A. §307(b).
        characterized these arguments as "Luddite": National Ass'n of Broadcasters v. FCC, 740 F.2d 1190 (D.C. Cir. 1984).
        FCC, to its credit: First Report and Order, Regulation of Domestic Receive-Only Satellite Earth Stations, 74 F.C.C.2d 205, 206, 217 (1979).
        pick their own legal labels: Report and Order, Inquiry into the Development of Regulatory Policy in Regard to Direct Broadcast Satellites for the Period Following the 1983 Regional Administrative Radio Conference, 90 F.C.C.2d 676, 706–709 (1982).

66   **told to take another look:** National Ass'n of Broadcasters v. FCC, 740 F.2d 1190, 1199–1206 (D.C. Cir. 1984).
        as "non-broadcast services": *See* Notice of ProposedRulemaking, Subscription Video Services, Gen. Dkt. No. 85-305, 51 Fed. Reg. 1817 (1986); Report and Order, Subscription Video, 2 F.C.C. Rec. 1001 (1987).
        approach was upheld: National Ass'n for Better Broadcasting v. FCC, 849 F.2d 665 (D.C. Cir. 1988).
        Congress halfheartedly reimposed: 47 U.S.C.A. §335(a).

66 **free to the general public:** National Ass'n for Better Broadcasting v. FCC, 849 F.2d 665, 668 (D.C. Cir. 1988); *see* 47 U.S.C.A. §153(o).

67 **smaller slices of satellite capacity:** *See* Memorandum Opinion, Order and Authorization, Domestic Fixed-Satellite Transponder Sales, 90 F.C.C.2d 1238 (1982); World Communications, Inc. v. FCC, 735 F.2d 1465 (D.C. Cir. 1984).

68 **finally approved commercial cellular:** Report and Order, An Inquiry into the Use of the Bands 825–845 MHz and 870–890 MHz for Cellular Communications Systems, 86 F.C.C.2d 469 (1981).

two cellular carriers in each market: Report and Order, An Inquiry Into the Use of the Bands 825–845 MHz and 870–890 MHz for Cellular Communications Systems, 86 F.C.C.2d 469 (1981).

a decade of meteoric growth: The Commission has already allocated 220 MHz of this spectrum. First Report and Order and Third Notice of Proposed Rulemaking, Amendment of the Commission's Rules to Establish New Personal Communications Services, 7 F.C.C. Rec. 6886 (1992). In addition, Congress directed the U.S. Secretary of Commerce to reallocate at least 200 MHz of additional spectrum previously reserved for government use to new wireless services. Omnibus Budget Reconciliation Act of 1993, Pub. L. No. 103-66, Title VI, §6001(a), 107 Stat. 312 (1993).

services in every geographic market: Each wireless market has been allocated 50 MHz of cellular spectrum (divided into two 25 MHz licenses) and 120 MHz of broadband PCS spectrum (divided into three 30 MHz licenses and three 10 MHz licenses). No firm can hold more than one 25 MHz cellular license, 40 MHz of PCS spectrum, or 45 MHz of total spectrum per market. Thus the spectrum aggregation rules provide for two cellular and at least three PCS carriers per market.

69 **at least a decade earlier:** Jeffrey H. Rohlfs, Charles L. Jackson, and Tracey E. Kelly, National Economic Research Associates, Estimate of Loss to the United States Caused by the FCC's Delay in Licensing Cellular Telecommunications 4 (Nov. 8, 1991). *See also* WEFA Group, Economic Impact of Deregulating U.S. Communications Industries 97 (Feb. 1995).

consumers lost at least $85 billion: Jeffrey H. Rohlfs, Charles L. Jackson, and Tracey E. Kelly, National Economic Research Associates, Estimate of Loss to the United States Caused by the FCC's Delay in Licensing Cellular Telecommunications 4 (Nov. 8, 1991). *But see* WEFA Group, Economic Impact of Deregulating U.S. Communications Industries 97 (Feb. 1995) (estimating loss at $25 billion between 1973 and 1983 in constant 1994 dollars).

state regulators can't stop them: *See* Second Report and Order, Implementation of Sections 3(n) and 332 of the Communications Act Regulatory Treatment of Mobile Services, 9 F.C.C. Rec. 1411, 1418 (1994).

using the subcarrier portions: Report and Order, Amendment of Parts 2 and 73 of the Commission's AM Broadcast Rules Concerning the Use of the AM Carrier, 100 F.C.C.2d 5 (1984).

vertical blanking interval: Amendment of Parts 2, 73, and 76 of the Commission's Rules to Authorize the Offering of Data Transmission Services on the Vertical Blanking Interval by TV Stations, 101 F.C.C.2d 973 (1985).

69   **resolving program format disputes:** Memorandum Opinion and Order,
        Development of Policy re: Changes in the Entertainment Formats of
        Broadcast Stations, 60 F.C.C.2d 858 (1976).

        shouldn't have any at all: The review had only "fortified our conviction"
        that FCC regulation of entertainment formats "would produce an unnec-
        essary and menacing entanglement in matters that Congress meant to leave
        to private discretion." Memorandum Opinion and Order, Development of
        Policy re: Changes in the Entertainment Formats of Broadcast Stations, 60
        F.C.C.2d 858, 865 (1976).

        appellate court disagreed: WNCN Listeners Guild v. FCC, 610 F.2d
        838 (D.C. Cir. 1979).

        formats to the marketplace: FCC v. WNCN Listeners Guild, 450 U.S.
        589 (1981).

70   **programming guidelines for both radio:** Report and Order, Deregula-
        tion of Radio, 84 F.C.C.2d 968 (1981).

        and broadcast television: *See* Action for Children's Television v. FCC,
        821 F.2d 741 (D.C. Cir. 1987).

        Prime Time Access Rule: Report and Order, Amendment of Part 73 of
        the Commission's Rules and Regulations with Respect to Competition and
        Responsibility in Network Television Broadcasting, 23 F.C.C.2d 382
        (1970). The prime-time hours were 7–11 P.M. Eastern and Pacific Time;
        6–10 P.M. Central and Mountain Time.

        finally repealed in 1995: Report and Order, In re Review of the Prime
        Time Access Rule, Section 73.658(k) of the Commission's Rules, 11
        F.C.C. Rcd 546 (1995).

        monitor programming to ensure: *See* Memorandum Opinion and Or-
        der, Revision of Programming and Commercialization Policies, 104
        F.C.C.2d 358 (1986).

        community issues each quarter: Memorandum Opinion and Order, De-
        regulation of Radio, 104 F.C.C.2d 505, 507 n.8 (1986).

        passive role of a common carrier: Decision, Applications of Fresno FM
        Limited Partnership, et al., for Construction Permit for a New FM Station
        on Channel 257A, Fresno, California, 6 F.C.C. Rec. 1570, 1572 (1991).

        generally be approved, at least for radio: Report and Order, Revision of
        Radio Rules and Policy, 7 F.C.C. Rec. 2755, 2773–2778, 2784, 2788 n. 124
        (1992). A survey of broadcast stations conducted by the Commission's
        Field Operations Bureau showed time brokerage is not widespread. Of 284
        stations surveyed, 17 (or 6 percent) engaged in time brokerage. Of those
        17, only 7 brokered more than half of their broadcast day, and only 2 radio
        stations (less than 1 percent) were engaged in local time brokerage. *Id.* at
        2788 n.127 (citing Public Notice, Broadcast Station Time Brokerage Sur-
        vey Completed, FCC, Mimeo No. 21878 (Feb. 14, 1992)).

        such things as wireless voice or data: Telecommunications Act of 1996
        §201 (to be codified at 47 U.S.C. §336); Fourth Further Notice of Pro-
        posed Rule Making and Third Notice of Inquiry, Advanced Television
        Systems and Their Impact Upon the Existing Television Broadcast Ser-
        vice, 10 F.C.C. Rec. 1054 (1995).

71   **sell it if you wish:** Arthur S. De Vany, Ross D. Eckert, Charles J. Meyers,
        Donald J. O'Hara, and Richard C. Scott, A Property System for Market

Allocation of the Electromagnetic Spectrum: A Legal-Economic-Engineering Study, 21 Stanford L. Rev. 1499 (1969).

71 **licenses come up for renewal:** Public Notice, Policy Statement Concerning Comparative Hearings Involving Regular Renewal Applicants, 22 F.C.C.2d 424, 425–426 (1970).

the courts resisted: *See, e.g.,* Citizens Communications Center v. FCC, 447 F.2d 1201 (D.C. Cir. 1971).

"substantial" service: *See, e.g.,* Memorandum Opinion and Order, United Broadcasting Co., 100 F.C.C.2d 1574 (1985).

"minimal or nonexistent": *See, e.g.,* Decision, Application of WIOO, Inc., 95 F.C.C.2d 974 (1983). *See also* FCC: Time to Modernize Comparative Renewal, Broadcasting, June 27, 1988 at 35.

radio licenses to seven: 47 U.S.C.A. §307(b).

challenge license renewals: In renewal proceedings, the new Act declares that "the Commission shall not consider whether the public interest, convenience, and necessity might be served by the grant of a license to a person other than the renewal applicant." Telecommunications Act of 1996, Pub. L. No. 104-104, §204(a), 110 Stat. 56 (1996) (to be codified at 47 U.S.C. §309(k)(4)). *See* Peter W. Huber, Michael Kellogg, and John Thorne, The Telecommunications Act of 1996 §2.3 (1996).

bad, not abominable: Telecommunications Act of 1996 §201 (to be codified at 47 U.S.C. §336(c)). *See* Peter W. Huber, Michael Kellogg, and John Thorne, The Telecommunications Act of 1996 §2.1 (1996).

Ten or more years later: No certain date is specified. The FCC has previously proposed a fifteen-year transition period. Memorandum Opinion and Order, Third Report and Order, Third Further Notice of Proposed Rulemaking, Advanced Television Systems and Their Impact upon the Existing Television Broadcast Services, 7 F.C.C. Rec. 6924, 6926 (1992).

72 **cellular-like networks:** 47 U.S.C.A. §309(j).

$600 million: *See* Edmund L. Andrews, Airwaves Auctions Bring $833 Million For U.S. Treasury, New York Times, July 30, 1994 at A1.

preauction projections: Each of the five 50-50 kHz paired nationwide licenses sold for $80 million. Winning bids for 50-12.5 kHz paired licenses ranged between $47.0 and $47.5 million. *See* Paul Kagan Associates, Inc., Wireless Telecom Investor at 11 (Aug. 23, 1994); Communications, PCS Auction Gains $650 Million, IVDS $216 Million For Treasury, Daily Report For Executives, Aug. 1, 1994 at A145.

topped $490 million: Included in the $490.9 million total is a $2 million penalty levied against Pagemart for withdrawing a high bid. Factoring in discounts to designated entities, the government's total earnings from this auction will be roughly $395 million. *See* Companies Offer $491 Million; 9 Bidders Win 30 Narrowband PCS Licenses As FCC Auction Closes, Communications Daily, Nov. 9, 1994 at 2; The Cutting Edge: Computing/Technology/Innovation; 9 Groups Win Paging Licenses at FCC Auction, Los Angeles Times, Nov. 9, 1994 at D6.

revenues exceeded $7 billion: L.A. Valued Highest; FCC Auction for PCS Licenses Ends with Proceeds Topping $7 Billion, Communications Daily, Mar. 14, 1995, at 1.

netted $10 billion: Entrepreneurs' C Block Auction Closes FCC Announces Winning Bidders in the Auction of 493 Licenses to Provide Broadband PCS in Basic Trading Areas: Auction Event No. 5, 1996 FCC Lexis 2435 (May 8, 1996).

72   **$12 billion between 1994 and 1998:** Second Report and Order, Implementation of Section 309(j) of the Communications Act—Competitive Bidding, 9 F.C.C. Rec. 2348, 2379 (1994).

$15 billion by mid-1996: FCC Hits $15 Billion Mark in Total Net Auction Revenues, 1996 FCC Lexis 584 (Feb. 6, 1996).

already bought and sold: *See* Ithiel de Sola Pool, Technologies of Freedom at 139–140 (1983).

New Zealand and Britain: New Zealand has made extensive use of competitive bidding to award spectrum licenses, and the United Kingdom has used it to award broadcasting rights. *See* Notice of Proposed Rule Making and Tentative Decision Making, Amendment of the Commission's Rules to Establish New Personal Communications Services; 7 F.C.C. Rec. 5676, 5710, 5711 (1992).

73   **government itself estimated:** Evan Kwerel and John R. Williams, Changing Channels: Voluntary Reallocation of UHF Television Spectrum, FCC, Office of Plans and Policy (OPP), Working Paper No. 27 (Nov. 1992).

Nextel was created: Memorandum Opinion and Order, Request of Fleet Call, Inc. for a Waiver and Other Relief to Permit Creation of Enhanced Specialized Mobile Radio System in Six Markets, 6 F.C.C. Rec. 1533 (1991).

74   **would have served better:** *See* Arthur S. DeVany et al., A Property System Approach to the Electromagnetic Spectrum (Cato Institute 1980).

George Gilder has developed: George Gilder's Telecosm, Forbes, Apr. 11, 1994 at 99.

75   **engineering and smart management:** *See generally* Mark S. Fowler and Daniel L. Brenner, A Marketplace Approach to Broadcast Regulation, 60 Tex. L. Rev. 207, 221–226 (1982).

Chapter 7

77   **operators were still being used:** *See* John Brooks, Telephone: The First Hundred Years at 244 (1975).

78   **on one substrate:** *See* T. R. Reid, The Chip: How Two Americans Invented the Microchip and Launched a Revolution (1984).

FCC progressively eliminated: Decision, Use of Carterfone Device in Message Toll Telephone Services, 13 F.C.C.2d 420 (1968). *See generally* Michael K. Kellogg, John Thorne, and Peter W. Huber, Federal Telecommunications Law §3.6 (1992).

79   **consumers would have saved over $3 billion:** *See* Progress for Freedom Foundation, The Telecom Revolution—An American Opportunity at 18 (May 1995).

barred from the radio broadcast: Radio Act of 1927, Pub. L. No. 632, 44 Stat. 1162 (1927).

80   **microwave systems comprised:** *See* Richard H. K. Vietor, AT&T and the Public Good: Regulation and Competition in Telecommunica-

tions, 1910–1987, in Future Competition in Telecommunications at 27, 52 (Bradley and Hausman eds. 1989).

80   **let them do so:** Allocation of Frequencies in Bands above 890 Mc, 27 F.C.C. 359 (1959).

between St. Louis and Chicago: *See* Peter Temin, The Fall of the Bell System: A Study in Pricing and Politics at 47–54 (1987).

special characteristics: *Quoted in* Peter Temin, The Fall of the Bell System: A Study in Pricing and Politics at 50 (1987).

slowly let them in: *See* Applications of Microwave Communications, Inc. for Construction Permits to Establish New Facilities in the Domestic Public Point to Point Microwave Service in Chicago, IL., St. Louis, MO., and Immediate Points, 18 F.C.C.2d 953 (1969).

adopted an open-entry policy: First Report and Order, Policy and Rules Concerning Rates for Competitive Carrier Services and Facilities Authorizations Therefor, 85 F.C.C.2d 1 (1980).

consumers would have saved $16 billion: *See* Progress and Freedom Foundation, The Telecom Revolution—An American Opportunity at 19 (May 1995).

81   **thus trumping state regulators:** *See, e.g.,* Memorandum Opinion and Order, Application of Iowa Network Access Division, 3 F.C.C. Rec. 1468 (1988).

large city in the country: *See, e.g.,* Memorandum Opinion and Order, Application of Teleport Communications, New York, 7 F.C.C. Rec. 5986 (1992).

already done so: *See* NARUC, Report on the Status of Competition in Intrastate Telecommunications (Sept. 23, 1994).

explicitly bar competitive entry: Telecommunications Act of 1996, Pub. L. No. 104-104 §101(a), 110 Stat. 56 (1996) (to be codified at 47 U.S.C. §253(a)). *See* Peter W. Huber, Michael Kellogg, and John Thorne, The Telecommunications Act of 1996 §1.1.1 (1996).

toll revenues nationwide: LECs account for approximately 80 percent of the short-haul toll market, or about $11.3 billion. By extrapolation, the size of the total short-haul toll market is about $14 billion. Competition in the Local Loop, Telecom Perspectives, July 1996 at 73; FCC, Statistics of Communications Common Carriers 1995/1996 at Table 1.4 (1996). However, this total is subject to access charges, making the net revenues $9 billion. FCC, Statistics of Communications Common Carriers 1995/1996 at Tables 6.2 and 1.4 (1996).

$54 billion a year: The total size of the toll market is $83.8 billion. Subtracting the $14 billion short-haul market from this total, we obtain a long-distance market of $69.8 billion. However, as we stated before, approximately $24.6 billion of this is paid to LECs in access charges, and is thus considered part of their revenues. Long-distance revenues then account for $45.2 billion. Similarly, the short-haul market net of access charges is approximately $9 billion. FCC, Statistics of Communications Common Carriers 1995/1996 at Tables 6.2 and 1.4 (1996).

82   **Computer Inquiry in 1980:** Final Decision, Amendment of Section 64.702 of the Commission's Rules and Regulations, 77 F.C.C.2d 384, 391 (1980).

82   **begin tearing it down:** Memorandum Opinion, Order and Statement of
        Principles, Communication Protocols under Section 64.702 of the Com-
        mission's Rules and Regulations, 95 F.C.C.2d 584 (1983).

        it was ready to abandon: *See* Memorandum Opinion and Order on Fur-
        ther Reconsideration, Amendment of Section 64.702 of the Commission's
        Rules and Regulations (Third Computer Inquiry), 3 F.C.C. Rec. 1135
        (1988).

        paid their own way: *See* Memorandum Opinion and Order on Further
        Reconsideration and Second Further Reconsideration, Amendment of
        Section 64.702 of the Commission's Rules and Regulations, 4 F.C.C. Rec.
        5927 (1989).

        regulatory superstructure: The 1996 Telecommunications Act knocks
        down one other serious obstruction to competition by authorizing local
        phone companies to provide long-distance connections as needed in con-
        nection with on-line services and video programming. Telecommunica-
        tions Act of 1996 §151(a) (to becodified at 47 U.S.C. §271(b)(3),(g)). *See*
        Peter W. Huber, Michael Kellogg, and John Thorne, The Telecommuni-
        cations Act of 1996 §1.2.4 (1996).

83   **sixteen years earlier:** Report and Order, Amendment of Part 76 of the
        Commission's Rules Concerning Carriage of Television Broadcast Signals
        by Cable Television Systems, 1 F.C.C. Rec. 864, 897 (1986).

        1992 Cable Act: Cable Television Consumer Protection and Competi-
        tion Act of 1992, Pub. L. No. 385, 106 Stat. 1460 (1992) (codifed at 47
        U.S.C.A. §§521-558).

        video fare for others: Second Report and Order, Recommendation to
        Congress, and Second Further Notice of Proposed Rulemaking, Tele-
        phone Company-Cable Television Cross-Ownership Rules, Sections
        63.54-63.58, 7 F.C.C. Rec. 5781, 5798, 5801–5802 (1992).

        handful of applications: As of December 1994 another commercial appli-
        cant had been waiting twenty-five months for the Commission to act, more
        than double the statutory maximum period.

        knocked down the ban: Chesapeake & Potomac Tel. Co. v. United
        States, 830 F. Supp. 909, 932 (E.D. Va. 1993).

        federal appellate court affirmed: Chesapeake & Potomac Tel. Co. v.
        United States, 42 F.3d 181 (4th Cir. 1994), *cert. granted* 1995 U.S. LEXIS
        4273 (June 26, 1995).

        Every other court that considered: *See* U S West, Inc. v. United States,
        1994 U.S. App. LEXIS 39121 (9th Cir. 1994); Southwestern Bell Corp.
        v. United States, No. 3:94-CV-0193-D (N.D. Tex. Mar. 27, 1995);
        United States Tel. Ass'n v. United States, No. 1:94CV01961 (D.D.C. Jan.
        27, 1995); GTE South, Inc. v. United States, No. 94-1588-A (E.D. Va.
        Jan. 13, 1995); NYNEX Corp. v. United States, No. 92-323-P-C (D. Me.
        Dec. 8, 1994); BellSouth Corp. v. United States, 868 F. Supp. 1335 (N.D.
        Ala. 1994); Ameritech Corp. v. United States, 867 F. Supp. 721 (N.D. Ill.
        1994).

        Supreme Court in December 1995: Chesapeake & Potomac Tel. Co. v.
        United States, 830 F. Supp. 909 (E.D. Va. 1993), *aff'd,* 42 F.3d 181 (4th
        Cir. 1994), *cert. granted,* 1995 U.S. LEXIS 4273 (June 26, 1995).

        tangled video-dialtone jurisprudence: Telecommunications Act of 1996

§302(a), 110 Stat. 56 (1996) (to be codified at 47 U.S.C. §651(a)(3)(A)). *See* Peter W. Huber, Michael Kellogg, and John Thorne, The Telecommunications Act of 1996 §3.3.2 (1996).

84   **between 1983 and 1992:** *See* Progress and Freedom Foundation, The Telecom Revolution—An American Opportunity at 24 (May1995).

technical statutory grounds: Southwestern Bell Tel. Co. v. FCC, 19 F.3d 1475, 1478, 1481 (D.C. Cir. 1994).

permission to stop: 47 U.S.C.A. §214(c).

85   **"engaged in broadcasting":** 47 U.S.C.A. §153(h).

providing any cable service: 47 U.S.C.A. §541(c).

under federal jurisdiction: Second Report and Order, Recommendation to Congress, and Second Further Notice of Proposed Rulemaking, Telephone Company-Cable Television Cross-Ownership Rules, Sections 63.54-63.58, 7 F.C.C. Rec. 5781, 5783 (1992).

no valid complaint: National Cable Television Ass'n v. FCC, 33 F.3d 66, 75 (D.C. Cir. 1994).

may not occupy more than one third: Unless there's no demand for the others. Telecommunications Act of 1996 §302(a)(to be codified at 47 U.S.C. §653(b)(1)(B)). *See* Peter W. Huber, Michael Kellogg, and John Thorne, The Telecommunications Act of 1996 §3.3.4 (1996).

86   **but no more:** Telecommunications Act of 1996 §302(a) (to be codified at 47 U.S.C. §653(c)(2)(B)). *See* Peter W. Huber, Michael Kellogg, and John Thorne, The Telecommunications Act of 1996 §3.3.4 (1996).

Chapter 8

88   **acquisition three years later:** United States v. AT&T, 1 Decrees & Judgments in Civil Federal Antitrust Cases 554 (D. Or. 1914) (No. 6082), *modified,* 1 Decrees & Judgments in Civil Federal Antitrust Cases 569 (D. Or. 1914), modified, 1 Decrees & Judgments in Civil Federal Antitrust Cases 572 (D. Or. 1918), *modified,* 1 Decrees & Judgments in Civil Federal Antitrust Cases 574 (D. Or. 1922).

federal code in 1890: Sherman Antitrust Act, 26 Stat. 204, ch. 647 (1890) (codified at 15 U.S.C.A. §1 et seq.).

89   **kept suing:** *See, e.g.,* Pastor v. AT&T, 76 F. Supp. 781 (S.D.N.Y. 1940); Carter v. AT&T, 365 F.2d 486 (5th Cir. 1966).

equipment used in providing telephone service: United States v. Western Elec. Co., 1956 Trade Cas. (CCH) ¶68,246, §IV(A) (D.N.J. 1956). This effectively barred Bell from participating in the infant computer industry that a Bell invention (the transistor) had created, and thus it set the stage for what would eventually become a massive antitrust suit against IBM.

other than common carriage: 1956 Decree §V. "Common carrier communications services" were defined by Section II(i) of the 1956 Decree as "communications services and facilities . . . the charges for which are subject to public regulation under the Communications Act of 1934 [or state laws]." 1956 Decree §II(i). AT&T was, however, permitted to supply services of any kind to the federal government. 1956 Decree §§IV(B)(3), V(a).

89   **$277 million verdict:** Litton Systems, Inc. v. AT&T, 700 F.2d 785 (2d Cir. 1983).

        AT&T fiercely litigated: *See, e.g.,* Phonetele, Inc. v. AT&T, 889 F.2d 224 (9th Cir. 1989).

        MCI sued Bell: *See* MCI v. AT&T, 708 F.2d 1081 (7th Cir. 1983).

        $113 million on appeal: MCI v. AT&T, 708 F.2d 1081 (7th Cir. 1983), *cert. denied,* 464 U.S. 891 (1984).

        appellate court affirmed: Southern Pacific Comm. Co. v. AT&T, 556 F. Supp. 825 (D.D.C. 1983), *aff'd,* 740 F.2d 980 (D.C. Cir. 1984), *cert. denied,* 470 U.S. 1005 (1985).

90   **ruling on Bell's motion:** United States v. AT&T, 524 F. Supp. 1336 (D.D.C. 1981).

        It capitulated: United States v. AT&T, 552 F. Supp. 226 (D.D.C. 1982).

        case against IBM: *See* Michael K. Kellogg, John Thorne, and Peter W. Huber, Federal Telecommunications Law §1.7.5 (1992).

        Watson trained as a salesman: *See* Regis McKenna, Who's Afraid of Big Blue? How Companies Are Challenging IBM—and Winning at 15–16 (1989).

        "Register" became "Machines": *See* Richard DeLamarter, Big Blue: IBM's Use and Abuse of Power at 15 (1986).

91   **punch card itself:** *See* Robert Sobel, I.B.M.: Colossus in Transition at 210 (1981).

        became prohibitively expensive: *See* Richard DeLamarter, Big Blue: IBM's Use and Abuse of Power at 19–23 (1986).

        new investment in software: *See* Regis McKenna, Who's Afraid of Big Blue? How Companies are Challenging IBM—and Winning at 22 (1989).

        abandoned in 1982: *See* Michael K. Kellogg, John Thorne, and Peter W. Huber, Federal Telecommunications Law §1.7.5 (1992).

        enter the computer business: In 1991 AT&T purchased NCR, the former National Cash Register, where Thomas Watson first learned how to sell business machines.

92   **shed a hundred thousand employees:** *See* John W. Verity, Deconstructing the Computer Industry, Business Week, Nov. 23, 1992 at 90.

        $52 by year's end 1992: *See* Joel Kurtzman, The End of I.B.M.'s Overshadowing Role, New York Times, Dec. 20, 1992, section 3 at 2.

        "The End of I.B.M.'s Overshadowing Role": Joel Kurtzman, The End of I.B.M.'s Overshadowing Role, New York Times, Dec. 20, 1992, section 3 at 2.

        deadlocked 2–2: The fifth commissioner was unable to vote due to stock ownership in a computer firm. *See* Stuart Taylor Jr., What to Do with the Microsoft Monster, The American Lawyer, Nov. 1993 at 72. Four months later, FTC commissioners deadlocked once again on the issue.

        in mid-1994: United States v. Microsoft Corp., No. 94-1564, Proposed Final Judgment §IV (D.D.C. July 15, 1994). The proposed consent decree was rejected by a U.S. District Court on February 14, 1995. United States v. Microsoft Corp., 159 F.R.D. 318 (D.D.C. 1995). On June 16, 1995, the court of appeals ordered approval of the decree and directed that the case be assigned to another judge on remand. United States v. Microsoft Corp., Nos. 95-5037, 95-5039 (D.C. Cir. June 16, 1995).

92   **its checkbook program:** *See* John Wilke and Viveca Novak, Microsoft's
        Plan to Acquire Intuit Sparks Closer Antitrust Scrutiny, Wall Street Jour-
        nal, Feb. 1, 1995 at B8. The deal wasabandoned three weeks after the
        Department sued. *See* Christian Hill and Don Clark, Undone Deal, Wall
        Street Journal, May 22, 1995 at A1.

93   **AP refused to sell:** Technically, the applicant could buy AP's services—
        but it had to obtain majority approval of the existing members and pay
        retroactive fees. The bylaws forbade members from furnishing news to
        nonmembers, required a member's competitor seeking membership to pay
        a percentage of assessments received from members since 1900, and forced
        those seeking membership to obtain a majority vote of members.

        halt the exclusive dealing: Associated Press v. United States, 326 U.S. 1,
        20 (1945).

        refusing to provide movies: *See, e.g.,* United States v. Paramount Pic-
        tures, 66 F. Supp. 323, 333 n. 1 (S.D.N.Y. 1946).

        forced to divest: *See, e.g.,* United States v. Interstate Circuit, Inc., 20 F.
        Supp. 868 (N.D. Tex. 1937); United States v. Fox West Coast Theaters,
        1932–1939 Trade Cas. (CCH) ¶55,018 (S.D. Cal. 1932).

        1949 consent decree: United States v. Loew's Inc., 1951 Trade Cas.
        (CCH) ¶62,765 (S.D.N.Y. 1951) (Loew's consent decree).

        decrees began to vanish: *See* John Thorne, Peter W. Huber, and Michael
        K. Kellogg, Federal Broadband Law §8.3.2 (1995).

        forced NBC to sell: *See* Jonathan W. Emord, The First Amendment
        Invalidity of FCC Ownership Regulations, 38 Cath. U. L. Rev. 401, 407
        (1989).

94   **added stricter conditions:** United States v. National Broadcasting Co.,
        449 F. Supp. 1127 (C.D. Cal. 1978); United States v. CBS Inc., 1980–1981
        Trade Cas. (CCH) ¶63,594 (C.D. Cal. 1980); United States v. American
        Broadcasting Co., 1980–1981 Trade Cas. (CCH) ¶64,150 (C.D. Cal.
        1980).

        clearly in decline: *See* United States v. National Broadcasting Co., 842 F.
        Supp. 402 (C.D. Cal. 1993).

        Two 1993 consent decrees: State of New York v. Primestar Partners,
        L.P., 1993-2 Trade Cas. (CCH) ¶70,403, §IV(A), (C) (S.D.N.Y. 1993);
        United States v. Primestar Partners, L.P., 1994-1 Trade Cas. (CCH)
        ¶70,562, §IV(C)(3) (S.D.N.Y. 1994).

        decrees duplicate and extend: 47 U.S.C.A. §§536(a), 522(12). These
        rules are supplemented by the terms of the consent decrees, which bar
        MSOs from retaliating against programmers that sell programming to
        competing distributors. United States v. Primestar Partners, L.P., No. 93-
        CV-9313, §IV(B) (S.D.N.Y. 1993); State of New York v. Primestar Part-
        ners, L.P., Civ. No. 93-3868, §IV(E)-(F) (S.D.N.Y. 1993).

        control of much more: The current Justice Department has argued that
        innovation itself may be a market subject to protection. *See, e.g.,* Speech of
        Anne K. Bingaman, Innovation and Antitrust, before the Commonwealth
        Club of California (July 29, 1994) (http://gopher.usdoj.gov/atr/atr.htm).

        Motion Picture Patents Company: *See* Ralph Cassady Jr., Monopoly in
        Motion Picture Production and Distribution: 1908–1915, 32 S. Cal. L.
        Rev. 325, 329-350 (1959).

95   **patents held by its members:** *See* Reese V. Jenkins, Images and Enterprise: Technology and the American Photographic Industry, 1839 to 1925
      at 285 (1975).

      lawsuits against infringers: *See* John Thorne, Peter W. Huber, and
      Michael K. Kellogg, Federal Broadband Law § 9.6.1(i) (1995).

      stripped the trust of its power: United States v. Motion Picture Patents
      Co., 225 F. 800, 811 (E.D. Pa. 1915).

      navy decreed a wartime moratorium: *See* Sydney W. Head and Christopher H. Sterling, Broadcasting in America: A Survey of Electronic Media
      at 38 (6th ed. 1990).

      more than four thousand patents: *See* Application of Radio Corp. of
      America, 13 F.R.D. 167, 168 (S.D.N.Y. 1952).

      Department of Justice charged them: *See* Application of Radio Corp. of
      America, 13 F.R.D. 167, 168 (S.D.N.Y. 1952).

      suit against AT&T alleged: Complaint, United States v. Western Elec.
      Co., No. 17-49 (D.N.J. Jan. 14, 1949).

      licenses to all comers: United States v. Western Elec. Co., 1956 Trade
      Cas. (CCH) ¶68,246, §X (D.N.J. 1956).

      created performing-rights societies: Many owners of copyright in musical compositions organized the Harry Fox Agency to license the mechanical reproduction of music. *See* Harry Fox Agency, Inc. v. Mills Music, Inc.,
      543 F. Supp. 844 (S.D.N.Y. 1982), *rev'd*, 720 F.2d 733 (2d Cir. 1983), *rev'd
      sub nom.* Mills Music, Inc. v. Snyder, 469 U.S. 153 (1985).

      unable to agree to one: United States v. ASCAP, 1940–1943 Trade Cas.
      (CCH) ¶56,104 (S.D.N.Y. 1941), *amended,* 1950–1951 Trade Cas. (CCH)
      ¶62,595 (S.D.N.Y. 1950).

96   **been overtly corrupted:** *See, e.g.,* Parker v. Brown, 317 U.S. 341 (1943).

      does not open the door: City of Columbia v. Omni Outdoor Advertising,
      Inc., 499 U.S. 365, 378 (1991).

      does not face antitrust liability: Paragould Cablevision, Inc. v. City of
      Paragould, 930 F.2d 1310, 1314 (8th Cir. 1991).

      authority to immunize local telephone mergers: Willis-Graham Act,
      ct. 20, 42 Stat. 27 (1921) (codified at 47 U.S.C.A. §221(a)).

      unless the Commission so ordered: 47 U.S.C.A. §201(a).

      alarm services out of business: Sonitrol of Fresno, Inc. v. AT&T, 629 F.
      Supp. 1089 (D.D.C. 1986).

      less vulnerable to antitrust attack: *See, e.g.,* MCI v. AT&T, 708 F.2d
      1081, 1124 (7th Cir. 1983). As the court put it, any conflict, "actual or potential, between an obligation imposed by the 1934 Act and an antitrust
      remedy" may block the antitrust prosecution. MCI v. AT&T, 708 F.2d
      1081, 1121 (7th Cir. 1983).

      approval of mergers and acquisitions: Telecommunications Act of 1996,
      Pub. L. No. 104-104, §601(b)(2), 110 Stat. 56 (1996) (repealing 47 U.S.C.
      §221(a)).

      a key 1943 holding: Parker v. Brown, 317 U.S. 341 (1943).

      affirmatively expressed: Southern Motor Carriers Rate Conference, Inc.
      v. United States, 471 U.S. 48, 57 (1985).

97   **chance to resolve it:** *See, e.g.,* Pan American World Airways v. United
      States, 371 U.S. 296 (1963).

97   **fact of market life:** MCI v. AT&T, 708 F.2d 1081, 1105 (7th Cir. 1983) (quoting ITT v. GTE Corp., 518 F.2d 913, 935–936 (9th Cir. 1975)).

fact-of-life defense may explain: MCI v. AT&T, 708 F.2d 1081, 1107 (7th Cir. 1983).

may refute the inference: *See* United States v. Aluminum Co. of America, 148 F.2d 416, 432 (2d Cir. 1945).

serve the whole market: *See* MCI v. AT&T, 708 F.2d 1081, 1108 (7th Cir. 1983).

Filed Tariff Doctrine: *See, e.g.,* Keogh v. Chicago & Northwestern Railway Co., 260 U.S. 156 (1922).

the company began losing: *See* Michael K. Kellogg, John Thorne, and Peter W. Huber, Federal Telecommunications Law §§3.4.1–3.5.4 (1992).

Cable operators likewise began losing: *See, e.g.,* Affiliated Capital Corp. v. City of Houston, 519 F. Supp. 991 (S.D. Tex. 1981).

98   **monopolized amateur photography:** United States v. Eastman Kodak Co., 226 F. 62 (W.D.N.Y. 1915).

decree was issued in 1916: United States v. Eastman Kodak Co., 230 F. 522 (W.D.N.Y. 1916). Kodak also faced another government suit claiming monopolization. Eastman Kodak Co. v. Federal Trade Comm., 7 F.2d 994 (2d Cir. 1925), *aff'd*, 74 U.S. 619 (1925).

Kodak settled: United States v. Eastman Kodak Co., 1954 Trade Cas. ¶67,920 (W.D.N.Y. 1954).

were the two decrees finally vacated: United States v. Eastman Kodak Co., 853 F. Supp. 1454 (W.D.N.Y. 1994).

consent decree in 1956: *See* Richard DeLamarter, Big Blue: IBM's Use and Abuse of Power at 23 (1986).

sued again in 1969: United States v. IBM, No. 69-200 (S.D.N.Y. Jan. 12, 1969).

case was dropped in 1982: In re International Business Machines Corp., 687 F.2d 591, 596–597 (2d Cir. 1982). The court subsequently issued a further writ of mandamus directing Judge Edelstein (1) to cease his consideration of whether the parties had to comply with the Tunney Act before their stipulation of dismissal became effective, and (2) to dispose promptly of any matters presented by the parties necessary to effectuate the conclusion of the litigation.

remove Judge Edelstein: In re International Business Machines Corp., 45 F.3d 641 (2d Cir. 1995).

forbidden to provide long-distance: Modification of Final Judgment, §III.D.3, United States v. AT&T, 552 F. Supp. 131, 225–234 (D.D.C. 1982).

supply equal access: Modification of Final Judgment, §II.A, United States v. AT&T, 552 F. Supp. 131, 225–227 (D.D.C. 1982).

99   **cajoled, hectored, and prosecuted:** *See* Michael K. Kellogg, John Thorne, and Peter W. Huber, Federal Telecommunications Law §7.1 et seq. (1992).

often took years: Judge Greene increasingly issued fact-specific waivers rather than decide declaratory ruling requests, noting that a limited waiver is better than "an undesirable precedent" regarding the scope of the decree. *See* United States v. Western Elec. Co., 578 F. Supp. 658, 661

(D.D.C. 1983); United States v. Western Elec. Co., 604 F. Supp. 256, 261 n.20 (D.D.C. 1984).

99 **private-line service was authorized:** Order, United States v. Western Elec. Co., No. 82-0192 (D.D.C. Dec. 16, 1988).

Pacific Bell is permitted: Order, United States v. Western Elec. Co., No. 82-0192 (D.D.C. Mar. 22, 1985).

Wisconsin Bell may provide: Order, United States v. Western Elec. Co., No. 82-0192 (D.D.C. Sept. 10, 1991).

1995 Justice Department proposal: Motion of the United States for a Modification of the Decree to Permit a Trial, at ¶¶40–43, 44–46, 37, 28–29, United States v. Western Elec. Co., No. 82-0192 (D.D.C. Apr. 3, 1995).

100 **$113 million on appeal:** MCI v. AT&T, 708 F.2d 1081 (7th Cir. 1983).

101 **automatically after ten years:** In 1979 the Department adopted a policy generally limiting the life of antitrust decrees it negotiates to no more than ten years. *See* Michael DeBow, Judicial Regulation of Industry: An Analysis of Antitrust Consent Decrees, 1987 U. Chi. L. Forum 353, 358 (1987).

can be vacated sooner: *See* United States v. Western Elec. Co., 900 F.2d 283, 305 (D.C. Cir. 1990).

Chapter 9

105 **still smaller margins today:** William Taylor, NERA, Effects of Competitive Entry in the U.S. Interstate Toll Markets: An Update at 4 (May 28, 1992).

seemed likely to fall: *See, e.g.,* AT&T Price Cap Order, 4 F.C.C. Rcd at 3047–3048; MCI Reply Comments at 20–22, Policy & Rules Concerning Rates for Dominant Carriers, No. 87-313 (FCC Dec. 4, 1987); Sprint Comments at 50–52, Policy & Rules Concerning Rates for Dominant Carriers, No. 87-313 (FCC Oct. 19, 1987).

reduce[d] customer choice: Statement of Alfred C. Sikes, FCC Chairman, June 19, 1991 (1991 FCC LEXIS 4212).

lose business to its rivals: Reply Comments of CompTel at 2–3, Competition in the Interstate Interexchange Marketplace, No. 90-132 (F.C.C. Sept. 18, 1990).

over half of all customers: AT&T's share of long distance toll revenue was 55 percent in 1995 and 58 percent in 1994. Ind. Analy. Div., FCC, Long Distance Market Shares: First Quarter 1996 at 14 (1996).

107 **million-customer mark in 1987:** Busy Signal a Welcome Sign in Cellular Telephone Industry, Chicago Tribune, Oct. 18, 1987 at 10C.

thirty million subscribers today: CTIA, The Wireless Factbook at 2 (Spring 1996).

assigned to cellular phones: R. G. Klugman, Painewebber Inc., Ind. Rep. No. 1537197, RBOCs and GTE 70 (Dec. 13, 1994).

108 **services within a few years:** Electric utilities have some eighteen thousand route miles of fiber-optic cable in place. Warren Causey, UTC '95 to Assess Utility Communications Networks, Telecom-Market Possibilities, Electrical World, July 27, 1995 at 41. Their fiber-optic networks are expected to expand by 1998 to forty thousand route miles. Jeffrey Sheldon,

Utilities Able to Provide Access to Nation's Information Highway, Radio Comm. Report, Apr. 24, 1995 at 10. Although at present most electric utility provision of telecommunications is limited to leasing excess fiber capacity to IXCs and CAPs, some utilities are becoming more aggressive as regulators allow them greater freedom. *See* Electric Utilities and Telecommunications, Connecticut Research Report on Competitive Telecommunications, Feb. 1, 1995 at 7.

109   **combine cable backbone networks:** J. Reif et al., Merrill Lynch Capital Markets, Co. Rep. No. 1559372, Sprint/TCI/Comcast/Cox 14 (Feb. 10, 1995).

145 million potential subscribers: *See* Public Notice, Commercial Mobile Radio Service Information: Announcing the Winning Bidders in the FCC's Auction of 99 Licenses to Provide Broadband PCS in Major Trading Areas (F.C.C. Mar. 13, 1995); Edmund L. Andrews, Winners of Wireless Auction to Pay $7 Billion, New York Times, Mar. 14, 1995 at D1. In addition, Sprint, Cox, and TCI (without Comcast) secured one other license—in Philadelphia—under the name PhillieCo. This adds another $85 million to their spending and another nine million potential subscribers to their population served.

fiber networks and rights-of-way: Warren Causey, UTC '95 to Assess Utility Communications Networks, Telecom-Market Possibilities, Electrical World, July 27, 1995 at 41. Texas Utilities Company has a 20 percent stake in the Texas licenses of PCS PrimeCo, a partnership between Airtouch, Bell Atlantic, NYNEX, and U S West. PCS PrimeCo and Texas Utilities Form Partnership to Deliver Wireless Communications, BusinessWire, May 9, 1995.

distant central offices: F. W. Moran, Salomon Brothers Inc., Co. Rep. No. 1572392, Cox Communications, Inc. 22 (Mar. 15, 1995).

Phones with these capabilities: GTE's Tele-Go, for example, is a handset that functions as an ordinary cordless phone at home and as an untethered cellular phone away from home. GTE's in Hot Pursuit of Residential Customers, Says New VP, Advanced Wireless Communications, July 5, 1995. GTE has invested more than $50 million in Tele-Go and currently serves more than 150,000 customers in the United States with the system. GTE Mobilnet Licenses Tele-Go to Bell Mobility, PCS Week, Aug. 23, 1995.

110   **fast Internet access:** Robin Gareiss, Cable Operators Play the Data Game, Data Communications, Aug. 1995 at 73; Larry J. Yokell, Cable TV Moves into Telecom Markets, Business Communications Review, Nov. 1994 at 43.

advanced information and two-way services: By the end of 1994, 30 percent of cable subscribers had been upgraded; the industry plans to have 60 percent upgraded by the end of 1996. P. J. Sirlin, Wertheim Schorder & Co., Co. Rep. No. 1545274, Tele-Communications, Inc. 10 (Jan. 9, 1995).

new 6 MHz blocks of spectrum: Chris McConnell, Turning Data Streams into Revenue Streams, Broadcasting & Cable, Apr. 10, 1995 at 32.

112   *School's Out:* School's Out: Hyperlearning, the New Technology, and the End of Education (1992).

112   **outsourcing and shrinking:** *See* John A. Byrne et al., The Virtual Corporation, Business Week, Feb. 8, 1993 at 98; David C. Churbuck and Jeffrey S. Young, The Virtual Workplace, Forbes,Nov. 23, 1992 at 184.

        outweighs the benefits: Ronald Coase, The Nature of the Firm, *in* The Firm, the Market, and the Law (1988).

        knitted together into an efficient whole: *See* Michael Schrage, Shared Minds: The New Technologies of Collaboration (1990).

        The Death of Money: Joel Kurtzman, The Death of Money: How the Electronic Economy Has Destabilized the World's Markets and Created Financial Chaos (1993); Gregory J. Millman, The Vandals' Crown: How Rebel Currency Traders Overthrew the World's Central Banks (1995).

113   **phesbian leminists:** George Orwell, The Road to Wigan Pier at 174 (1956). *See* Howard Rheingold, The Virtual Community: Homesteading on the Electronic Frontier (1993); Michael Schrage and Alun Anderson, Computer Tools for Thinking in Tandem, Science, Aug. 2, 1991 at 505.

        spreading out: *See* Peter Huber, Tele-City on a Hill, Forbes, Feb. 27, 1995 at 64.

        The Twilight of Sovereignty: Walter B. Wriston, The Twilight of Sovereignty: How the Information Revolution Is Transforming Our World (1992).

114   **crossword puzzle fans:** George Orwell, England, Your England, in George Orwell: A Collection of Essays at 255 (1946).

Chapter 10

118   **jurisdiction in 1910:** Mann-Elkins Act of 1910, ch. 309, 36 Stat. 539 (1910).

        "unjust or unreasonable": 47 U.S.C.A. §201(b).

        preferred stock, and common equity: *See* El Paso Natural Gas Co. v. Federal Power Commission, 449 F.2d 1245, 1250 (5th Cir. 1971).

        switched and unswitched, and so on: *See* Peter W. Huber, The Geodesic Network: 1987 Report on Competition in the Telephone Industry at 3.53 (1987).

        federal and state authorities: 47 U.S.C.A. §152.

        Ozark Plan of 1970: Prescriptions of Procedures for Separating and Allocating Plant Investment, Operating Expenses, Taxes and Reserve Between the Intrastate and Interstate Operations of Telephone Companies, 26 F.C.C.2d 247 (1970).

        subsidies grew and grew: *See* Michael K. Kellogg, John Thorne, and Peter W. Huber, Federal Telecommunications Law §9.4 (1992).

        8 percent of access line usage: *See* Gerald R. Faulhaber, Telecommunications in Turmoil: Technology and Public Policy at 73 (1987).

        to local exchange companies: *See* Gerald R. Faulhaber, Telecommunications in Turmoil: Technology and Public Policy at 73 (1987).

        some $11 billion a year: *See* Alfred E. Kahn and William B. Shew, Current Issues in Telecommunications Regulation: Pricing, 4 Yale J. on Reg. 191, 197 (1987).

119   **on the telephone itself:** *See* Michael K. Kellogg, John Thorne, and Peter W. Huber, Federal Telecommunications Law §§1.2, 10.2 (1992).

119   **its Red network:** *See* Michael Rothschild, Stagecoach Days on the Info-
        highway, Forbes, Feb. 28, 1994, at 25.
120   **Radio Act of 1927:** Radio Act of 1927, Pub. L. No. 632, 44 Stat. 1162
        (1927).
        cable operators themselves: First Report and Order, Amendment of Part
        74, Subpart K, of the Commission's Rules and Regulations Relative to
        Community Antenna Television Systems, 20 F.C.C.2d 201 (1969).
        to regulate cable rates: Cable Television Report and Order, Amendment
        of Part 74, Subpart K, of the Commission's Rules and Regulations Relative
        to Community Antenna Television Systems, 36 F.C.C.2d 143, 209 (1972).
        premium cable services: *See* Report and Order, Amendment of Subpart
        C of Part 76 of the Commission's Rules and Regulations Regarding the
        Regulations of Cable Television System Regular Subscriber Rates, 60
        F.C.C.2d 672, 685 (1976).
        completely if they chose: *See* Report and Order, Amendment of Subpart
        C of Part 76 of the Commission's Rules and Regulations Regarding the
        Regulations of Cable Television System Regular Subscriber Rates, 60
        F.C.C.2d 672, 685 (1976).
        per-program or per-channel charges: Clarification of the Cable Televi-
        sion Rules and Notice of Proposed Rulemaking and Inquiry, 46 F.C.C.2d
        175, 199 (1974).
        loosely defined basic tier: Memorandum Opinion and Order, Commu-
        nity Cable TV, Inc. Petition for Special Relief, 95 F.C.C.2d 1204,
        1206–1207, 1216 (1983).
121   **these deregulatory initiatives:** 47 U.S.C.A. §543(a), (g).
        subject to "effective competition": 47 U.S.C.A. §543(b)(1); 47 C.F.R.
        §76.33(a)(2).
        broadcast signals were competition enough: 47 C.F.R. §76.33(1)(2).
        immediately deregulated: *See* S. Rep No. 92, 102nd Cong., 1st Sess.
        (1992).
        service mounted sharply: *See* National League of Cities, The State of
        America's Cities Ninth Annual Opinion Survey of Municipal Elected Of-
        ficials at 9 (Jan. 1993).
        "a dominant national video medium": Cable Television Consumer Pro-
        tection and Competition Act of 1992 §2(a)(3), 102d Cong., 2d Sess., Pub.
        L. No. 385, 106 Stat. 1460 (1992).
        proved they were serious: 47 U.S.C.A. §543(a)(3)-(5).
        FCC would take charge: 47 U.S.C.A. §§543(a)(2)(A)-(B), 543(a)(6).
        new set of pricing regulations: Report and Order and Proposed Rule-
        making, Implementation of Sections of the Cable Television Consumer
        Protection and Competition Act of 1992: Rate Regulation, 8 F.C.C. Rec.
        5631 (1993).
        10 percent less than others: Report and Order and Proposed Rulemak-
        ing, Implementation of Sections of the Cable Television Consumer Pro-
        tection and Competition Act of 1992: Rate Regulation, 8 F.C.C. Rec.
        5631, 5770–5774, 5881–5883 (1993).
        5.9 percent: *See* Cable Services Bureau, FCC, Report and Summary, FCC
        Cable Regulation Impact Survey, Changes in Cable Television Rates Be-
        tween April 5, 1993–September 1, 1993 at 3 (Feb. 22, 1994).

121   **savings of $1 billion a year:** Report and Order and Proposed Rulemaking, Implementation of Sections of the Cable Television Consumer Protection and Competition Act of 1992: Rate Regulation, 8 F.C.C. Rec. 5631, 5990 (1993).

        jiggered their services: *See* Cable Services Bureau, FCC, Report and Summary, FCC Cable Regulation Impact Survey, Changes in Cable Television Rates Between April 5, 1993–September 1, 1993 at 3 (Feb. 22, 1994).

122   **below the no-competition average:** Second Rate Regulation Reconsideration Order, Implementation of Sections of the Cable Television Consumer Protection and Competition Act of 1992; Rate Regulation, 9 F.C.C. Rec. 4119, 4166, 4173, 4176 (1994).

        Nashville, Tennessee, was not: *Compare* Memorandum Opinion and Order, District Cablevision Cost of Service Filing to Support Cable Programming Service Rates, 9 F.C.C. Rec. 7167 (1994), *with* Memorandum Opinion and Order, Viacom Cable Nashville, Tennessee Benchmark Filing to Support Cable Programming Service Price, DA 94-1151, 1994 FCC LEXIS 5688 (1994).

        in step with price rollbacks: *See* Thomas W. Hazlett, Predation on Local Cable TV Markets; Recent Competition Issues in Telecommunications, 40 Antitrust Bulletin 609 (1995).

        deregulated in 1983: Fourth Report and Order, Policy and Rules Concerning Rates for Competitive Common Carrier Services and Facilities Authorizations Therefor, 95 F.C.C.2d 554, 575 (1983).

123   **set their own prices:** 47 U.S.C.A. §543(a)(1). *See* Report and Order, Definition of a Cable Television System, 5 F.C.C. Rec. 7638, 7638 (1990).

        microwave is also deregulated: Notice of Proposed Rulemaking, Order, Tentative Decision and Order on Reconsideration, Rulemaking to Amend Part 1 and Part 21 of the Commission's Rules to Redesignate the 27.5 GHz Frequency Band and to Establish Rules and Policies for Local Multipoint Distribution Service, 8 F.C.C. Rec. 557, 558 (1993).

        common carriage by phone companies: Telecommunications Act of 1996, Pub. L. No. 104-104, §302(a), 110 Stat. 56 (1996) (to be codified at 47 U.S.C. §651(a)(4)). The Act requires that the FCC promulgate rules by September 1996 to ensure that the rates operators charge to transport independently supplied programming are reasonable and "not unjustly or unreasonably discriminatory." *Ibid.*

        through retiering or otherwise: 47 U.S.C.A. §543(h).

        found to be evasive: Third Order on Reconsideration, Implementation of Sections of the Cable Television Consumer Protection and Competition Act of 1992: Rate Regulation and Buy-Through Provisions, 9 F.C.C. Rec. 4316, 4364–4365 (1994).

        payments are unregulated: *See* Thomas W. Hazlett, Free Markets for Telecom: How Home-Shopping Became King of Cable, Wall Street Journal, July 14, 1994 at A10.

        rates for current services: Report and Order and Further Notice of Proposed Rulemaking, Implementation of Sections of the Cable Television Consumer Protection and Competition Act of 1992; Rate Regulation, 9 F.C.C. Rec. 4527, 4677–4680 (1994).

        interactive cable services: Second Rate Regulation Reconsideration Order, Implementation of Sections of the Cable Television Consumer Protection and Competition Act of 1992: Rate Regulation, 9 F.C.C. Rec. 4119, 4131 (1994).

123 **providing competitive video services:** Telecommunications Act of 1996 §301(b) (to be codified at 47 U.S.C. §543(c)). *See* Peter W. Huber, Michael Kellogg, and John Thorne, The Telecommunications Act of 1996 §3.1 (1996).

124 **"streamlined" regulatory treatment:** First Report and Order, Policy and Rules Concerning Rates for Competitive Common Carrier Services and Facilities Authorizations Therefor, 85 F.C.C.2d 1 (1980).

filing tariffs altogether: Sixth Report and Order, Policy and Rules Concerning Rates for Competitive Common Carrier Services and Facilities Authorizations Therefor, 99 F.C.C.2d 1020 (1985).

mandate of the 1934 Communications Act: MCI Telecommunications Corp. v. FCC, 765 F.2d 1186, 1192 (1985).

1934 Act notwithstanding: Notice of Proposed Rulemaking, Tariff Filing Requirements for Non-Dominant Common Carriers, 8 F.C.C. Rec. 1395 (1993).

nothing left to the exercise: 47 C.F.R. §61.23(c); Memorandum Opinion and Order, Tariff Filing Requirements for Non-Dominant Common Carriers, 8 F.C.C. Rec. 6752, 6756 (1993).

company's rates as well: Order, In the Matter of Motion of AT&T Corp. to be Reclassified as a Non-Dominant Carrier, 11 F.C.C. Rec. 3271 (1995).

regulation with price caps: Report Card's Out: Some States Still Drag Heels on Deregulation, State Telephone Regulation Report (Apr. 6, 1995).

higher than ever: *See* Industry Analysis Division, FCC, Trends in Telephone Service (Aug. 7, 1991).

regulatory picture entirely: Final Decision, Amendment of Section 64.702 of the Commission's Rules and Regulations (Second Computer Inquiry), 77 F.C.C.2d 384, 452 (1980).

125 **price-deregulated across the board:** A few states require the filing of informational tariffs. The FCC recently declared that rate regulation of the new PCS services would be counterproductive. Second Report and Order, Implementation of Sections 3(n) and 332 of the Communications Act; Regulatory Treatment of Mobile Services, 9 F.C.C. Rec. 1411, 1418 (1994).

126 **because it contains so few:** *See* OPP Working Paper No. 24, Through the Looking Glass: Integrated Broadband Networks, Regulatory Policies and Institutional Change, 4 F.C.C. Rec. 1306, 1313 (1988).

128 **copying of sound recordings:** *See* Alan Latman et al., Copyright for the Nineties at 592-593 (1989).

have been equally unsuccessful: *See, e.g.,* Sony Corp. of America v. Universal City Studios, 464 U.S. 417 (1984).

Chapter 11

130 **Web accessible to all:** *See* Information Infrastructure Task Force, The National Information Infrastructure: Agenda for Action, Tab B at 7–8 (Sept. 15, 1993).

130 **cut loose from the future:** *See* Clinton Administration White Paper on Communications Act Reforms (issued Jan. 27, 1994), *reprinted in* Daily Rep. for Executives (BNA) No. 18, at M-1, M-4 (Jan. 28, 1994).

demand that doesn't exist: *See* Robert S. Boyd, Fear of Technology Phobia of the '90s; Is Your VCR Flashing 12:00? Survey Says You're Not Alone, Houston Chronicle, May 9, 1994, Discovery section at 6.

131 **too much, in any event:** *See, e.g.,* Leland L. Johnson and David P. Reed, Residential Broadband Services by Telephone Companies? at 13 (1990).

bereft of any common language: Benjamin Barber, The Second American Revolution, Channels, Feb.-Mar. 1982 at 23–24.

132 **served by two providers:** *See* Milton Mueller, Universal Service in Telephone History: A Reconstruction, Telecommunications Policy at 362–363 (July 1993).

133 **Willis-Graham Act of 1921:** Willis-Graham Act of 1921, ch. 20, 42 Stat. 27 (1921).

seventy UHF bands for the new medium: Sixth Report and Order, In the Matter of Amendment of Section 3.606 of the Commission's Rules and Regulations, 41 F.C.C. 148 (1952).

one television station: Report and Order, Amendment of Part 3 of the Commission's Rules and Regulations Governing Television Broadcast Stations, 13 Rad. Reg. (P & F) 1571, 1572 (1956).

all it could to kill it: *See, e.g.,* Decision, Application of Carter Mountain Transmission Corp., 32 F.C.C. 459 (1962).

enemy of universal service: *See* Joseph R. Fogarty and Marcia Spielholz, FCC Cable Jurisdiction: From Zero to Plenary in Twenty-Five Years, 37 Fed. Com. L. J. 113 (1985).

subscribership soared: *See* Video Media Competition: Regulation, Economics, and Technology at 14 (E. Noam ed. 1985).

every home in the country: NCTA, Cable Television Developments at 1-A (April 1994).

capacity has grown rapidly, too: NCTA, Cable Television Developments at 1, 10 (Spring 1996).

134 **television's $25.8 billion:** U.S. Dep't of Commerce, U.S. Industrial Outlook 1994 at 31-6 (1994).

only the affluent suburbs: Cable Television Report and Order, Amendment of Part 74, Subpart K, of the Commission's Rules and Regulations Relative to Community Antenna Television Systems, 36 F.C.C.2d 143, 208 (1972).

wired would be wired: Clarification of the Cable Television Rules and Notice of Proposed Rulemaking and Inquiry, Amendment of Part 76 of the Commission's Rules and Regulations Relative to the Advisability of Federal Preemption of Cable Television Technical Standards or the Imposition of a Moratorium on Non-Federal Standards, 46 F.C.C.2d 175, 192–193 (1974).

cable construction back to local authorities: Report and Order, Amendment of Subparts B and C of Part 76 of the Commission's Rules Pertaining to Applications for Certificates of Compliance and Federal-State/Local Regulatory Relationships, 66 F.C.C.2d 380, 392-393 (1977).

too remote to wire economically: Report and Order, Amendment of

Parts 1, 63, and 76 of the Commission Rules to Implement the Provisions of the Cable Communications Policy Act of 1984, 1985 FCC LEXIS 3475 at *62-63 (1985).

134   **much service as the first:** *See, e.g.,* Calif. Gov't Code §653066.3 (West 1995).

backed by the courts: *See, e.g.,* Joint Appendix at 261–262, Suburban Cablevision v. Earth Satellite Communications, Inc., No. C-1554-83E (N.J. Super. Ct. Ch. Div. 1983).

deregulated receive-only facilities: First Report and Order, Regulation of Domestic Receive-Only Satellite Earth Stations, 74 F.C.C.2d 205, 206, 217 (1979).

DBS, in late 1980: Inquiry into the Development of Requesting Policy in Regard to Direct Broadcast Satellite for the Period Following the 1983 Regional Administrative Radio Conference, 45 Fed. Reg. 72, 719 (Nov. 3, 1980).

135   **siphoning once again:** National Ass'n of Broadcasters v. FCC, 740 F.2d 1190 (D.C. Cir. 1984).

reducing advertising support: *See* Memorandum Opinion and Order, Application of Satellite Television Corporation for Authority to Construct an Experimental Direct Broadcast Satellite System, 91 F.C.C.2d 953, 974, 975 n.51 (1982).

profits of existing licensees: Report and Order, Inquiry into the Development of Regulatory Policy in Regard to Direct Broadcast Satellites for the Period Following the 1983 Regional Administrative Radio Conference, 90 F.C.C.2d 676, 680, 689 (1982).

provide nationwide coverage: Memorandum Opinion and Order, Applications of Continental Satellite Corporation, et al., 4 F.C.C. Rec. 6292 (1989).

the universal footprint: Report and Order, Potential Uses of Certain Orbital Allocations by Operators in the Direct Broadcast Satellite Service, 6 F.C.C. Rec. 2581 (1991).

137   **Commission claimed victory:** *See* Gerry Butters, The Future of Universal Service in Telecommunications, Special Report: Universal Service, Ready for the 21st Century? 1991 Annual Review of the Institute for Information Studies, 6 Edge 75, Dec. 2, 1991.

should include programming: National Information Infrastructure Universal Service Hearing, Albuquerque, New Mexico (Dec. 16, 1993) (statement of Carol Clifford, assistant attorney general, New Mexico's Consumer Protection Division).

public access: National Information Infrastructure Universal Service Hearing, Albuquerque, New Mexico (Dec. 16, 1993) (statement of Jon Cooper, general manager, public broadcasting station KNME-TV; statement of Fernando Moreno, executive director, Quote . . . Unquote, Inc.).

access for the disabled: National Information Infrastructure Universal Service Hearing, Albuquerque, New Mexico (Dec. 16, 1993) (statement of Robert Geesey, executive director, New Mexico Committee for the Deaf and Hard of Hearing).

education and training: National Information Infrastructure Universal Service Hearing, Albuquerque, New Mexico (Dec. 16, 1993) (statement of

Gary Tydings, executive director, Professional Engineering Development, Dep't. of Engineering, University of New Mexico; statement of Erich Strebe, STARS program coordinator, New Mexico Small Business Development Center).

139   **the 1996 Telecommunications Act:** Telecommunications Act of 1996, Pub. L. No. 104-104, §6101(a), 110 Stat. 56 (1996) (to be codified at 47 U.S.C. §6254). *See* Peter W. Huber, Michael Kellogg, and John Thorne, The Telecommunications Act of 1996 §1.3.5 (996).

Chapter 12

142   **uniform rates announced in advance:** National Ass'n of Regulatory Util. Comm'rs v. FCC, 525 F.2d 630, 641 (D.C. Cir. 1975).
advertising alongside: *See, e.g.,* New York Times v. Sullivan, 376 U.S. 254 (1964).
special duties and special privileges: In one of the few things it got mostly right, the 1996 Telecommunications Act encourages telephone companies to deploy "open" video platforms by promising them the traditional privileges of common carriers if they do. Any operator of an open video system qualifies "for reduced regulatory burdens." Telecommunications Act of 1996, Pub. L. No. 104-104, §302(a) 110 Stat. 56 (1996) (to be codified at 47 U.S.C. §653(a)(1)). *See* Peter W. Huber, Michael Kellogg, and John Thorne, The Telecommunications Act of 1996 §3.3.4 (1996).

143   **acquired by Bell, or they folded:** *See* Glen O. Robinson, The Federal Communications Act: An Essay on Origins and Regulatory Purpose, reprinted in A Legislative History of the Communications Act of 1934 at 7 (Paglin ed. 1989).
accept each other's traffic: *See* People ex rel. Western Union Telegraph Co. v. Public Service Commission, 129 N.E. 220 (1920).
links to independent phone companies: Letter from Nathan C. Kingsbury, AT&T, to James C. McReynolds, Attorney General at 3–4 (Dec. 19, 1913).
consent decree in 1914: United States v. AT&T, 1 Decrees & Judgments in Civil Federal Antitrust Cases 554 (D. Ore. 1914) (No. 6082), *modified*, 1 Decrees & Judgments in Civil Federal Antitrust Cases 569 (D. Ore. 1914), *modified*, 1 Decrees & Judgments in Civil Federal Antitrust Cases 572 (D. Ore. 1918), *modified*, 1 Decrees & Judgments in Civil Federal Antitrust Cases 574 (D. Ore. 1922).
"carriers' carriers": *See, e.g.,* Home Tel. Co. v. Granby & Neosho Tel. Co., 126 S.W. 773 (Mo. 1910), *overruled by* Home Tel. Co. v. Sarcoxie Light & Tel. Co., 139 S.W. 108 (Mo. 1911).
several others didn't: *See, e.g.,* Pacific Tel. & Tel. Co. v. Anderson, 196 F. 699 (E.D. Wash. 1912).

144   **jurisdiction of the ICC:** Commerce Court (Mann-Elkins) Act, Pub. L. No. 218, ch. 309, §7, 36 Stat. 539 (1910) (codified as amended at 49 U.S.C.A. §1 et seq.).
when the FCC so ordered: Communications Act of 1934, 43 Stat 1064 (1934) (codified at 47 U.S.C.A. §201(a)).
Carterfone decision of 1968: Use of the Carterphone Service in Message Toll Telephone Services, 13 F.C.C.2d 430 (1967).

145   **interconnect with MCI's long-distance services:** Decision, Application of Microwave Communications, Inc. for Construction Permits to Establish New Facilities in the Domestic Public Point-to-Point Microwave Radio Service at Chicago, Ill. 18 F.C.C.2d 953 (1969).

independently of the breakup: *See, e.g.,* Report and Order, An Inquiry into the Use of the Bands 825–845 MHz and 870–890 MHz for Cellular Communications Systems, 86 F.C.C.2d 469, 495–496 (1981).

feared that Bell would monopolize: *See* Ithiel de Sola Pool, Technologies of Freedom at 136 (1983).

common carrier obligations on broadcasters: 47 U.S.C.A. §153(h).

commercial messages to fill them: *See* Policy Statement, Petition for Issuance of Policy Statement or Notice of Inquiry on Part-Time Programming, 82 F.C.C.2d 107 n. 2 (1980).

time brokering might be tolerated: Findings of Fact and Conclusions of the Commission, Metropolitan Broadcasting Corp. et al., 8 F.C.C. 557 (1941).

broker was forbidden: Decision, Application of Continental Broadcasting, Inc., 15 F.C.C.2d 120, 127 (1968).

too much like a phone company: *See* Policy Statement, Petition for Issuance of Policy Statement or Notice of Inquiry on Part-Time Programming, 82 F.C.C.2d 107, 120 (1980); Decision, Applications of Fresno FM Limited Partnership, et al., 6 F.C.C. Rec. 1570, 1572 (1991); Report and Order, Revision of Radio Rules and Policy, 7 F.C.C. Rec. 2755, 2773–2778 (1992); 47 C.F.R. §73.3556.

146   **importance to the public:** Great Lakes Broadcasting v. Federal Radio Comm'n, 3 F.R.C. Ann. Rep. 32, 33 (1929).

centrally in every proceeding: *See, e.g.,* Trinity Methodist Church, South v. Federal Radio Comm'n, 62 F.2d 850 (D.C. Cir. 1932).

Fairness Doctrine in 1949: Report of the Commission, Editorializing by Broadcast Licensees, 13 F.C.C. 1246 (1949).

if no one else would: *See* Dempsey v. Albuquerque Broadcasting Co., 6 Rad. Reg. (P & F) 615 (1950).

147   **amendments to the Communications Act:** 47 U.S.C. §312(a)(7). Congress did not, however, expressly codify the fairness doctrine. *See* Telecommunications Research and Action Ctr. v. FCC, 801 F.2d 501, 516–517 (D.C. Cir. 1986).

First Amendment principle at all: Red Lion Broadcasting Co. v. FCC, 395 U.S. 367 (1969).

codified the doctrine in 1959: Fairness Report, The Handling of Public Issues Under the Fairness Doctrine and the Public Interest Standards of the Communications Act, 48 F.C.C.2d 1 (1974).

engaged the Fairness Doctrine, too: *See* Fairness Report, The Handling of Public Issues under the Fairness Doctrine and the Public Interest Standards of the Communications Act, 48 F.C.C.2d 1, 24 (1974).

limited its holding to cigarettes: Complaint Directed to WCBS-TV, New York, NY, Concerning Fairness Doctrine, 8 F.C.C.2d 381 (1967).

federal appellate court affirmed: Banzhaf v. FCC, 405 F.2d 1082 (D.C. Cir. 1968).

court overruled: Friends of the Earth v. FCC, 449 F.2d 1164 (D.C. Cir. 1971).

147   **controversial issue of public importance:** Fairness Report, The Han-
        dling of Public Issues under the Fairness Doctrine and the Public Interest
        Standards of the Communications Act, 48 F.C.C.2d 1, 23, 26 (1974).
        court affirmed: Public Interest Research Group v. FCC, 522 F.2d 1060
        (1st Cir. 1975).
        FCC threw in the towel: Report and Order, Deregulation of Radio, 84
        F.C.C.2d 968 (1981).
        the First Amendment, too: Report, Inquiry into Section 73.1910 of the
        Commission's Rules and Regulations Concerning the General Fairness
        Doctrine Obligations of Broadcast Licensees, 102 F.C.C.2d 145, 196–217
        (1985).
        pending a two-year review: *See* Continuing Appropriations for 1987,
        Pub. L. No. 500, 100 Stat. 1783 (1986).
        Judge Bork shredded the scarcity logic: Telecommunications Research
        and Action Ctr. v. FCC, 801 F.2d 501, 508, 517 (D.C. Cir. 1986). *See* Red
        Lion Broadcasting Co. v. FCC, 395 U.S. 367 (1969).

148   **Fairness Doctrine from scratch:** Meredith Corp. v. FCC, 809 F.2d 863
        (D.C. Cir. 1987).
        unconstitutional to boot: Syracuse Peace Council, 63 Rad. Reg. 2d (P &
        F) 541 (1987).
        declined to reach the second: Syracuse Peace Council v. FCC, 867 F.2d
        654 (D.C. Cir. 1989).
        reinstating the Fairness Doctrine: Fairness in Broadcasting Act of 1987,
        H.R. 1934, S.742, 100th Cong., 1st Sess. (1987).
        Reagan vetoed it: *See* Veto of the Fairness in Broadcasting Act of 1987,
        Message to the Senate Returning S.742 Without Approval, 23 Weekly
        Comp. Pres. Doc. 715 (June 19, 1987).
        Commission declined: Memorandum Opinion and Order, Frontier
        Broadcasting Co. v. Collier, 24 F.C.C. 251, 255 (1958).
        households not served by cable: Decision, Application of Carter Moun-
        tain Transmission Corp., 32 F.C.C. 459, 464–465 (1962).
        import distant broadcast signals: First Report and Order, Amendment
        of Subpart L, Part 11, to Adopt Rules and Regulations to Govern the
        Grant of Authorization in the Business Radio Services for Microwave Sta-
        tions to Relay Television Signals to Community Antenna Systems, 38
        F.C.C. 683, 713–714 (1965).
        broadcast signals of any kind: Second Report and Order, Amendment of
        Subpart L, Part 91, to Adopt Rules and Regulations to Govern the Grant
        of Authorizations in the Business Radio Service for Microwave Stations for
        Relay Signals for Community Antenna Systems, 2 F.C.C.2d 725, 746,
        752–753 (1966).

149   **should fit in the marketplace:** Notice of Inquiry, Inquiry into the Eco-
        nomic Relationship between Television Broadcasting and Cable Televi-
        sion, 65 F.C.C.2d 9, 14 (1977).
        survived intact for the next decade: Report, Inquiry into the Economic
        Relationship Between Television Broadcasting and Cable Television, 71
        F.C.C.2d 632, 653 (1979).
        cable service was not common carriage: 47 U.S.C.A. §541(c).
        on its electronic pages: Century Communications Corp. v. FCC, 835
        F.2d 292 (D.C. Cir. 1987).

149 **rules against constitutional challenge:** Cable Television Consumer Protection Act of 1992, H.R. Rep. No. 862, 102d Cong., 2d. Sess. §2(a)(16) (1992).

commercial stations are to be carried: 47 U.S.C.A. §534(b)(6).

"retransmission consent" rights if they prefer: 47 U.S.C.A. §325(b)(1).

tenuous hold on life: Turner Broadcasting System v. FCC, 810 F. Supp. 1308 (D.D.C. 1992), *vacated and remanded,* 114 S. Ct.2445 (1994), *reh'g denied,* 115 S. Ct. 30 (1994), *claim dismissed, summ. judgment granted on remand,* Turner Broadcasting v. FCC, 910 F. Supp. 734, 1995 U.S. Dist. LEXIS 18611 (D.D.C. 1995), *petition for cert. filed,* Dec. 21, 1995.

"public, educational, and government" (PEG) purposes: 47 U.S.C.A. §531.

outright lease to independent programmers: 47 U.S.C.A. §532.

subject to the Fairness Doctrine, too: First Report and Order, Amendment of Part 74 Subpart K of the Commission's Rules and Regulations Relative to Community Antenna Television Systems, 20 F.C.C.2d 201 (1969).

150 **do not control the content at all:** Order, Amendment of Part 76 of the Commission's Rules and Regulations Concerning the Cable Television Channel Capacity and Access Channel Requirements of Section 76.251, 83 F.C.C.2d 147, 148 (1980).

"essential facilities" doctrine: United States v. Terminal Railroad Association, 224 U.S. 383 (1912).

between Chicago and St. Louis: Decision, Applications of Microwave Communications, Inc. for Construction Permits to Establish New Facilities in the Domestic Public Point-to-Point Microwave Radio Service at Chicago, Ill., St. Louis, Mo., and Intermediate Points, 18 F.C.C.2d 953, 966 (1969).

AT&T had refused in bad faith: MCI v. AT&T, 708 F.2d 1081, 1132-1133 (7th Cir. 1982).

federal district judge found for AT&T: Southern Pacific Comm. Co. v. AT&T, 556 F. Supp. 825, 1096-1199 (D.D.C. 1983).

not required to interconnect with MCI: A federal appellate court agreed. Southern Pacific Comm. Co. v. AT&T, 740 F.2d 980 (D.C. Cir. 1984).

breakup of the Bell System a decade later: Indeed, MCI shared its discovery materials with the federal government. *See* AT&T v. Grady, 594 F.2d 594 (7th Cir. 1978).

blanket immunity from the antitrust laws: United States v. AT&T, 524 F. Supp. 1336, 1347–1348, 1352–1353 (D.D.C. 1981).

151 **Judge Greene announced a similar requirement:** Order, United States v. Western Elec. Co., No. 82-0192 (D.D.C. Aug. 24, 1982).

was shoehorned in later on: United States v. Western Elec. Co., 673 F. Supp. 525 (1987).

152 **already in place for terminal equipment:** First Report and Order, Proposals for New or Revised Classes of Interstate and Foreign Message Toll Telephone Service (MTS) and Wide Area Telephone Service (WATS), 56 F.C.C.2d 593 (1975).

wireless phone service: Inquiry into the Use of the Bands 825–845 MHz for Cellular Communications Systems, 89 F.C.C.2d 58, 80–82 (1982);

Amendment of the Commission's Rules to Establish New Personal Communications Services, 7 F.C.C. Rec. 5676, 5715 (1992).

152   **competitive access providers:** Report and Order and Notice of Proposed Rulemaking, Expanded Interconnection with Local Telephone Company Facilities, 7 F.C.C. Rec. 7369, 7381 (1992); Second Report and Order and Third Notice of Proposed Rulemaking, Expanded Interconnection with Local Telephone Company Facilities, 8 F.C.C. Rec. 7374 (1993); Memorandum Opinion and Order, Expanded Interconnection with Local Telephone Company Facilities, 9 F.C.C. Rec. 5154 (1994).

Open Network Architecture proceeding: Report and Order, Amendment of Section 64.702 of the Commission's Rule and Regulations (Third Computer Inquiry), 104 F.C.C.2d 958 (1986), *vacated*, California v. FCC, 905 F.2d 1217 (9th Cir. 1990).

makes unbundling the key thing: Telecommunications Act of 1996 §151(a) (to be codified at 47 U.S.C. §271(c)(2)(b)).

Chapter 13

157   **banned cable/broadcast cross-ownership:** *See* Notice of Inquiry, Acquisition by Television Licensees, Community Antenna Television Systems, 29 Fed. Reg. 5,416 (1964). The Commission determined that restrictions on such ownership were not warranted at that time, and the issue was treated on an ad hoc basis for several years. *See, e.g.,* Decision, Applications of Lorain Community Broadcasting et al., 13 F.C.C.2d 106 (1968). The FCC has granted limited waivers to these vertical restrictions when the network's request is for areas outside the local service area of television stations licensed to it. *See* Memorandum Opinion and Order, CBS Inc., Petition for Special Relief, 87 F.C.C.2d 587 (1981).

codified the ban in 1984: 47 U.S.C.A. §533(a). A federal appellate court upheld the ban against First Amendment challenge in 1986. Marsh Media, Ltd. v. FCC, 798 F.2d 772, 776–777 (5th Cir. 1986).

directs the FCC to revise its rules: Telecommunications Act of 1996, Pub. L. No. 104-104, §§202(f), 202(i)(1), 110 Stat. 56 (1996). *See* Peter W. Huber, Michael Kellogg, and John Thorne, The Telecommunications Act of 1996 §2.2.3 (1996).

Chapter 14

165   **every form of diseased intelligence:** George Orwell, Benefits of Clergy: Some Notes on Salvador Dali, in Decline of the English Murder and Other Essays at 27 (1953).

166   **lascivious, filthy, or indecent:** 47 U.S.C.A. §223; Denver Area Educ. Telecoms. Consortium, Inc. v. FCC, 116 S. Ct. 2374 (1996).

obscene materials from the mails: *See* Public Clearing House v. Coyne, 194 U.S. 497, 507 (1904); Enterprise Sav. Ass'n v. Zurnstein, 67 F. 1000, 1004 (6th Cir. 1895); United States v. Wilson, 58 F. 768 (N.D. Cal. 1893); United States v. Gaylord, 17 F. 438 (S.D. Ill. 1803); United States v. Loftis, 12 F. 671 (D. Or. 1802).

166   **six million calls a month:** *See* Sable Communication of California, Inc. v. FCC, 492 U.S. 115, 120, n. 3 (1989).

no law barred dial-a-porn: Application for Review of Complaint Filed by Peter F. Cohalan, FCC File No. E-83-14, May 13, 1983.

immediately passed one that did: 47 U.S.C.A. §223(b).

part of that law as unconstitutional: Carlin Communications, Inc. v. FCC, 837 F.2d 546 (2d Cir. 1988).

Congress passed another: 47 U.S.C.A. §223(b).

power to censor broadcasts: Radio Act of 1927 §29, codified at 47 U.S.C.A. §109, repealed June 19, 1934, c. 652, §602(a), 48 Stat. 1102 (1934).

profane language on the air: Radio Act of 1927 §§14, 33. *See also* 18 U.S.C.A. §1464.

fourteen kinds of unacceptable material: *See generally* C. Sterling and J. Kittross, Stay Tuned: A Concise History of American Broadcasting at 189 (1978).

small, mostly urban stations: *See* Memorandum Opinion and Order, Sonderling Broadcasting Corp., 41 F.C.C.2d 777.

how-to discussion of oral sex: Sonderling Broadcasting Corp., 27 Rad. Reg. 2d. (P & F) 285 (1973).

never to be uttered on radio or television: *See* FCC v. Pacifica Foundation, 438 U.S. 726 (1978).

may be in the audience: Memorandum Opinion and Order, Citizen's Complaint Against Pacifica Foundation Station WBAI (FM), New York, N.Y. Declaratory Order, 56 F.C.C.2d 98 (1975).

a ban round the clock: Pub. L. No. 459, §608, 102 Stat. 2228 (1988).

rulings flew thick and fast: *See* John Thorne, Peter W. Huber, and Michael K. Kellogg, Federal Broadband Law §11.9 (1995).

"good character" of licensees: 47 U.S.C.A. §§308(b), 319(a); 47 C.F.R. §73.24(d).

167   **members of the family find a place:** *See* Application of Great Lakes Broadcasting Co., 3 FRC Annual Rep. 32 (1929), *quoted in* Charles D. Ferris, Frank W. Lloyd and Thomas J. Casey, Cable Television Law §2.06[2][a] (1993).

cars, tobacco, and nuclear power: Report and Order (Proceeding Terminated), Deregulation of Radio, 84 F.C.C.2d 968 (1981).

to a bottle in front of me: Broadcast of Programs Advertising Alcoholic Beverages, Letter to Senator Edwin C. Johnson, 43 F.C.C. 446 (1949).

regulate advertising of lotteries: Use of Sirens and Other Alarming Sound Effects in Announcements, 26 F.C.C.2d 275 (1970); Policy Statement and Memorandum Opinion and Order, Elimination of Unnecessary Broadcast Regulation, 54 Rad. Reg. 2d (P & F) 1043 (1983).

horse races: Report and Order, Elimination of Unnecessary Broadcast Regulation, 56 Rad. Reg. 2d (P & F) 976 (1984).

cigarettes: 15 U.S.C.A. §1335.

advertising of any kind: *See, e.g.,* FCC, Public Service Responsibility of Broadcast Licensees, Report by Federal Communications Commission (Mar. 7, 1946).

program-length "infomercials": Public Notice, Applicability of Commission Policies on Program-Length Commercials, 44 F.C.C.2d 985 (1974).

167   **advertising aimed at children:** H.R. 1677, 101st Cong., 2nd Sess., Pub. L. No. 437 (1990).

educate the nation's youth: *See* Edmund L. Andrews, "Flintstones" and Programs Like It Aren't Educational, F.C.C. Says, New York Times, Mar. 4, 1993 at A1.

curtailed that power a bit: 47 U.S.C.A. §§544, 545(a)(1)(B), 545(b)(3), 546(c)(1).

also barred cable indecency: Cable Television Report and Order, Amendment of Part 74, Subpart K, of the Commission's Rules and Regulations Relating to Community Antenna Television Systems, 36 F.C.C.2d 143, 238 (1972).

in the manner of *Wayne's World:* 47 U.S.C.A. §532(b).

giveaway channels as well: 47 C.F.R. §76.215.

168   **said that was unconstitutional:** Midwest Video Corp. v. FCC, 571 F.2d 1025, 1057 (8th Cir. 1978).

talk show featuring porn stars: Suzanne Oliver, The Porn Mandate, Forbes, August 28, 1995 at 46.

transmissions from public access channels: Pub. L. No. 385, §10(c), 28,106 Stat. 1460, 1486 (1992); 47 U.S.C.A. §531 (Historical and Statutory Notes).

keep it off leased channels: 47 U.S.C.A. §532(h).

authorized more of the same: Communications Decency Act of 1996, Publ. L. No. 104-104, §506, 110 Stat. 56 (1996) (to be codified at 47 U.S.C. §531(e)). *See* Peter W. Huber, Michael Kellogg, and John Thorne, The Telecommunications Act of 1996 §4.3 (1995).

socialist magazines from the mails: Ex parte Jackson, 96 U.S. 727 (1877).

however else it pleased: Public Clearing House v. Coyne, 194 U.S. 497, 506 (1904).

depraved pages of Esquire magazine: Hannegan v. Esquire, 327 U.S. 146 (1945).

Once rationing by commission is accepted: National Broadcasting Company v. United States, 319 U.S. 190 (1943).

courts had upheld general content prescriptions: *See* KFKB Broadcasting Ass'n, Inc. v. FRC, 47 F.2d 670 (D.C. Cir. 1931).

unanimously, in 1969: Red Lion Broadcasting Co. v. FCC, 395 U.S. 367 (1969).

169   **High Court approved:** FCC v. Pacifica Foundation, 438 U.S. 726, 749 (1978).

upheld cable censorship accordingly: *See* Black Hills Video Corp. v. FCC, 399 F.2d 65 (8th Cir. 1968); Community Communication Company, Inc. v. City of Boulder, 660 F.2d 1370 (10th Cir. 1981).

one court pointed out in 1985: Cruz v. Ferre, 755 F.2d 1415, 1420 n. 6 (11th Cir. 1985).

cable under the broadcast precedent: Turner Broadcasting System, Inc. v. FCC, 114 S. Ct. 2445, 2457, 2460 (1994).

struck down a dial-a-porn ban: Sable Communications v. FCC, 492 U.S. 115 (1989).

169   **Supreme Court is poised to review:** American Civil Liberties Union v. Janet Reno, 929 F. Supp. 824 (E.D. Pa. 1996).

170   **Supreme Court failed even to note:** In 1996, in yet another tangle of concurrences and dissents, the High Court struck down some provisions of the 1992 Cable Act that simply returned to cable operators the power to censor indecency on public-access and leased access channels. The Court upheld a similar return of control over indecency on commercially leased channels. Denver Area Educ. Telcoms. Consortium, Inc. v. FCC, 116 S. Ct. 2374 (1996).

171   **to be installed in televisions:** Communications Decency Act of 1996 §551(c) (to be codified at 47 U.S.C. §303(x)). *See* Peter W. Huber, Michael Kellogg, and John Thorne, The Telecommunications Act of 1996 §4.2 (1996).

        block coded programs: *See* James Heavey, Decisions on TV Violence, San Francisco Examiner, Feb. 3, 1994 at A-16.

        some degree of "time, place, and manner": Perry Education Ass'n v. Perry Local Educators' Ass'n, 460 U.S. 37, 45 (1983).

        audience is likely to react: Chaplinsky v. New Hampshire, 315 U.S. 568, 571-573 (1942).

172   **"contemporary community standards":** Miller v. California, 413 U.S. 15, 24 (1973).

        unite residents of both: *See* United States v. Thomas, Dkt. No. 94-20019 (W.D. Tenn. July 28, 1994).

        cripple the media themselves: Sable Communications of California, Inc. v. FCC, 492 U.S. 115, 125 (1989).

        state anti-obscenity statute: Ala. Code §13A-I 2-200.2 (1989).

        has acknowledged as much: Sable Communications v. FCC, 492 U.S. 115, 128 (1989).

        outside that network community: *But see* Paris Adult Theatre I, et al. v. Slaton, 413 U.S. 49 (1973).

173   **but blocked to all viewers in 39000:** This is technically feasible; some for-pay satellite subscriptions are already sold only to viewers in zip codes where cable television is not available. *See* 17 U.S.C.A. §119(a)(2)(B).

        a few modest steps in this direction: Communications Decency Act of 1996 §509 (to be codified at 47 U.S.C. §230). *See* Peter W. Huber, Michael Kellogg, and John Thorne, The Telecommunications Act of 1996 §4.1.2 (1996).

        copycat crime four days later: *See* Olivia N. v. Nat'l Broadcasting Co., Inc., 126 Col. App. 3d 488 (1981).

174   **may disturb the public peace:** The Works of Benjamin Franklin at 134 (J. Bigelow ed. 1907).

        discrimination in a commercial context: Suits for "negligent publication" are also speech-related, although these generally assert the creation of a physical danger as well as reputational harm. Braun v. Soldier of Fortune Magazine, Inc., 968 F.2d 1110 (11th Cir. 1992).

        suit brought by a public official in Montgomery, Alabama: New York Times Co. v. Sullivan, 376 U.S. 254 (1964).

175   **not just government officials:** Curtis Publ. Co. v. Butts, 388 U.S. 130 (1967).

175   **definition of "public figure":** Gertz v. Robert Welch, Inc., 418 U.S. 323 (1974).

               Producers of a movie about gangs: Bill v. Superior Court, 137 Cal. App. 3d 1002 (1982).

               causal nexus was too speculative: Zamora v. Columbia Broadcasting System, 480 F. Supp. 199, 202 (S.D. Fla. 1979).

               third driver into a fatal accident: Weirum v. RKO General, Inc., 539 P.2d 36 (Cal. 1975).

               have in the libel cases: Brandenburg v. State of Ohio, 395 U.S. 444, 447 (1969); Schenk v. United States, 249 U.S. 47, 52 (1919); Dennis v. United States, 341 U.S. 494 (1951); Hess v. State of Indiana, 414 U.S. 105, 108 (1973).

               even from private tort suits: R.A.V. v. City of Saint Paul, 112 S. Ct. 2538, 2547 (1992).

               shown on the *Mickey Mouse Club* show: Walt Disney Productions, Inc. v. Shannon, 276 S.E.2d 580 (Ga. 1981).

               the *Born Innocent* case: Olivia N. v. Nat'l Broadcasting Co., Inc., 126 Col. App. 3d 488 (1981).

               stunt he saw on the *Tonight Show*: DeFilippo v. National Broadcasting Co., 446 A.2d 1036 (R.I. 1982).

177   **the chorus of raspberries:** George Orwell, The Art of Donald McGill, *in* George Orwell: A Collection of Essays at 114 (1946).

Chapter 15

178   **implies a right to exclude:** White-Smith Music Publishing Co. v. Apollo Co., 209 U.S. 1, 19 (1908).

               assign it to others: A Transcript of the Registers of the Worshipful Company of Stationers, 1640–1708 A.D. at 494–496 (Eyre and Rivington eds., 1914).

               the times therein mentioned: 8 Anne, c. 19 (1710). The statute granted copyright protection to new books in fourteen-year increments.

               that inheres in copyright: U.S. Const. art. I, §8, cl. 8.

               to perform or display it: 17 U.S.C.A. §§101, 102(a)(1)-(8), 106(1), (3)-(5), 117.

179   **doctrine was first articulated:** Folsom v. Marsh, 9 F. Cas. 342 (D. Mass. 1841).

               codified it in 1976: 17 U.S.C.A. §110.

               majority of the Court concluded: Sony Corp. v. Universal City Studios, Inc., 464 U.S. 417, 423 (1984).

180   **hinged instead on a common-law tort:** International News Service v. The Associated Press, 248 U.S. 215, 239, 250 (1918).

               it can be done again: *See* RCA Mfg. Co. v. Whiteman, 114 F.2d 86 (2d Cir. 1940)

               codified it in 1976: 17 U.S.C.A. §111(a)(3).

               broadcast is a "public performance": Jerome H. Remick & Co. v. American Automobile Accessories, 5 F.2d 411 (6th Cir. 1925).

181   **pay record companies:** Act of July 17, 1952, 66 Stat. 752 (1952) (amending §1(c) of the 1909 Act).

181 **right in her recorded songs:** 17 U.S.C.A. §§402, 114.

movies that they don't own: *See* 17 U.S.C.A. §106(4).

to all rooms in the hotel: Buck v. Jewell-LaSalle Realty Corp., 283 U.S. 191, 199 n.5 (1931).

Supreme Court in 1975: Twentieth Century Music Corp. v. Aiken, 422 U.S. 151 (1975).

Congress agreed that small commercial establishments: H.R. Rep. No. 1476 at 8, 94th Cong., 2d Sess. 52 (1976), *reprinted in* 1976 U.S.C.C.A.N. 5659.

no charge within their buildings: 17 U.S.C.A. §111(a)(1).

been blacked out locally: National Football League v. McBee & Bruno's, Inc., 621 F. Supp. 880 (D. Mo. 1985).

bar had gone too far: National Football League v. McBee & Bruno's, Inc., 792 F.2d 726, 731 (8th Cir. 1986).

182 *Fortnightly v. United Artists Television:* 392 U.S. 390, 392 n.6, 399 (1968).

Teleprompter Corp. v. CBS: 415 U.S. 394 (1974).

183 **not one it could resolve:** *See* Second Further Notice of Proposed Rule-making, Amendment of Part 74, Subpart K, of the Commission's Rules and Regulations Relative to Community Antenna Television Systems, 24 F.C.C.2d 580 585, 589 (App. A) (1970).

sharp limits on cable's right: Notice of Proposed Rulemaking and Notice of Inquiry, Amendment of Part 74, Subpart K of the Commission's Rules and Regulations Relative to Community Antenna Television Systems, 15 F.C.C.2d 417, 461 (1968).

"break new ground": "Letter of Intent" to Congress, Commission Proposals for Regulation of Cable Television, 31 F.C.C.2d 115, 117 (1971).

abandoned retransmission consent: Cable Television Report and Order, Amendment of Part 74, Subpart K, of the Commission's Rules and Regulations Relative to Community Antenna Television Systems, 36 F.C.C.2d 143, 153, 173–175 (1972).

rules covering cable imports of syndicated: Cable Television Report and Order, Amendment of Part 74, Subpart K, of the Commission's Rules and Regulations Relative to Community Antenna Television Systems, 36 F.C.C.2d 143, 165–170 (1972).

FCC began to amend and backtrack: *See, e.g.,* Report and Order, Amendment of Part 76, Subpart F of the Commission's Rules and Regulations to Exempt Smaller Cable Television Systems, 55 F.C.C.2d 529, 536–537 (1975).

were just too cumbersome: H.R. Rep. No. 1476 at 89, 94th Cong., 2d Sess. 52 (1976), *reprinted in* 1976 U.S.C.C.A.N. 5659.

Commission-prescribed prices: 17 U.S.C.A. §111.

Copyright Royalty Tribunal: 17 U.S.C.A. §§801-810 (1976) (now codified at 17 U.S.C.A. §§801–803). The Royalty Tribunal's functions were quietly transferred to the Copyright Office and the Librarian of Congress in 1993, but the basic rate-setting and distribution scheme remained the same. Copyright Royalty Tribunal Act of 1993, 103 Pub. L. No. 198, 1993 HR 2840, 107 Stat 2304 (1993) (codified at 17 U.S.C.A. §803 et seq.).

184 **royalty fee schedules:** 17 U.S.C.A. §111(d)(1)(B).

184   **adjustments as deemed appropriate:** 17 U.S.C.A. §§801, 803.

gross receipts from subscribers: 17 U.S.C.A. §111(d)(1)(B)(i).

Each then pays a bit more: 17 U.S.C.A. §111(f).

in contracting with the networks: *See* H.R. Rep. No. 1476 at 90, 94th Cong., 2d Sess. 52 (1976), *reprinted in* 1976 U.S.C.C.A.N. 5659.

Receipts are distributed: 17 U.S.C.A. §111(d)(2), (3).

takes three to five years: *See* National Ass'n of Broadcasters v. CRT, 675 F.2d 367 (D.C. Cir. 1982).

3.25 percent to television stations: The remaining fees were distributed among public television broadcasters (5.25 percent), and music claimants (4.5 percent). *See* National Ass'n of Broadcasters v. CRT, 675 F.2d 367 (D.C. Cir. 1982).

this allocation in 1982: National Ass'n of Broadcasters v. CRT, 675 F.2d 367 (D.C. Cir. 1982).

again upheld the award: National Ass'n of Broadcasters v. CRT, 809 F.2d 172 (2d Cir. 1986).

$30 billion market for cable-delivered video programming: *See* Report, Compulsory Copyright License for Cable Retransmission, 4 F.C.C. Rec. 6711 (1989).

absent contractual agreement: 47 U.S.C.A. §325(b)(2).

whatever the market will bear: Report and Order, Implementation of the Cable Television Consumer Protection and Competition Act of 1992, 8 F.C.C. Rec. 2965, 3004–3006 (1993).

cable channels that they owned: *See* New News Channel; Cable Believes CBS Surrender Ends Retransmission Consent War, Comm. Daily, Aug. 27, 1993 at 2.

185   **wire and radio transmissions:** 47 U.S.C.A. §605(a).

police or fire department dispatches: *See* Lavritz S. Helland, Section 705(a) in the Modern Communications World: A Response to Di Geronimo, 40 Fed. Com. B. J. 115 (1988).

was expressly permitted: 47 U.S.C.A. §605(a).

FCC grudgingly allowed some stations: Report and Order, Amendment of Parts 2, 3 and 4 of the Commission's Rules and Regulations and the Standards of Good Engineering Practice, 11 Rad. Reg. (P & F) 1590, 1599 (1956).

sued the manufacturers of decoders: *See* ON/TV of Chicago v. Julien, 763 F.2d 839 (7th Cir. 1985).

1934 Act permitted interception: 47 U.S.C.A. §605(a).

subscription television a "broadcast" service: Further Notice of Proposed Rulemaking and Notice of Inquiry, Amendment of Part 73 of the Commission's Rules and Regulations (Radio Broadcast Services) to Provide for Subscription Television Service, 3 F.C.C.2d 1, 9 (1966).

pay-TV operators were protected anyway: Federal Communication Commission Public Notice, 43 Fed. Reg. 46,581 (1978).

courts eventually agreed: *See, e.g.,* California Satellite Systems v. Seimon, 767 F.2d 1364 (9th Cir. 1985) *and cases cited therein.*

turned on the operator's intent: *See, e.g.,* National Subscription Television v. S&H TV, 644 F.2d 820, 824–825 (9th Cir. 1981).

those who "assist in receiving": *See, e.g.,* United States v. Beale, 681 F. Supp. 74, 75 (D. Me. 1988).

185   **device is ultimately used to intercept:** *See, e.g.,* Chartwell Communications Group v. Westbrook, 637 F.2d 459, 465, 467 (6th Cir. 1980).
        includes criminal sanctions: 47 U.S.C.A. §501.

186   **personal use as well as commercial use:** 47 U.S.C.A. §605.
        broader than ordinary copyright: The Electronic Communications and Privacy Act of 1986 (ECPA), 18 U.S.C.A. §2512(1)(b). *See* United States v. Herring, 993 F.2d 784, 789 (11th Cir. 1993) *and cases cited therein.*
        Congress endorsed these legal developments: *See* 130 Cong. Rec. S14,287 (Oct. 11, 1984) (statement of Sen. Packwood), *reprinted in* 1984 U.S.C.C.A.N. at 4746.
        raised the civil and criminal penalties: 47 U.S.C.A. §605(e)(1).
        gave private parties expanded authority: 47 U.S.C.A. §605(e)(3)(A).
        were prohibited by the wiretap laws: FCC, Public Notice, 43 Fed. Reg. 46,581 (1978).
        NFL sued sports bars: *See, e.g.,* National Football League v. Cousin Hugo's, Inc., 600 F. Supp. 84, 87 (E.D. Mo. 1984).
        "satellite cable programming": 47 U.S.C.A. §605(d)(1).
        establishes a system for selling it: 47 U.S.C.A. §605(b).
        cable networks promptly did both: *See* Report, Inquiry into the Scrambling of Satellite Signals, 2 F.C.C. Rec. 1669, 1689-1694 (1987).
        copy-tap protections to cable: *See, e.g.,* Ciminelli v. Cablevision, 583 F. Supp. 158, 164 (E.D.N.Y. 1984) *and cases cited therein.*
        Congress followed suit in 1984: 47 U.S.C.A. §553(a)-(b).

187   **is still identified as HBO:** *See, e.g.,* Herald Publishing Co. v. Florida Antennavision, Inc., 173 So. 2d 469, 473–474 (Fla. Dist. Ct. App. 1965).
        courts have been more liberal: *See, e.g.,* Data Cash Systems Inc. v. JS&A Group, Inc., 480 F. Supp. 1063, 1070 (N.D. Ill. 1979).
        display HBO programming in Denver: American Television and Communications Corp. v. Manning, 651 P.2d 440 (Colo. Ct. App. 1982).
        a related precedent: KMLA Broadcasting Corp. v. 20th Century Cigarette Vendors Corp., 264 F. Supp. 35, 44 (C.D. Cal. 1967).
        misappropriation had been established: American Television and Communications Corp. v. Manning, 651 P.2d 440, 444 (Colo. Ct. App. 1982).

Chapter 16

190   **disagreeable person keep his distance:** Ambrose Bierce, The Devil's Dictionary at 257 (1978).

191   **repeated, or nonconsensual calls:** *See* Annotation, Validity, Construction, and Application of State Criminal Statute Forbidding Use of Telephone to Annoy or Harass, 95 A.L.R.3d 411 (1979).
        ring, with intent to harass: 47 U.S.C.A. §223(a)(1).
        conduct that would be protected: NAACP v. Button, 371 U.S. 415, 433 (1963).
        bars automatically dialed: Automated Telephone Consumer Protection Act, Pub. L. No. 243 (1991) (codified at 47 U.S.C.A. §228).
        ordinarily object to receiving: S. Rep. No. 177, 102d Cong., 2nd Sess. at 5–6 (1991).
        consistent with the free speech protections: Automated Telephone Consumer Protection Act §2(13), Pub. L. No. 243 (1991). Students of his-

tory may be forgiven, however, for fearing that this is not absolutely certain to occur.

192   **no general rules of this kind:** *See* Bigelow v. Virginia, 421 U.S. 809 (1975); Virginia Bd. of Pharmacy v. Virginia Consumer Council, 425 U.S. 748 (1976).

   unwanted solicitation on the rebound: *See* Glenn C. Smith, We've Got Your Number! (Is It Constitutional to Give It Out?): Caller Identification and the Right to Informational Privacy, 37 U.C.L.A. L. Rev. 145, 149 (1989).

   Pennsylvania Supreme Court concluded: Barasch v. PUC, 529 Pa. 523 (1992). The Pennsylvania General Assembly passed a law in 1993 that permits Caller ID service, but only if it allows callers to block their numbers on both a per-call and a per-line basis. 66 Pa. Cons. Stat. §2906 (1996).

   have supported the service: Sylvia Moreno, Public Hearings Place Caller ID Service on Hold Privacy, Price to Be Reviewed, Dallas Morning News, Aug. 1, 1993 at 45A.

   mandated the passage of interstate Caller ID: Memorandum Opinion and Order on Reconsideration, Second Report and Order and Third Notice of Proposed Rulemaking, In the Matter of Rules and Policies Regarding Calling Number Identification Service—Caller ID, 10 F.C.C. Rec. 11700 (1995).

   installation the accepted norm: *See* Encryption Standards and Procedures Act of 1994, H.R. 5199, 103rd Cong., 2nd. Sess. §103(b)(2), (3) (1994).

193   **purchased for unclassified communications:** E. Kennedy, Office of Technology Assessment, Protect Personal Property, Congressional Press Releases, Sep. 23, 1994.

   the Digital Telephony Act: Communications Assistance for Law Enforcement Act, Pub. L. No. 414, 108 Stat. 4279 (1994).

   substance, purport, effect, or meaning: 47 U.S.C.A. §605(a).

   a new Wiretap Act: Wire Interception and Interception of Oral Communications, 18 U.S.C.A. §§2510–2520 (1970).

   oral communications may be authorized: S. Rep. 1097, *reprinted in* 1968 U.S.C.C.A.N. 2112, 2153.

   by anyone but common carriers: 18 U.S.C.A. §2510(1) (1988).

   store's in-house phone system: United States v. Christman, 375 F. Supp. 1354 (N.D. Cal. 1974).

   protect all "electronic communications": 18 U.S.C.A. §2510(12) (1988).

   cordless phones still weren't covered: 18 U.S.C.A. §2510(1), (12)(A) (1988).

   intercepting cellular phones: The Telephone Disclosure and Dispute Resolution Act of 1992, Pub. L. No. 556, 106 Stat. 4181 (1992), codified at 15 U.S.C.A. §§5701, 5711-5714, 5721-5724, 47 U.S.C.A. §§227, 228, 302a.

195   **"search" or "seizure" at all:** Olmstead v. United States, 277 U.S. 438, 464–466 (1928).

   wrote a foreboding dissent: Olmstead v. United States, 277 U.S. 438, 474 (1928) (Brandeis, J., dissenting).

195 **any Fourth Amendment concern, either:** Goldman v. United States, 316 U.S. 129, 134–136 (1942).

"reasonable expectation of privacy": Katz v. United States, 389 U.S. 347, 351 (1967).

the publicity side of privacy: Whalen v. Roe, 429 U.S. 589, 599 (1977); Nixon v. Administrator of General Services, 433 U.S. 425, 457 (1977); California Bankers Assn. v. Schultz, 416 U.S. 21 (1974).

196 **right to individual privacy as such:** *See* W. Prosser and R. Keeton, Prosser & Keeton on the Law of Torts §117 at 849 (5th ed. 1984).

splashed across the pages of the Boston tabloids: *See* A. Miller, The Assault on Privacy: Computers, Data Banks, andDossiers at 170 (1971).

article in the Harvard Law Review: Samuel D. Warren and Louis D. Brandeis, The Right to Privacy, 4 Harv. L. Rev. 193 (1890).

still failed to recognize such a tort: *See* Note, Tort Recovery for Invasion of Privacy, 59 Neb. L. Rev. 808, 809–810 (1980).

may evolve out of them: *See, e.g.,* B-W Acceptance Corp. v. Callaway, 162 S.E.2d 430 (Ga. 1968).

an unwitting Marilyn Monroe: *See* W. Prosser and R. Keeton, Prosser & Keeton on the Law of Torts at 809 *(citing* Daily Times Democrat v. Grahm, 162 So.2d 474 (Ala. 1964)).

Unsafe at Any Speed: Nader v. General Motors Corp., 255 N.E.2d 765, 307 (N.Y. 1970).

American citizens and individuals in the Soviet Union: Birnbaum v. United States, 588 F.2d 319 (2d Cir. 1978).

decided in New York in 1902: Roberson v. Rochester Folding Box Co., 64 N.E. 442 (N.Y. 1902).

"Here's Johnny" product: Carson v. Here's Johnny Portable Toilets, Inc., 698 F.2d 831 (6th Cir. 1983).

197 **aired it on the local news:** Zacchini v. Scripps-Howard Broadcasting Co., 433 U.S. 562 (1977).

the U.S. Supreme Court disagreed: Zacchini v. Scripps-Howard Broadcasting Co., 351 N.E.2d 454 (Ohio 1976), *rev'd*, 433 U.S. 562 (1977).

broadcast the victim's name: Cox Broadcasting Corp. v. Cohn, 420 U.S. 469 (1975).

reenact the family's ordeal: Time, Inc. v. Hill, 385 U.S. 374 (1967).

Chapter 17

199 **Gutenberg Galaxy:** Marshall McLuhan, The Gutenberg Galaxy: The Making of the Typographic Man (1962).

200 **for trucks and newsracks:** *See* Miami Herald Publishing Co. v. Tornillo, 418 U.S. 241 (1974); City of Lakewood v. Plain Dealer Publishing Co., 486 U.S. 750 (1988).

constitutionally regulate network broadcasting: National Broadcasting Co. v. United States, 319 U.S. 190 (1943).

constitutionality of the FCC's Fairness Doctrine: Red Lion Broadcasting Co. v. FCC, 395 U.S. 367 (1969).

constitutionality of licensing DBS: National Ass'n of Broadcasters v. FCC, 740 F.2d 1190 (D.C. Cir. 1984).

200   **video programming by phone companies:** *See* Chesapeake & Potomac
        Tel. Co. v. United States, 42 F.3d 181 (4th Cir. 1994), *aff'g* Chesapeake &
        Potomac Tel. Co. v. United States, 830 F. Supp. 909, (E.D. Va. 1994); U S
        West, Inc. v. United States, 1994 U.S. App. LEXIS 39121 (9th Cir. 1994),
        aff'g U S West, Inc. v. United States, 855 F. Supp. 1184 (W.D. Wash.
        1994); Southwestern Bell Corp. v. United States, No. 3:94-CV-0193-D
        (N.D. Tex. Mar. 27, 1995); USTA v. United States, No. 1:94CV01961
        (D.D.C. Jan. 27, 1995); GTE South, Inc. v. United States, No. 94-1588-A
        (E.D. Va. Jan. 13, 1995); NYNEX Corp. v. United States, No. 92-323-P-
        C (D. Me. Dec. 8, 1994); BellSouth Corp. v. United States, 868 F. Supp.
        1335 (N.D. Ala. 1994); Ameritech Corp. v. United States, 867 F. Supp. 721
        (N.D. Ill. 1994).

        to carry broadcast signals: Turner Broadcasting System, Inc. v. FCC,
        114 S. Ct. 2445 (1994), *reh'g denied*, 115 S. Ct. 30 (1994).

201   ***United States v. O'Brien:*** 391 U.S. 367 (1968).

        to further that government interest: United States v. O'Brien, 391 U.S.
        367, 377 (1968).

202   **or any part of government:** The Constitution of Pennsylvania, Septem-
        ber 28, 1776, ¶38, *reprinted in* S. E. Morison, Sources and Documents Il-
        lustrating the American Revolution, 1764–1788, and the Formation of the
        Federal Constitution at 162, 173 (2d ed. 1929).

        requires much the same today: *See, e.g.,* Jerome A. Barron, Freedom of
        the Press for Whom? The Right of Access to Mass Media (1973); Jerome
        A. Barron, Access to the Press—A New First Amendment Right, 80 Harv.
        L. Rev. 1641 (1967).

        discussing public questions: Hague v. Committee for Indus. Org., 307
        U.S. 496, 515 (1939).

203   **not to salute, not to pledge:** *See* West Virginia Bd. of Educ. v. Barnette,
        319 U.S. 624 (1943).

        the political speech of others: *See generally* Laurence H. Tribe, American
        Constitutional Law, §12.4 at 589 (1978).

        regulate the price of the *Washington Post:* Cable plaintiffs have
        launched a frontal attack on the rate regulating provisions of the 1992 Ca-
        ble Act. Daniels Cablevision, Inc. v. United States, 835 F. Supp. 1, 7
        (D.D.C. 1993), *vacated and remanded sub nom.,* Turner Broadcasting Sys. v.
        FCC, 114 S. Ct. 2445 (1994), *claim dismissed, summ. judgment granted*, 910
        F. Supp. 734 (D.D.C. 1995), *vacated and remanded sub nom.,* National In-
        terfaith Cable v. FCC, 114 S. Ct. 2730 (1994). *See also* Time Warner En-
        tertainment Co., L.P. v. FCC, 810 F. Supp. 1302 (D.D.C. 1992); Time
        Warner Entertainment Co., L.P. v. FCC, 1996 U.S. App. LEXIS 22387
        (D.C. Cir. Aug. 30, 1996).

        defense of Barry Goldwater: Red Lion Broadcasting Co. v. FCC, 395
        U.S. 367 (1969).

        newspaper is more than a passive receptacle or conduit: Miami Herald
        Publishing Co. v. Tornillo, 418 U.S. 241, 258 (1974).

        maintain peace and quiet on his own: In 1980 the Supreme Court up-
        held a California state law permitting solicitation of signatures in the
        courtyard of a privately owned mall, but only because the value and use of
        the shopping center had not been measurably impaired. Pruneyard Shop-

ping Ctr. v. Robins, 447 U.S. 74 (1980). Telephone companies won a 1994 takings challenge to an FCC order that required them to permit physical collocation of competitors' wires and switches on telephone company premises. Bell Atlantic Tel. Co. v. FCC, 24 F.3d 1441 (D.C. Cir. 1994).

204   **instrument of censorship:** *See, e.g.,* Benjamin Kaplan, An Unhurried View of Copyright at 3 (1967).

to suppress books worldwide: The transfer of rights under copyright may be "by any means of conveyance," including a will, or "by operation of law." 17 U.S.C.A. §201(d)(1). This does not include, however, government seizure from an unwilling author. 17 U.S.C.A. §201(e).

to limit free speech: By its terms, the Copyright Act is intended not to displace the First Amendment. Pub. L. No. 650, Tit. VI, §609, 104 Stat. 5132 (1990). The Supreme Court has addressed the tension between the First Amendment and copyright in a number of cases. *See e.g.,* Mazer v. Stein, 347 U.S. 201, 217-218 (1954).

Privacy rights limit it, too: *See* Laurence H. Tribe, American Constitutional Law at 796 (2d ed. 1988).

205   **uniquely legitimate offspring of censorship:** Paul Goldstein, Copyright and the First Amendment, 70 Colum. L. Rev. 983, 983 (1970).

206   **road to serfdom:** Friedrich Hayek, The Road to Serfdom (1943).

adventurous, irresponsible, ungenteel ways: George Orwell, Review, Herman Melville, *by* Lewis Mumford, in 1 The Collected Essays of George Orwell at 21 (1968).

unquenchable sense of freedom and opportunity: George Orwell, Riding Down from Bangor, *in* The Penguin Essays of George Orwell at 406, 407 (1984).

Index